SHAKESPEARE
QUOTATIONS

SHAKESPEARE QUOTATIONS

G. F. Lamb

LAROUSSE

LAROUSSE
Larousse plc
43–45 Annandale Street, Edinburgh EH7 4AZ
Larousse Kingfisher Chambers Inc.
95 Madison Avenue, New York, New York 10016

Published by W & R Chambers Ltd 1992
Copyright © Introduction and selection G F Lamb 1992

First published under the Larousse imprint 1994
Copyright © Larousse plc 1994

10 9 8 7 6 5 4 3 2 1

British Library Cataloguing in Publication Data
for this book is available from the British Library

Library of Congress Catalog Card Number: 94-75738

ISBN 0-7523-5004-8

Cover illustration *William Shakespeare*, from a portrait attributed to
John Taylor, courtesy National Portrait Gallery, London

Typeset by Buccleuch Printers Ltd, Hawick
Printed in England by Clays Ltd, St Ives plc

CONTENTS

Introduction vi

List of Topics vii

Quotations 1

Dictionary of Characters 313

Shakespeare and the Stage 338

Shakespeare: A Brief Biography 344

Chronological List of Plays 345

Index 347

INTRODUCTION

It is no longer necessary to regard William Shakespeare as a kind of deity who is above all criticism. The generally accepted view today is that he was a very practical playwright who, often under pressure, wrote a great many plays, which are variable in quality and by no means free from imperfections. Nonetheless he remains one of the greatest figures in English literature, and is internationally respected. He is also the most quotable and quoted writer in the English language.

For this book I have gathered over 2 000 quotations from his works, some as familiar as old proverbs, others known to the Shakespeare specialist alone. But the book differs from most quotation books in one important respect: each quotation has been given a brief note, indicating not only the source but also the speaker and (where relevant) the person addressed, or other information which could help to give the words a context. Inevitably, what is informative to some readers will be obvious and unnecessary to others. I have aimed at brevity, because this is not a book *about* Shakespeare but a compilation of his own words, which I hope will provide interest and pleasure for a wide range of readers and browsers.

To avoid tedious repetition, a **Dictionary of Characters** has been included, offering a few basic facts about each character mentioned in the explanatory notes.

Entries are arranged under 197 topic headings, which are in alphabetical order. Plays are in alphabetical order within each topic, followed by poems. There are sections on **Shakespeare and the Stage** (quotations about Shakespeare and Shakespearean performances), a brief account of his life and a chronological list of his plays. The index is in the form of an alphabetical list of plays and poems, with a page number and topic reference for each quotation.

Acknowledgements are offered, with thanks, to *Chambers Quick Facts* (1991) for the list of plays, and to the *Larousse Biographical Dictionary* (Fifth Edition, 1990), from which the short account of Shakespeare's life has been abbreviated and adapted. I am also indebted to my wife for her help in checking the details of each quotation.

G. F. LAMB

LIST OF TOPICS

1	Absence	40	Drinking
2	Action	41	Duelling
3	Affection	42	Duty
4	Age	43	Earth
5	Ambition	44	Eating
6	Angel	45	Enemy
7	Anger	46	England
8	Animals	47	Eyes
9	Arms and Armour	48	Face
10	Ass	49	Farewell
11	Beauty	50	Fate
12	Bed	51	Father
13	Bells	52	Fear
14	Birds	53	Flowers
15	Blood	54	Folly
16	Books	55	Fortune
17	Candour	56	Friendship
18	Care	57	Freedom
19	Cats	58	Gentleman
20	Cause	59	Gifts
21	Change	60	God
22	Charms	61	Gods
23	Chastity	62	Gold
24	Children	63	Goodness
25	Comfort	64	Grief
26	Conquest	65	Hair
27	Courage	66	Hand
28	Dancing	67	Happiness
29	Danger	68	Harm
30	Daughters	69	Haste
31	Day	70	Hate
32	Death	71	Heart
33	Deeds	72	Heat
34	Delight	73	Heaven
35	Destiny	74	Hell
36	Devil	75	Home
37	Dogs	76	Honesty
38	Dreams	77	Honour
39	Dress	78	Hope

79	Horse	123	Oratory
80	Hours	124	Pardon
81	Husband	125	Patience
82	Hypocrisy	126	Peace
83	Ignorance	127	People
84	Inconstancy	128	Perfection
85	Ingratitude	129	Philosophy
86	Injury	130	Pity
87	Innocence	131	Place
88	Jealousy	132	Plays and Players
89	Jewels	133	Poetry
90	Joy	134	Poison
91	Judgement	135	Possessions
92	Justice	136	Poverty
93	King	137	Power
94	Kisses	138	Praise
95	Knighthood	139	Prayer
96	Knowledge	140	Pride
97	Lady	141	Prison
98	Law	142	Prophecy
99	Life	143	Punishment
100	Lips	144	Quarrels
101	Love	145	Queen
102	Madness	146	Rain
103	Magic	147	Reason
104	Malice	148	Remedy
105	Man	149	Repentance
106	Marriage	150	Reputation
107	Medicine	151	Rest
108	Memory	152	Revenge
109	Mirth	153	Reward
110	Misfortune	154	Roaring
111	Money	155	Rome
112	Months	156	Seasons
113	Moon	157	Silence
114	Morning	158	Sin
115	Murder	159	Slander
116	Music	160	Sleep
117	Name	161	Smiles
118	Nature	162	Sorrow
119	Necessity	163	Soul
120	Night	164	Sport
121	Oaths	165	Stars
122	Offence	166	Stone

167	Storm	183	Unkindness
168	Story	184	Valour
169	Suicide	185	Victory
170	Sun	186	Villainy
171	Talk	187	Virtue
172	Teaching	188	War
173	Tears	189	Weeping
174	Theft	190	Welcome
175	Thought	191	Wife
176	Time	192	Wit
177	Tomorrow	193	Woman
178	Touch	194	Wooing
179	Travel	195	Words
180	Treason	196	The World
181	Trees	197	Youth
182	Truth		

1 ABSENCE

1   There is no living, none,
If Bertram be away.
All's Well That Ends Well I, 1
Helena to herself, concerning the man she loves

2   Shall I abide
In this dull world, which in thy absence is
No better than a sty?
Antony and Cleopatra IV, 15
Cleopatra to dying Antony

3 My lord, your nobles, jealous of your absence,
Seek through your camp to find you.
Henry V IV, 1
Henry has been going among his troops, incognito, talking with
his soldiers

4 There is not one among them but I dote on his very absence,
and I wish them a fair departure.
The Merchant of Venice I, 2
Portia to Nerissa, concerning her unwelcome suitors

5 When you depart from me, sorrow abides, and happiness takes
his leave.
Much Ado About Nothing I, 1
Leonato to Don Pedro

6 What, keep a week away? Seven days and nights?
Eight score eight hours? and lovers' absent hours
More tedious than the dial eight score times?
A weary reckoning!
Othello III, 4
Bianca to Cassio

7   O absence, what a torment wouldst thou prove,
Were it not thy sour leisure gave sweet leave
To entertain the time with thoughts of love.
Sonnet 39

8   How like a Winter hath my absence been
From thee, the pleasure of the fleeting year!
What freezings have I felt, what dark days seen!
Sonnet 97

9   From you have I been absent in the spring,
When proud pied April (dress'd in all his trim)
Hath put a spirit of youth in everything.
Sonnet 98

10   O never say that I was false of heart,
Though absence seem'd my flame to qualify.
Sonnet 109

---

2   ACTION

---

1   In such business
Action is eloquence, and the eyes of the ignorant
More learned than the ears.
Coriolanus III, 2
Volumnia to Coriolanus. The business is bowing and scraping
to the crowd

2   What a piece of work is man! . . . in form and moving how
express and admirable! in action how like an angel!
Hamlet II , 2
Hamlet to Rosencrantz and Guildenstern

3   Suit the action to the word, the word to the action.
Hamlet III, 2
Hamlet, giving advice to the Players

4   We must not stint
Our necessary actions, in the fear
To cope malicious censurers.
Henry VIII I, 2
Wolsey to the king, on taxation

5   Things done well
And with a care, exempt themselves from fear.
Henry VIII I, 2
The king to Wolsey

6   After my death I wish no other herald,
No other speaker of my living actions, . . .
But such an honest chronicler as Griffith.
Henry VIII IV, 2
Queen Katherine, after hearing his impartial assessment of
Wolsey

7   If it were done when 'tis done, then 'twere well
It were done quickly.
Macbeth I, 7
Macbeth, trying to decide whether to murder King Duncan

8   If to do were as easy as to know what were good to do, chapels
had been churches, and poor men's cottages princes' palaces.
The Merchant of Venice I, 2
Portia to Nerissa

9   So smile the heavens upon this holy act
That after-hours with sorrow chide us not.
Romeo and Juliet II, 6
Friar Laurence to Romeo, before marrying him to Juliet

10   Thus the native hue of resolution
Is sicklied o'er with the pale cast of thought,
And enterprises of great pith and moment
With this regard their currents turn awry,
And lose the name of action.
Hamlet III, 1
Hamlet, soliloquizing

3   AFFECTION

1   Your affections are
A sick man's appetite, who desires most that
Which would increase his evil.
Coriolanus I, 1
Coriolanus, voicing his low opinion of the citizens of Rome

2   He hath, my lord, of late made many tenders of his affection to
me.
Hamlet I, 3
Ophelia to Polonius, regarding Hamlet

3   Keep you in the rear of your affection,
Out of the shot and danger of desire.
Hamlet I, 3
Laertes, giving advice to Ophelia

4   I do perceive
My king is tangled in affection to
A creature of the queen's, Lady Anne Bullen.
Henry VIII III, 2
Duke of Suffolk, reporting the words of Cardinal Wolsey

5   To my judgement, your highness is not entertained with that
ceremonious affection as you were wont.
King Lear I, 4
A knight, after Lear has handed over his kingdom to his elder daughters

6   They say, too, that she will rather die than give any sign of
affection . . . I will be horribly in love with her.
Much Ado About Nothing II, 3
Benedick to himself, concerning Beatrice

7   Preferment goes by letter and affection
And not by old gradation.
Othello I, 1
Iago, jealous of Cassio's advancement

8   Then let thy love be younger than thyself,
Or thy affection cannot hold the bent.
Twelfth Night II, 4
Duke Orsino to Viola, believing her to be a youth

9   Had she affections and warm youthful blood,
She would be swift in motion as a ball.
Romeo and Juliet II, 5
Juliet, on her nurse's slowness in bringing a message from Romeo

10   Affection is a coal that must be cool'd;
Else, suffer'd, it will set the heart on fire.
Venus and Adonis Stanza 65

4 AGE

1   For we are old, and on our quick'st decrees
The inaudible and noiseless foot of Time
Steals ere we can effect them.
All's Well That Ends Well V, 3
King of France

2   Age cannot wither her, nor custom stale
Her infinite variety.
Antony and Cleopatra II, 2
Enobarbus, describing Cleopatra

3   Age from folly could not give me freedom.
Antony and Cleopatra I, 3
Cleopatra

4   Though I look old, I am strong and lusty;
For in my youth I never did apply
Hot and rebellious liquors . . .
Therefore my age is as a lusty winter.
As You Like It II, 3
Adam, offering to continue helping his young master

5   Second childishness and mere oblivion,
    Sans teeth, sans eyes, sans taste, sans everything.
    As You Like It II, 7
    Jaques's sardonic view of old age

6   I see thy age and dangers make thee dote.
    The Comedy of Errors V, 1
    Duke of Ephesus to Aegeon

7   The satirical rogue says here that old men have grey beards, that their faces are wrinkled, their eyes purging thick amber and plum-tree gum, and that they have a plentiful lack of wit.
Hamlet II, 2
Hamlet to the elderly politician, Polonius

8   You cannot call it love, for at your age
    The hey-day in the blood is tame.
    Hamlet III, 4
    Hamlet reproving his mother for her second marriage.

9   Your lordship, though not clean past your youth, hath yet some smack of age in you, some relish of the saltness of time.
2 Henry IV I, 2
Falstaff to the Chief Justice

10   I know thee not, old man: fall to thy prayers;
    How ill white hairs become a fool and jester!
    2 Henry IV V, 5
    The newly-crowned Henry V rejects Falstaff and his dissolute companions

11   Lord, Lord, how subject we old men are to this vice of lying.
2 Henry IV III, 2
Falstaff to himself

12   O, father Abbot,
    An old man, broken with the storms of state,
    Is come to lay his weary bones among ye;
    Give him a little earth for charity!
    Henry VIII IV, 2
    Cardinal Wolsey's words at Leicester Abbey, after his downfall

13   The gods today stand friendly, that we may,
Lovers in peace, lead on our days to age!
Julius Caesar V, 1
Cassius to Brutus

14   As you are old and reverend, you should be wise.
King Lear I, 4
Goneril to her furiously indignant father

15   O, sir, you are old;
Nature in you stands on the very verge
Of her confine.
King Lear II, 4
Criticism from Lear's other daughter, Regan

16   Pray, do not mock me:
I am a very foolish fond old man,
Fourscore and upward, not an hour more nor less.
King Lear IV, 7
Lear, having lost his wits, to Cordelia

17   I have lived long enough: my way of life
Is fallen into the sear, the yellow leaf,
And that which should accompany old age,
As honour, love, obedience, troops of friends,
I must not look to have.
Macbeth V, 3
Macbeth to himself

18   As they say, when the age is in, the wit is out.
Much Ado About Nothing III, 5
Dogberry concerning Verges

19   Give me a staff of honour for mine age,
But not a sceptre to control the world.
Titus Andronicus I, 1
Titus to his brother Marcus

20   Age, I do abhor thee; youth, I do adore thee.
The Passionate Pilgrim Stanza 12

21 Respect and reason wait on wrinkled age.
The Rape of Lucrece Stanza 39

5   AMBITION

1   I hold ambition of so airy and light a quality that it is but a shadow's shadow.
Hamlet II, 2
Rosencrantz to Hamlet

2   Ill-weav'd ambition, how much art thou shrunk!
1 Henry IV V, 4
Prince Henry to Hotspur's dead body

3   Virtue is choked with foul ambition
And charity chased hence with rancour's hand.
2 Henry VI III, 1
Humphrey of Gloucester, defending himself against his detractors

4   The devil speed him! no man's pie is freed
From his ambitious finger.
Henry VIII I, 1
Duke of Buckingham, criticizing Cardinal Wolsey

5   Cromwell, I charge thee, fling away ambition:
By that sin fell the angels: how can man, then,
The image of his Maker, hope to win by it?
Henry VIII III, 2
Wolsey to Thomas Cromwell

6   Ambition's debt is paid.
Julius Caesar II, 1
Brutus, announcing the killing of Caesar to the people

7   He hath brought many captives home to Rome,
    Whose ransoms did the general coffers fill:
    Did this in Caesar seem ambitious?
    When that the poor have cried, Caesar hath wept:
    Ambition should be made of sterner stuff.
    Julius Caesar III, 2
    Antony's speech over Caesar's body

8   Thou wouldst be great;
    Art not without ambition; but without
    The illness should attend it.
    Macbeth I, 5
    Lady Macbeth, musing on her husband

9   I have no spur
    To prick the sides of my intent, but only
    Vaulting ambition, which o'erleaps itself.
    Macbeth I, 7
    Macbeth to himself

10 Thriftless ambition, that wilt ravin up
    Thine own life's means.
    Macbeth II, 4
    Ross to Macduff

11 Farewell the plumed troop and the big wars
    That make ambition virtue!
    Othello III, 3
    Othello, mentally disturbed by accusations concerning his wife's
    virtue

6   ANGEL

1   By Jupiter, an angel! or if not
    An earthly paragon.
    Cymbeline III, 6
    Belarius to his sons, concerning Fidele's appearance

2 Angels and ministers of grace defend us!
   Hamlet I, 4
   Hamlet, on seeing his father's ghost

3 Good night, sweet prince,
   And flights of angels sing thee to thy rest.
   Hamlet V, 2
   Horatio, as Hamlet dies

4 Thou hast the sweetest face I ever look'd on,—
   Sir, as I have a soul, she is an angel.
   Henry VIII IV, 1
   A gentleman watching Anne Bullen's wedding procession

5 An angel is like you, Kate, and you are like an angel.
   Henry V V, 2
   Henry to the French princess whom he later marries

6 Brutus, as you know, was Caesar's angel.
   Julius Caesar III, 2
   Antony to the crowd, concerning Brutus's part in Caesar's
   assassination

7   They have in England
   A coin that bears the figure of an angel
   Stamped in gold.
   The Merchant of Venice II, 7
   Prince of Morocco, choosing a casket

8 What angel wakes me from my flowery bed?
   A Midsummer Night's Dream III, 1
   Titania to Bottom, despite his ass's head

9 God for his Richard hath in heavenly pay
   A glorious angel: then if angels fight,
   Weak men must fall, for heaven still guards the right.
   Richard II III, 2
   Richard to his followers, trying to bolster up his fighting spirit

10   O speak again, bright angel! for thou art
As glorious to this night, being o'er my head,
As is a winged messenger of heaven.
Romeo and Juliet II, 2
Romeo to himself, overhearing Juliet on her balcony

11   Two loves have I of comfort and despair,
Which like two spirits do suggest me still:
The better angel is a man right fair,
The worser spirit a woman colour'd ill.
Sonnet 144

7 ANGER

1   Never anger
Made good guard for itself.
Antony and Cleopatra IV, 1
Maecenas to Octavius Caesar, concerning Antony

2 Put him to choler straight . . . being once chafed he cannot
Be rein'd again to temperance.
Coriolanus III, 3
The two tribunes, plotting the downfall of Coriolanus

3 Anger's my meat: I sup upon myself,
And so shall starve with feeding.
Coriolanus IV, 2
Volumnia to Menenius

4 What, drunk with choler? Stay and pause awhile.
1 Henry IV I, 3
Earl of Northumberland to his excitable son, Hotspur

5   Anger is like
A full-hot horse; who being allow'd his way,
Self-mettle tires him.
Henry VIII I, 1
Duke of Norfolk, calming Duke of Buckingham's anger towards
Wolsey

6   What sudden anger's this? how have I reap'd it?
He parted frowning from me, as if ruin
Leap'd from his eyes.
Henry VIII III, 2
Cardinal Wolsey to himself, regarding King Henry

7   O Cassius, you are yoked with a lamb
That carries anger as the flint bears fire,
Who, much enforced, shows a hasty spark
And straight is cold again.
Julius Caesar IV, 3
Brutus, following a quarrel with Cassius

8   Touch me with noble anger,
And let not women's weapons, water-drops,
Stain my man's cheeks.
King Lear II, 4
Lear calls on the gods for help against his ungrateful daughters

9   The moon, the governess of floods,
Pale in her anger, washeth all the air.
A Midsummer Night's Dream II, 1
Titania to Oberon

10   I tell thee, Kate, 'twas burnt and dried away;
And I expressly am forbid to touch it,
For it engenders choler, planteth anger.
And better 'twere that both of us did fast,
Since, of ourselves, ourselves are choleric.
The Taming of the Shrew IV, 1
Petruchio, taming Kate by starvation

8   ANIMALS

1   Our dungy earth alike
Feeds beast as man.
Antony and Cleopatra I, 1
Antony to Cleopatra

2   A poor sequester'd stag
That from the hunter's aim had ta'en a hurt,
Did come to languish, and indeed, my lord,
That wretched animal heav'd forth such groans
That their discharge did stretch his leathern coat.
As You Like It II, 1
A Lord to Duke Senior

3   Nature teaches beasts to know their friends.
Coriolanus II, 1
Sicinius to Menenius

4   Why, let the stricken deer go weep,
The hart ungalled play.
Hamlet III, 2
Hamlet to Horatio

5   That island of England breeds very valiant creatures; their
mastiffs are of unmatchable courage.
Henry V III, 7
Rambures to other French officers and nobles

6   Is not this a lamentable thing, that the skin of an innocent lamb
should be made parchment?
2 Henry VI IV, 2
Jack Cade to the mob in his attack on lawyers

7   But mice and rats and such small deer
Have been Tom's food for seven long year.
King Lear III, 4
Edgar, posing as mad

8   Some men there are love not a gaping pig;
Some, that are mad if they behold a cat.
The Merchant of Venice IV, 1
Shylock to the Duke in the court scene

9   *Demetrius:* I'll run from thee and hide me in the
brakes,
And leave thee to the mercy of wild
beasts.
Helena: The wildest hath not such a heart as you.
A Midsummer Night's Dream II, 1
Lovesick Helena, at this stage of the play unloved by Demetrius

10   A lion among ladies is a most dreadful thing.
A Midsummer Night's Dream III, 1
Bottom to his fellow actors

11   Lions make leopards tame.
Richard II I, 1
Richard to Mowbray, optimistically thinking of himself as the
lion

9   ARMS AND ARMOUR

1   Such was the very armour he had on
When he the ambitious Norway combated.
Hamlet I, 1
Horatio to Marcellus, about the Ghost of Hamlet's father

2   Whether 'tis nobler in the mind to suffer
The slings and arrows of outrageous fortune,
Or to take arms against a sea of troubles,
And by opposing end them,
Hamlet III, 1
Hamlet, soliloquizing

3 I saw young Harry with his beaver on,
   His cuisses on his thighs, gallantly arm'd.
   1 Henry IV IV, 1
   Vernon to Hotspur, concerning Prince Hal

4 Now thrive the armourers, and honour's thought
   Reigns solely in the breast of every man.
   Henry V Prologue II
   Chorus on the preparations for battle

5 The armourers, accomplishing the knights,
   With busy hammers closing rivets up,
   Give dreadful note of preparation.
   Henry V Prologue IV
   Chorus

6 Their armours, that march'd hence so silver-bright,
   Hither return all gilt with Frenchmen's blood.
   King John II, 1
   English herald, after an English victory

7 Come, put mine armour on; give me my staff . . .
   Come, sir, dispatch.
   Macbeth V, 3
   Macbeth to his attendant

8 I have known where he would have walked ten mile a-foot to
   see a good armour; and now he will lie ten nights awake
   carving the fashion of a new doublet.
   Much Ado About Nothing II, 3
   Benedick to himself, concerning Claudio in love

9 Now are our brows bound with victorious wreaths;
   Our bruised arms hung up for monuments.
   Richard III I, 1
   Richard of Gloucester, soliloquizing

10   Stand, stand, thou Greek; thou art a goodly mark.
     No? wilt thou not? I like thy armour well:
     I'll frush it, and unlock the rivets all,
     But I'll be master of it.
     Troilus and Cressida V, 6
     Hector to a Greek soldier in sumptuous armour
     frush 'break it up'

10   ASS

1   Your dull ass will not mend his pace with beating.
    Hamlet V, 1
    First gravedigger to his fellow

2   Though we lay these honours on this man,
    To ease ourselves of divers slanderous loads,
    He shall but bear them as the ass bears gold,
    To groan and sweat under the business . . .
    And having brought our treasure where we will,
    Then take we down his load and turn him off,
    Like to the empty ass.
    Julius Caesar IV, 1
    Antony, speaking contemptuously of Lepidus to Octavius
    Caesar

3   Like an ass whose back with ingots bows,
    Thou bear'st thy heavy riches but a journey,
    And death unloads thee.
    Measure for Measure III, 1
    Duke to Claudio

4   I do begin to perceive that I am made an ass.
    The Merry Wives of Windsor V, 5
    Falstaff to Ford and others

5   I am such a tender ass, if my hair do but tickle me, I must
scratch.
A Midsummer Night's Dream IV, 1
Bottom, inflicted with an ass's head

6   My Oberon! what visions have I seen!
I thought I was enamour'd of an ass.
A Midsummer Night's Dream IV, 1
Titania, released from the love charm that made her idolize
Bottom

7   Remember that I am an ass; though it be not written down, yet
forget not that I am an ass.
Much Ado About Nothing IV, 2
The foolish constable, Dogberry, indignant at having been called an ass by
someone he is arresting

8   I was not made a horse;
And yet I bear a burden like an ass,
Spur-gall'd and tir'd by jauncing Bolingbroke.
Richard II V, 5
Richard after his abdication

11   BEAUTY

1   What danger will it be to us,
Maids as we are, to travel forth so far!
Beauty provoketh thieves sooner than gold.
As You Like It I, 3
Rosalind to Celia, as they prepare to flee to the Forest of Arden

2   She's beautiful, and therefore to be woo'd;
She is a woman, therefore to be won.
1 Henry VI V, 3
Earl of Suffolk concerning Princess Margaret of Anjou

3 The chariest maid is prodigal enough
If she unmask her beauty to the moon.
Hamlet I, 3
Laertes to Ophelia

4 Beauty's princely majesty is such,
Confounds the tongue and makes the senses rough.
1 Henry VI V, 3
Earl of Suffolk to Margaret

5 Could I come near your beauty with my nails,
I'd set my ten commandments in your face.
2 Henry VI I, 3
Duchess of Gloucester, who has just been struck by Queen
Margaret

6 The fairest hand I ever touched! O beauty,
Till now I never knew thee!
Henry VIII I, 4
King Henry to Anne Bullen

7 Beauty doth vanish age as if new born.
Love's Labour's Lost IV, 3
Biron to King of Navarre

8   Look on beauty
And you shall see 'tis purchased by the weight.
The Merchant of Venice III, 2
Bassanio, choosing the lead casket

9   Beauty is a witch
Against whose charms faith melteth into blood.
Much Ado About Nothing II, 1
Claudio, believing that his friend, Don Pedro, has stolen Hero

10 Her face, like heaven, enticeth thee to view
Her countless glory.
Pericles I, 1
King of Antioch concerning his daughter

11 O, she doth teach the torches to burn bright . . .
    Beauty too rich for use, for earth too dear!
    Romeo and Juliet I, 5
    Romeo on his first sight of Juliet

12 Here lies Juliet, and her beauty makes
    This vault a feasting presence full of light.
    Romeo and Juliet V, 3
    Romeo, entering the tomb where Juliet lies

13 'Tis beauty truly blent, whose red and white
    Nature's own sweet and cunning hand laid on:
    Lady, you are the cruellest she alive
    If you will lead these graces to the grave
    And leave the world no copy.
    Twelfth Night I, 5
    Viola as Cesario, to Olivia

14 Beauty is but a vain and doubtful good;
    A shining gloss that fadeth suddenly;
    A flower that dies when first it 'gins to bud;
    A brittle glass that's broken presently.
    The Passionate Pilgrim Stanza 13

15 Beauty itself doth of itself persuade
    The eyes of men without an orator.
    The Rape of Lucrece Stanza 5

16 Thy beauty hath ensnared thee to this night.
    The Rape of Lucrece Stanza 70

17 If I could write the beauty of your eyes
    And in fresh numbers, number all your graces,
    The age to come would say 'This poet lies;
    Such heavenly touches ne'er touch'd earthly faces'.
    Sonnet 17

18 O! how much more doth beauty beauteous seem
    By that sweet ornament which truth doth give!
    Sonnet 54

19   That thou art blamed shall not be thy defect,
For slander's mark was ever yet the fair;
The ornament of beauty is suspect.
Sonnet 70

20   To me, fair friend, you never can be old
For as you were when first your eye I eyed,
Such seems your beauty still.
Sonnet 104

12 BED

1   How bravely thou becomest thy bed! fresh lily!
And whiter than the sheets!
Cymbeline II, 2
Iachimo to the sleeping Imogen

2   Let not the royal bed of Denmark be
A couch for luxury and damned incest.
Hamlet I, 4
Ghost to Hamlet

3   Go not to my uncle's bed;
Assume a virtue if you have it not.
Hamlet III, 4
Hamlet to his mother

4   I would 'twere bed-time, Hal, and all well.
1 Henry IV V, 1
Falstaff, just before battle

5   What does gravity out of his bed at midnight?
1 Henry IV II, 4
Falstaff, on an elderly nobleman acting as messenger

6   I will show you a chamber with a bed; which bed, because it
shall not speak of your pretty encounters, press it to death!
Troilus and Cressida III, 2
Pandarus to Troilus and Cressida

7   To be up after midnight and to go to bed then, is early.
Twelfth Night II, 3
Sir Toby Belch to Sir Andrew Aguecheek

8   Although the sheet were big enough for the bed of Ware.
Twelfth Night III, 2
Sir Toby Belch's reference is to the largest bed in England

9   I was in love with my bed.
The Two Gentlemen of Verona II, 1
Speed to Valentine

10   Weary with toil I haste me to my bed,
The dear repose for limbs with travel tired.
Sonnet 27

11   Misery acquaints a man with strange bedfellows.
The Tempest II, 2
Trinculo, sheltering under Caliban's gaberdine

12   Into the chamber wickedly he stalks
And gazeth on her yet unstained bed.
The Rape of Lucrece Stanza 53

13   BELLS

1   If ever you have look'd on better days,
If ever been where bells have knoll'd to church . . .
Let gentleness my strong enforcement be.
As You Like It II, 7
Orlando, asking Duke Senior and his companions for help

2 I, of ladies most deject and wretched . . .
Now see that noble and most sovereign reason,
Like sweet bells jangled out of tune and harsh.
Hamlet III, 1
Ophelia, believing Hamlet to be mad

3 The first bringer of unwelcome news
Hath but a losing office, and his tongue
Sounds ever after as a sullen bell,
Remember'd tolling a departing friend.
2 Henry IV I, 1
Earl of Northumberland, receiving news of Hotspur's death

4 Why ring not out the bells throughout the town?
1 Henry VI I, 6
Reignier to Dauphin, on the relief of Orleans from the English

5 Hark! hark! the Dauphin's drum, a warning bell,
Sings heavy music to thy timorous soul.
1 Henry VI IV, 2
French General to Lord Talbot, the far from timorous English
commander

6 Bell, book, and candle shall not drive me back,
When gold and silver becks me to come on.
King John III, 3
Philip the Bastard to the king

7 Go bid thy mistress, when my drink is ready,
She strike upon the bell.
Macbeth II, 1
Macbeth, awaiting the signal to murder Duncan

8 Let us all ring fancy's knell;
I'll begin it — Ding, dong, bell.
The Merchant of Venice III, 2
Song while Bassanio examines caskets

14 BIRDS

1 I saw Jove's bird, the Roman eagle, wing'd
   From the spongy south to this part of the west,
   There vanish'd in the sunbeams.
   Cymbeline IV, 2
   Soothsayer, offering a favourable omen

2 Hark! hark! the lark at heaven's gate sings,
   And Phoebus 'gins arise.
   Cymbeline II, 3
   Song to wake Imogen

3 The cock, that is the trumpet to the morn,
   Doth with his lofty and shrill-sounding throat
   Awake the god of day.
   Hamlet I, 1
   Horatio to Marcellus, after the ghost of Hamlet's father has
   suddenly vanished

4 Some say that ever 'gainst that season comes
   Wherein our Saviour's birth is celebrated,
   The bird of dawning singeth all night long.
   Hamlet I, 1
   Marcellus to Horatio

5   The morning cock crew loud,
   And at the sound it shrunk in haste away,
   And vanish'd from our sight.
   Hamlet I, 2
   Horatio to Hamlet, concerning the ghost

6 The croaking raven doth bellow for revenge.
   Hamlet III, 2
   Hamlet to the murderer in the 'Mousetrap' play

7 Being fed by us, you used us so
   As that ungentle gull, the cuckoo's bird
   Useth the sparrow.
   1 Henry IV V, 1
   Earl of Worcester to Henry

8   Let frantic Talbot triumph for a while,
And like a peacock sweep along his tail;
We'll pull his plumes and take away his train.
1 Henry VI III, 3
Joan of Arc to the Dauphin

9   So doth the swan her downy cygnets save,
Keeping them prisoners underneath her wings.
1 Henry VI V, 3
Earl of Suffolk to the French princess, Margaret. Though his
prisoner, she captivates him by her beauty

10   But what a point, my lord, your falcon made,
And what a pitch she flew above the rest.
2 Henry VI II, 1
Henry to Duke of Suffolk

11   I have seen a swan
With bootless labour swim against the tide,
And spend her strength with over-matching waves.
3 Henry VI I, 4
Duke of York to himself

12   The hedge-sparrow fed the cuckoo so long
That it had its head bit off by its young.
King Lear I, 4
Fool to Lear

13   The raven himself is hoarse
That croaks the fatal entrance of Duncan
Under my battlements.
Macbeth I, 5
Lady Macbeth, soliloquizing

14   The guest of summer,
The temple-haunting martlet, does approve,
By his lov'd mansionry, that the heaven's breath
Smells wooingly here.
Macbeth I, 6
Banquo, arriving with Duncan at Macbeth's castle

15   It was the owl that shriek'd, the fatal bellman,
Which gives the stern'st good night.
Macbeth II, 2
Lady Macbeth to herself, while Macbeth is killing Duncan

16   Light thickens; and the crow
Makes wing to the rooky wood.
Macbeth III, 2
Macbeth to his wife

17   The crow doth sing as sweetly as the lark
When neither is attended.
The Merchant of Venice V, 1
Portia to Nerissa

18   The bird was fledged; and then it is the complexion of them all
to leave the dam.
The Merchant of Venice III, 1
Salanio to Salarino and Shylock, concerning Jessica

19   I will aggravate my voice so that I will roar you as gently as any
sucking dove; I will roar you an 'twere any nightingale.
A Midsummer Night's Dream I, 2
Bottom, insisting that his lion's roar will not alarm the ladies

20   The finch, the sparrow, and the lark,
The plain-song cuckoo grey,
Whose note full many a man doth mark,
And dares not answer nay.
A Midsummer Night's Dream III, 1
Bottom, singing to Titania

21   Look where Beatrice, like a lapwing, runs
Close by the ground, to hear our conference.
Much Ado About Nothing III, 1
Hero to Ursula

22   It was the nightingale, and not the lark,
That pierc'd the fearful hollow of thine ear;
Nightly she sings on yond pomegranate tree.
Romeo and Juliet III, 5
Juliet, reluctant to part from Romeo

23   Dost thou love hawking? thou hast hawks will soar
Above the morning lark.
The Taming of the Shrew Induction 2
Lord to Christopher Sly

24   The swallow follows not summer more willing than we your
lordship.
Timon of Athens III, 6
A lord to Timon

25   The eagle suffers little birds to sing,
And is not careful what they mean thereby,
Knowing that with the shadow of his wings
He can at pleasure stint their melody.
Titus Andronicus IV, 4
Tamora to Saturninus

26   Birds never limed no secret bushes fear.
The Rape of Lucrece Stanza 13

27   Bare ruin'd choirs, where late the sweet birds sang.
Sonnet 73

28   Then my state
Like to the lark at break of day arising
From sullen earth, sings hymns at heaven's gate.
Sonnet 29

29   Lo! here the gentle lark, weary of rest,
From his moist cabinet mounts up on high,
And wakes the morning.
Venus and Adonis Stanza 143

15 BLOOD

1   Many will swoon when they do look on blood.
As You Like It IV, 3
Oliver to Rosalind, who has just done so

2   The blood more stirs
To rouse a lion than to start a hare.
1 Henry IV I, 3
Hot-blooded Hotspur

3   If we may pass, we will: if we be hinder'd,
We shall your tawny ground with your red blood
Discolour.
Henry V III, 6
Henry to French herald

4   There is not work enough for all our hands;
Scarce blood enough in all their sickly veins
To give each naked curtle-axe a stain.
Henry V IV, 2
Constable of France, sneering at the small English force

5   He today that sheds his blood with me
Shall be my brother, be he ne'er so vile.
Henry V IV, 3
Henry to Earl of Westmoreland

6   Woe to the hand that shed this costly blood!
Julius Caesar III, 1
Antony over Caesar's body

7   He that steeps his safety in true blood
Shall find but bloody safety and untrue.
King John III, 4
Cardinal Pandulph to Dauphin

8   Here lay Duncan,
His silver skin lac'd with his golden blood . . .
      there, the murderers
Steep'd in the colour of their trade, their daggers
Unmannerly breech'd with gore.
Macbeth II, 3
Macbeth, professing to believe that Duncan's grooms were
guilty of his murder

9 Who would have thought the old man to have had so much
blood in him?
Macbeth V, 1
Lady Macbeth sleep-walking, the murder of Duncan on her mind

10   I am in blood
Stepp'd in so far that, should I wade no more,
Returning were as tedious as go o'er.
Macbeth III, 4
Macbeth to his wife

11 We'll mingle our bloods together in the earth,
From whence we had our being and our birth.
Pericles I, 2
Helicanus promises to defend Tyre against any attack while
Pericles is away

16 BOOKS

1 In nature's infinite book of secrecy
A little I can read.
Antony and Cleopatra I, 2
Soothsayer to Charmian

2 Small have continual plodders ever won,
Save base authority from others' books.
Love's Labour's Lost I, 1
Biron to King of Navarre

3   He hath never fed of the dainties that are bred in a book.
Love's Labour's Lost IV, 2
Sir Nathaniel to Holofernes, concerning Dull

4   We turned over many books together.
The Merchant of Venice IV, 1
Bellario, writing to recommend Balthasar to the Duke of Venice

5   Who has a book of all that monarchs do,
He's more secure to keep it shut than shown.
Pericles I, 1
Pericles to Antiochus

6   Knowing I lov'd my books, he furnish'd me
From mine own library with volumes that
I prize above my dukedom.
The Tempest I, 2
Prospero, paying tribute to Gonzalo

7   And deeper than did ever plummet sound,
I'll drown my book.
The Tempest V, 1
Prospero, preparing to abandon his magic

8   I have unclasp'd
To thee the book even of my secret soul.
Twelfth Night I, 4
Orsino to Viola as Cesario

9   O let my books be then the eloquence
And dumb presages of my speaking breast.
Sonnet 23

10 The painful warrior famoused for fight,
After a thousand victories, once foiled
Is from the book of honour razed quite.
Sonnet 25

17   CANDOUR

1   What I think I utter, and spend my malice in my breath.
Coriolanus II, 1
Menenius to the tribunes

2   This rudeness is a sauce to his good wit,
Which gives men stomach to digest his words
With better appetite.
Julius Caesar I, 2
Cassius to Brutus on Casca

3   He was wont to speak plain and to the purpose, like an honest
man and a soldier; and now his words are a very fantastical
banquet.
Much Ado About Nothing II, 3
Benedick, concerning Claudio, who has fallen in love

4   Rise, prithee, rise: thou art no flatterer:
I thank thee for it; and heaven forbid
That kings should let their ears hear their faults hid.
Pericles I, 2
Pericles to Helicanus

5   Why, sir, I trust I may have leave to speak;
And speak I will; I am no child, no babe:
Your betters have endured me say my mind,
And if you cannot, best you stop your ears.
The Taming of the Shrew IV, 3
Kate to Petruchio

6   Your plainness and your shortness please me well.
The Taming of the Shrew IV, 4
Baptista to Pedant, pretending to be Lucentio's father

7   Fear not my truth; the moral of my wit
Is 'plain and true'; there's all the reach of it.
Troilus and Cressida IV, 4
Troilus to Cressida

18 CARE

1   The care you have of us,
To mow down thorns that would annoy our foot,
Is worthy praise.
2 Henry VI III, 1
Henry to assembled noblemen

2   O polish'd perturbation! golden care!
That keeps the ports of slumber open wide
To many a watchful night.
2 Henry IV IV, 5
Prince Henry, regarding the crown on the pillow of his dying
father

3   My life itself, and the best heart of it,
Thanks you for this great care: I stood i' the level
Of a full-charged confederacy, and give thanks
To you that choked it.
Henry VIII I, 2
Henry to Wolsey, who has unmasked an alleged plot against the
king

4   What watchful cares do interpose themselves
Betwixt your eyes and night?
Julius Caesar II, 1
Brutus to the conspirators against Caesar

5   'Tis our fast intent
To shake all cares and business from our age,
Conferring them on younger strengths.
King Lear I, 1
Lear, preparing to hand over control of his kingdom to his
children

6   Though care killed a cat, thou hast mettle enough in thee to
kill care.
Much Ado About Nothing V, 1
Claudio to Benedick

7   The care I had and have of subjects' good
    On thee I lay, whose wisdom's strength can bear it.
    Pericles I, 2
    Pericles, about to travel, to Helicanus

8   Say, is my kingdom lost? why, 'twas my care;
    And what loss is it to be rid of care?
    Richard II III, 2
    Richard, preparing himself to face bad news

9   Things past redress are now with me past care.
    Richard II II, 3
    Duke of York, hoping to remain neutral between the king and
    Bolingbroke

10 Care keeps his watch in every old man's eye.
    Romeo and Juliet II, 3
    Friar Lawrence to Romeo

19   CATS

1   I could endure anything before but a cat, and now he's a cat to
    me.
    All's Well That Ends Well IV, 3
    Bertram concerning Parolles

2   I am as vigilant as a cat to steal cream.
    1 Henry IV IV, 2
    Falstaff to Prince Hal

3   Thrice the brinded cat hath mewed.
    Macbeth IV, 1
    First Witch, chanting a charm

4 Letting 'I dare not' wait upon, 'I would',
Like the poor cat i' the adage.
Macbeth I, 7
Lady Macbeth urging Macbeth to murder Duncan
The adage refers to the cat that would eat fish but fears to wet its
paws

5 A harmless necessary cat.
The Merchant of Venice IV, 1
Shylock to Duke

6 What though care killed a cat, thou hast mettle enough in thee
to kill care.
Much Ado About Nothing V, 1
Claudio to Benedick

7 They'll take suggestion as a cat laps milk.
The Tempest II, 1
Antonio to Sebastian

20 CAUSE

1 And now remains
That we find out the cause of this effect,
Or rather say, the cause of this defect.
Hamlet II, 2
Polonius, being facetious about Hamlet's supposed madness

2 God befriend us, as our cause is just!
1 Henry IV V, 1
King to Prince Henry, before meeting a powerful force of rebels

3 I could not die anywhere so contented as in the king's
company; his cause being just and his quarrel honourable.
Henry V IV, 1
King Henry, incognito, to some soldiers

4 There is occasions and causes why and wherefore in all things.
Henry V V, 1
Fluellen to Gower

5 By virtue of that ring, I take my cause
Out of the gripes of cruel men and give it
To a most noble judge, the king my master.
Henry VIII V, 3
Archbishop Cranmer to accusing councillors, revealing a
protective ring given him by King Henry

6 What need we any spur but our own cause
To prick us to redress.
Julius Caesar II, 1
Brutus to other conspirators against Caesar

7 I know no personal cause to spurn at him,
But for the general. He would be crown'd.
Julius Caesar II, 1
Brutus, soliloquizing on Caesar

8   For certain
He cannot buckle his distemper'd cause
Within the belt of rule.
Macbeth V, 2
Caithness to Scottish noblemen, on Macbeth

9 It is the cause, it is the cause, my soul.
Othello V, 2
Othello to himself, before murdering Desdemona

10 Cousin of Hereford, as thy cause is right,
So be thy fortune in this royal fight.
Richard II I, 3
Richard to Bolingbroke

21 CHANGE

1   This world is not for aye, nor 'tis not strange
    That even our loves should with our fortunes change.
    Hamlet III, 2
    Player King to Player Queen in the 'Mousetrap' play

2   This is the state of man: he puts forth
    The tender leaves of hopes; tomorrow blossoms,
    And bears his blushing honours thick upon him;
    The third day comes a frost, a killing frost,
    And when he thinks, good easy man, full surely
    His greatness is a-ripening, nips his root,
    And then he falls, as I do.
    Henry VIII III, 2
    Cardinal Wolsey to himself

3   Hark, in thine ear. Change places, and handy-dandy, which is
    the justice, which is the thief?
    King Lear IV, 6
    Lear, suffering madness, to Earl of Gloucester

4   The love of wicked friends converts to fear;
    That fear to hate, and hate turns one or both
    To worthy danger and deserved death.
    Richard II V, 1
    Richard to Earl of Northumberland, who has helped
    Bolingbroke depose him

5   Our solemn hymns to sullen dirges change;
    Our bridal flowers serve for a buried corse,
    And all things change them to the contrary.
    Romeo and Juliet IV, 5
    Capulet, believing Juliet to have died suddenly

6   If once I find thee ranging,
    Hortensio will be quit with thee by changing.
    The Taming of the Shrew III, 1
    Hortensio to himself, concerning Bianca, who favours Lucentio

7   Old fashions please me best.
    The Taming of the Shrew III, 1
    Bianca to Hortensio

8   Now the melancholy god protect thee, and the tailor make thy
    doublet of changeable taffeta, for thy mind is a very opal.
    Twelfth Night II, 4
    Clown Feste to Duke Orsino

9   Sure this robe of mine
    Doth change my disposition.
    The Winter's Tale IV, 4
    Perdita to Florizel. A supposed shepherdess, she is wearing a
    regal fancy dress

10 For thy sweet love remember'd such wealth brings
    That then I scorn to change my state with kings.
    Sonnet 29

22   CHARMS

1   Damsel of France, I think I have you fast:
    Unchain your spirits now with spelling charms,
    And try if they can gain your liberty.
    1 Henry VI V, 3
    Duke of York to Joan of Arc, captured

2   Here stood he in the dark, his sharp sword out,
    Mumbling of wicked charms, conjuring the moon.
    King Lear II, 1
    Edmund, lying about his brother Edgar to their father

3   Thrice to thine, and thrice to mine,
    And thrice again, to make up nine.
    Peace! the charm's wound up.
    Macbeth I, 3
    The three witches' charm

4   I, the mistress of your charms,
The close contriver of all harms.
Macbeth III, 5
Hecate, chief of the witches

5   I bear a charmed life, which must not yield
To one of woman born.
Macbeth V, 8
Macbeth, believing himself protected

6 We are simple men; we do not know what's brought to pass under the profession of fortune-telling. She works by charms, by spells.
The Merry Wives of Windsor IV, 2
Ford, concerning Mrs Ford's maid's aunt

7   I will a round unvarnish'd tale deliver
Of my whole course of love: what drugs,
    what charms,
What conjuration, and what mighty magic.
Othello I, 3
Othello ridicules the idea that he has used charms to win Desdemona

8   Your charm so strongly works 'em,
That if you now beheld them, your affections
Would become tender.
The Tempest V, 1
Ariel to Prospero, whose magic charms have brought his usurping brother and companions to his island

9   Now my charms are all o'erthrown
And what strength I have's mine own.
The Tempest Epilogue
Prospero

10 By some illusion see thou bring her here:
I'll charm his eyes against she do appear.
A Midsummer Night's Dream III, 2
Oberon to Puck, wishing to bring Helena and Demetrius together

23   CHASTITY

1   Virginity is peevish, proud, idle, made of self-love, which is the most inhibited sin in the canon. Keep it not.
All's Well That Ends Well I, 1
Parolles to Helena

2   My chastity's the jewel of our house,
Bequeathed down from many ancestors;
Which were the greatest obloquy i' the world
In me to lose.
All's Well That Ends Well IV, 2
Diana to Bertram

3   I thought her
As chaste as unsunn'd snow.
Cymbeline II, 5
Posthumus, soliloquizing on his wife

4   Weigh what loss your honour may sustain
If with too credent ear you list his songs,
Or lose your heart, or your chaste treasure open
To his unmaster'd importunity.
Hamlet I, 3
Laertes to Ophelia, concerning Hamlet

5   Then, Isabel, live chaste, and, brother, die;
More than our brother is our chastity.
Measure for Measure II, 4
Isabella, as a novice-nun, deciding that her virtue is more
important than her brother's life

6   If I live to be as old as Sibylla, I will die as chaste as Diana, unless I be obtained by the manner of my father's will.
The Merchant of Venice I, 2
Portia to Nerissa

7   If I know more of any man alive
Than that which maiden modesty doth warrant,
Let all my sins lack mercy!
Much Ado About Nothing IV, 1
Hero to Friar Francis

8   You, my lord, best know . . .
                    my past life
Hath been as continent, as chaste, as true,
As I am now unhappy.
The Winter's Tale III, 2
Hermione to Leontes

9   There my white stole of chastity I daff'd,
Shook off my sober guards and civil fears.
A Lover's Complaint Stanza 43

10 Pure chastity is rifled of her store,
And Lust, the thief, far poorer than before.
The Rape of Lucrece Stanza 99

11 Therefore, despite of fruitless chastity,
Love-lacking vestals and self-loving nuns,
That on the earth would breed a scarcity
And barren dearth of daughters and of sons,
Be prodigal.
Venus and Adonis Stanza 126

24   CHILDREN

1   'Tis such fools as you
That makes the world full of ill-favour'd children.
As You Like It III, 5
Rosalind to Silvius, who unduly flatters his scornful mistress

2   O that it could be proved
That some night-tripping fairy had exchanged
In cradle-clothes our children where they lay!
1 Henry IV I, 1
The king, regretting that his son's reputation is inferior to
Hotspur's

3 How sharper than a serpent's tooth it is
To have a thankless child.
King Lear I, 4
King Lear to Goneril

4 Bring forth men children only;
For thy undaunted mettle should compose
Nothing but males.
Macbeth I, 7
Macbeth to his wife

5 It is a wise father that knows his own child.
The Merchant of Venice II, 2
Launcelot Gobbo to his blind father

6 'Tis not good that children should know any wickedness.
The Merry Wives of Windsor II, 2
Mrs Quickly to Falstaff

7 Woe to that land that's govern'd by a child.
Richard III II, 3
A citizen, before the murder of the two young princes

8 Your children were vexation to your youth,
But mine shall be a comfort to your age.
Richard III IV, 4
Richard to former queen, wife to Edward IV

9 If children pre-decease progenitors,
We are their offspring, and they none of ours.
The Rape of Lucrece Stanza 251

10 A decrepit father takes delight
To see his active child do deeds of youth.
Sonnet 37

25   COMFORT

1   He that doth the ravens feed,
Yea, providently caters for the sparrow,
Be comfort to my age!
As You Like It II, 3
The old servant, Adam, is offering to help his young master,
Orlando

2   Thou art all the comfort
The gods will diet me with.
Cymbeline III, 4
Imogen, who is helped by Pisanio when her husband wrongly
accuses her of unfaithfulness

3   Society is no comfort
To one not sociable.
Cymbeline IV, 2
Imogen to Guiderius

4 *Capucius:*   The king
                Sends you his princely commendations
                And heartily entreats you take good
                comfort.
Katharine: O my good lord, that comfort comes too
                late;
                'Tis like a pardon after execution.
Henry VIII IV, 2
The ambassador of Charles V is visiting King Henry's wife

5   Entreat the north
To make his bleak winds kiss my parched lips,
And comfort me with cold . . .
I beg cold comfort.
King John V, 7
The king to his son, Henry

6 My soul hath her content so absolute
That not another comfort like to this
Succeeds.
Othello II, 1
Othello to Desdemona

7   The heavens forbid
But that our loves and comforts should increase,
Even as our days do grow.
Othello II, 1
Desdemona to Othello

8   What comfort have we now?
By heaven, I'll hate him everlastingly
That bids me be of comfort any more.
Richard II III, 2
Richard, after receiving increasingly bad news

9 Comfort's in heaven, and we are on the earth,
Where nothing lives but crosses, cares, and griefs.
Richard II II, 2
Duke of York, the king's supporter, unhappy with his position

10 All comfort that the dark night can afford
Be to thy person.
Richard III V, 3
Earl of Richmond to the Earl of Derby

---

26 CONQUEST

---

1   You did know
How much you were my conqueror, and that
My sword, made weak by my affection, would
Obey it on all cause.
Antony and Cleopatra III, 11
Antony to Cleopatra

2   He that can endure
To follow with allegiance a fall'n lord
Does conquer him that did his master conquer.
Antony and Cleopatra III, 13
Enobarbus to himself

3 So it should be, that none but Antony
   Should conquer Antony.
   Antony and Cleopatra IV, 15
   Cleopatra to Antony

4 A peace is of the nature of a conquest;
   For then both parties nobly are subdued,
   And neither party loser.
   2 Henry IV IV, 2
   Archbishop of York to Prince John of Lancaster and others

5 He saw me and yielded; that I may justly say, with the hook-
   nosed fellow of Rome, 'I came, saw, and overcame'.
   2 Henry IV IV, 3
   Falstaff compares his capture of Sir John Colevile to Caesar's conquest of
   Britain

6 O mighty Caesar! dost thou lie so low?
   Are all thy conquests, glories, triumphs, spoils,
   Shrunk to this little measure?
   Julius Caesar III, 1
   Antony, over Caesar's body

7 Wherefore rejoice? What conquest brings he home?
   Julius Caesar I, 1
   Marullus, denigrating Caesar

8 If we be conquered, let men conquer us,
   And not those bastard Bretons, whom your fathers
   Have in their own land beaten, bobb'd, and thump'd.
   Richard III V, 3
   Richard in his boastful oration to his troops before the battle of
   Bosworth

9 That England, that was wont to conquer others,
   Hath made a shameful conquest of itself.
   Richard II II, 1
   John of Gaunt, criticizing the state of England

27 COURAGE
see also **Valour** 184

1   He did look far
Into the service of the time, and was
Discipled of the bravest.
All's Well That Ends Well I, 2
King of France concerning Bertram's father

2   What's brave, what's noble,
Let's do it after the high Roman fashion,
And make death proud to take us.
Antony and Cleopatra IV, 15
Cleopatra, after Antony's death

3   Husband, I come:
Now to that name my courage prove my title.
Antony and Cleopatra V, 2
Cleopatra to herself, thinking of Antony

4   As heart can think: there is not such a word
Spoke of in Scotland as this term of fear.
1 Henry IV IV, 1
Douglas to Hotspur

5   Full bravely hast thou flesh'd
Thy maiden sword.
1 Henry IV V, 4
Prince Henry to his brother, John of Lancaster

6   Gloucester, 'ts true that we are in great danger;
The greater therefore should our courage be.
King Henry V IV, 1
King to Duke of Gloucester, before the battle of Agincourt

7   Fearless minds climb sooner unto crowns.
3 Henry VI IV, 7
Duke of Gloucester, later Richard III

8 Why, courage, then! what cannot be avoided
   'Twere childish weakness to lament or fear.
   3 Henry VI V, 4
   Queen Margaret to Lords

9 By how much unexpected, by so much
   We must awake endeavour for defence;
   For courage mounteth with occasion.
   King John II, 1
   Duke of Austria to King of France

10 Screw your courage to the sticking-place
   And we'll not fail.
   Macbeth I, 7
   Lady Macbeth to her husband

11 He hath borne himself beyond the promise of his age, doing, in
   the figure of a lamb, the feats of a lion.
   Much Ado About Nothing I, 1
   Messenger concerning Claudio

---

28 DANCING

---

1   So, to your pleasures:
   I am for other than dancing measures.
   As You Like It V, 4
   Jaques to his companions

2 They bid us to the English dancing-schools,
   And teach lavoltas high and swift corantos;
   Saying our grace is only in our heels.
   Henry V III, 5
   Duke of Bourbon, complaining of the attitude of French ladies
   to French nobles

3   Your Grace,
I fear, with dancing is a little heated . . .
              There's fresher air, my lord,
In the next chamber.
Henry VIII I, 4
Wolsey to King Henry

4   Say to her, we have measured many miles
To tread a measure with her on this grass.
Love's Labour's Lost V, 2
King of Navarre to Boyet, concerning Rosaline

5   If you will patiently dance in our round,
And see our moonlight revels, go with us.
A Midsummer Night's Dream II, 1
Titania to Oberon

6   Sound, music! Come, my queen, take hands with me,
And rock the ground whereon these sleepers be.
A Midsummer Night's Dream IV, 1
Oberon to Titania

7   Come now, what masques, what dances shall we have,
To wear away this long age of three hours?
A Midsummer Night's Dream V, 1
Theseus to Lysander and others

8 Let's have a dance ere we are married, that we may lighten our
own hearts, and our wives' heels.
Much Ado About Nothing V, 4
Benedick to Claudio and others

9   You have dancing shoes with nimble soles.
Romeo and Juliet I, 4
Romeo to Mercutio

10 You and I are past our dancing days.
Romeo and Juliet I, 5
Capulet to his cousin

11 When you do dance, I wish you
  A wave o' the sea, that you might ever do
  Nothing but that.
  The Winter's Tale IV, 4
  Florizel to Perdita

12 Bid me discourse, I will enchant thine ear . . .
  Or like a nymph with long dishevell'd hair,
  Dance on the sands, and yet no footing seen.
  Venus and Adonis Stanza 25

29 DANGER

1   You must not think
  That we are made of stuff so flat and dull
  That we can let our beard be shook with danger
  And think it pastime.
  Hamlet IV, 7
  King Claudius to Laertes, with reference to Hamlet

2 For, though I am not splenetive and rash,
  Yet have I in me something dangerous,
  Which let thy wisdom fear.
  Hamlet V, 1
  Hamlet, warning Laertes during a struggle

3 Out of this nettle, danger, we pluck this flower, safety.
  1 Henry IV II, 3
  Hotspur, defying a warning letter

4 There's not a dangerous action can peep out his head, but I am
thrust upon it.
  2 Henry IV I, 2
  Falstaff, professing heroism

5   I must go and seek my danger there
Or it will seek me in another place,
And find me worse provided.
2 Henry IV II, 3
Earl of Northumberland to his wife and daughter

6   Now thou art come unto a feast of death,
A terrible and unavoided danger.
1 Henry VI IV, 5
Lord Talbot to his son, before battle

7   Into what dangers would you lead me, Cassius,
That you would have me seek into myself
For that which is not in me?
Julius Caesar I, 2
Brutus to Cassius

8   Yond Cassius has a lean and hungry look;
He thinks too much: such men are dangerous.
Julius Caesar I, 2
Caesar to Antony

9   Danger knows full well
That Caesar is more dangerous than he.
Julius Caesar II, 2
Caesar to his wife

10   Go closely in with me:
Much danger do I undergo for thee.
King John IV, 1
Hubert de Burgh to young Arthur, having disobeyed the king's
order to kill the boy

11   She loved me for the dangers I had passed,
And I loved her that she did pity them.
Othello I, 3
Othello, on his early contact with Desdemona

30 DAUGHTERS

1   I am by birth a shepherd's daughter
    My wit untrain'd in any kind of art.
    1 Henry VI I, 2
    Joan of Arc to Dauphin

2   Thy youngest daughter does not love thee least;
    Nor are those empty-hearted whose low sound
    Reverbs no hollowness.
    King Lear I, 1
    Earl of Kent to Lear, in defence of Cordelia

3   The dear father
    Would with his daughter speak.
    King Lear II, 4
    Lear, ironically, angry at Regan's failure to welcome him

4   I prithee, daughter, do not make me mad.
    King Lear II, 4
    Lear to Goneril

5   Alack, what heinous sin is it in me
    To be ashamed to be my father's child!
    But though I am a daughter to his blood,
    I am not to his manners.
    The Merchant of Venice II, 3
    Jessica to Launcelot Gobbo, Shylock's servant

6   I would my daughter were dead at my foot.
    The Merchant of Venice III, 1
    Shylock, on learning that Jessica has stolen his treasure

7   O thou foul thief, where hast thou stow'd my
        daughter?
    Damn'd as thou art, thou hast enchanted her.
    Othello I, 2
    Brabantio to Othello, on learning of Desdemona's marriage to
    him

8 Thou hast bewitch'd my daughter, and thou art
A villain.

Pericles II, 5
Simonides to Pericles. Fortunately the anger was only assumed

9 *Baptista:* What, will my daughter prove a good
musician?
Hortensio: I think she'll sooner prove a soldier!

The Taming of the Shrew II, 1
Katherina has broken a lute over Hortensio's head

10 Call you me daughter? now, I promise you
You have shown a tender fatherly regard,
To wish me wed to one half lunatic,

The Taming of the Shrew II, 1
Katherina, after her first meeting with Petruchio

11 My father had a daughter loved a man,
As it might be, perhaps, were I a woman,
I should your lordship.

Twelfth Night II, 4
Viola, as the youth Cesario, to Duke Orsino

---

31 DAY
see also **Morning** 114

---

1 The bright day is done,
And we are for the dark.

Antony and Cleopatra V, 2
Iras to Cleopatra. Antony is dead, and Cleopatra the captive of
Octavius Caesar

2 I tell thee truly, herald,
I know not if the day be ours or no.

Henry V IV, 7
Henry to French herald at the battle of Agincourt

3 If it be a hot day and I brandish anything but a bottle, I would I might never spit white again.
2 Henry IV I, 2
Falstaff to the Chief Justice

    4 It is the bright day that brings forth the adder,
      And that craves wary walking.
    Julius Caesar II, 1
    Brutus, meditating on Caesar

5 The posterior of this day, which the rude multitude call the afternoon.
Love's Labour's Lost V, 1
Armado to Holofernes

    6 So foul and fair a day I have not seen.
    Macbeth I, 3
    Macbeth, returning with Banquo from battle

    7   Come, seeling night,
      Scarf up the tender eye of pitiful day.
    Macbeth III, 2
    Macbeth, before the murder of Banquo

    8 The nightingale, if she should sing by day,
      When every goose is cackling, would be thought
      No better a musician than the wren.
    The Merchant of Venice V, 1
    Portia to Nerissa

    9 Fair love, you faint with wandering in the wood,
      And to speak truth, I have forget our way;
      We'll rest us, Hermia, if you think it good,
      And tarry for the comfort of the day.
    A Midsummer Night's Dream II, 2
    Lysander, helping Hermia in a flight from a forced marriage

    10 Night's candles are burnt out, and jocund day
      Stands tiptoe on the misty mountain-tops.
    Romeo and Juliet III, 5
    Romeo, reluctantly aware of the dawn

11   The busy day,
Waked by the lark hath rous'd the ribald crows,
And dreaming night will hide our joys no longer.
Troilus and Cressida IV, 2
Troilus to Cressida

---

32 DEATH

1 Golden lads and girls all must,
As chimney-sweepers, come to dust.
Cymbeline IV, 2
Song by Guiderius

2 The dread of something after death —
The undiscover'd country from whose bourn
No traveller returns.
Hamlet III, 1
Hamlet, meditating on suicide

3 He is dead and gone, lady,
 He is dead and gone;
At his head a grass-green turf,
 At his heels a stone.
Hamlet IV, 5
Ophelia, singing a mad song

4 This fell sergeant, Death,
Is strict in his arrest.
Hamlet V, 2
Hamlet, dying, to Horatio

5 Death, as the psalmist saith, is certain to all: all shall die.
2 Henry IV III, 2
Justice Shallow reflects on the number of his old acquaintances who are now dead

6   A man can but die once; we owe God a death.
2 Henry IV III, 2
Feeble, a recruit who belies his name, to Bardolph

7   But now the arbitrator of despair,
Just death, kind umpire of men's miseries,
With sweet enlargement doth dismiss me hence.
1 Henry VI II, 5
Edmund Mortimer, approaching death, to his gaolers

8   Death, a necessary end,
Will come when it will come.
Julius Caesar II, 2
Caesar to his wife

9   He that cuts off twenty years of life
Cuts off so many years of fearing death.
Julius Caesar III, 1
Cassius, attempting to prove that killing Caesar was doing him a kindness

10   Have I not hideous death within my view,
Retaining but a quantity of life
Which bleeds away.
King John V, 4
A wounded French lord on the battlefield

11   Men must endure
Their going hence, even as their coming hither:
Ripeness is all.
King Lear V, 2
Edgar to his father

12   Duncan is in his grave;
After Life's fitful fever he sleeps well.
Macbeth III, 2
Macbeth, almost envying the man he has murdered

13   Nothing in his life
Became him like the leaving of it: he died
As one that had been studied in his death,
To throw away the dearest thing he owed.
Macbeth I, 4
Malcolm, reporting to Duncan the execution of the Thane of
Cawdor

14   The weariest and most loathed worldly life
That age, ache, penury, and imprisonment
Can lay on nature is a paradise
To what we fear of death.
Measure for Measure III, 1
Claudio, under sentence of death, to his sister

15 A man that apprehends death no more dreadfully but as a
drunken sleep.
Measure for Measure IV, 2
Provost to the Duke, concerning a hardened criminal

16   Death's a great disguiser.
Measure for Measure IV, 2
Duke to the Provost

17   Cry woe, destruction, ruin and decay;
The worst is death, and death will have his day.
Richard II III, 2
Richard, trying to be philosophical over his misfortunes

18   'Tis a vile thing to die, my gracious lord,
When men are unprepared and look not for it.
Richard III III, 2
Sir William Catesby to Lord Hastings, who, unknown to
himself, will shortly be executed

19   Death, that hath suck'd the honey of thy breath,
Hath had no power yet upon thy beauty.
Romeo and Juliet V, 3
Romeo to Juliet, believing her dead

20 He that dies pays all debts.
The Tempest III, 2
Stephano, alarmed by mysterious sounds

21 Come away, come away, death,
And in sad cypress let me be laid;
Fly away, fly away, breath;
I am slain by a cruel fair maid.
Twelfth Night II, 4
Feste, singing to Orsino

22 If thou survive my well-contented day
When that churl Death my bones with dust shall
    cover . . .
O, then vouchsafe me but this loving thought.
Sonnet 32

33 DEEDS

1   It is great
To do that thing that ends all other deeds.
Antony and Cleopatra V, 2
Cleopatra, awaiting capture by Octavius Caesar

2   He covets less
Than misery itself would give: rewards
His deeds with doing them.
Coriolanus II, 2
Cominius, stressing Coriolanus's freedom from greed

3   Foul deeds will rise,
Though all the earth o'erwhelm them, to men's eyes.
Hamlet I, 2
Hamlet to himself, after being told that the ghost of his father
has been seen

4 'Tis a kind of good deed to say well:
   And yet words are no deeds.
   Henry VIII III, 2
   The king to Cardinal Wolsey

5 They that have done this deed are honourable.
   Julius Caesar III, 2
   Antony over Caesar's body, with hidden irony

6 *Macbeth:* How now, you secret, black, and midnight
                   hags!
               What is't you do?
   Witches: A deed without a name.
   Macbeth IV, 1
   The deed is the brewing of charms

7   No boasting like a fool;
   This deed I'll do before the purpose cool.
   Macbeth IV, 1
   Macbeth, deciding to attack Macduff

8 I give thee thanks in part of thy deserts,
   And will with deeds requite thy gentleness.
   Titus Andronicus I, 1
   Saturninus to Titus

9 Go in and cheer the town: we'll forth and fight,
   Do deeds worth praise, and tell you them at night.
   Troilus and Cressida V, 3
   Hector to Priam

10 They look into the beauty of thy mind,
    And that, in guess, they measure by thy deeds.
    Sonnet 69

34 DELIGHT

1 The business that we love we rise betime,
And go to't with delight.
Antony and Cleopatra IV, 4
Antony, discussing war with a soldier

2 Man delights not me; no, nor woman neither.
Hamlet II, 2
Hamlet to Rosencrantz

3 All delights are vain; but that most vain,
Which, with pain purchased, doth inherit pain.
Love's Labour's Lost I, 1
Biron to King of Navarre

4 I pray thee, let us go and find him out,
And quicken his embraced heaviness
With some delight or other.
The Merchant of Venice II, 8
Salanio to Salarino, concerning Antonio

5 The labour we delight in physics pain.
Macbeth II, 3
Macbeth, conducting Macduff to the door of King Duncan's
room

6 I know a bank whereon the wild thyme blows . . .
There sleeps Titania some time of the night,
Lull'd in these flowers with dances and delight.
A Midsummer Night's Dream II, 1
Oberon to Puck

7 Say, what abridgement have you for this evening? . . .
How shall we beguile
The lazy time, if not with some delight?
A Midsummer Night's Dream V, 1
Duke Theseus to Master of the Revels

8 These violent delights have violent ends.
Romeo and Juliet II, 6
Friar Laurence to Romeo

9 I know she taketh most delight
In music, instruments, and poetry.
The Taming of the Shrew I, 1
Baptista on Bianca

10   The isle is full of noises,
Sounds and sweet airs, that give delight and hurt not.
The Tempest III, 2
Caliban, strangely poetical, to Stephano and Trinculo

11 Music to hear, why hear'st thou music sadly?
Sweets with sweets war not, joy delights in joy.
Sonnet 8

35 DESTINY
see also **Fate 50**

1 Imperious Caesar, dead and turn'd to clay,
Might stop a hole to keep the wind away.
Hamlet V, 1
Hamlet at Ophelia's graveside

2 There's a divinity that shapes our ends,
Rough-hew them how we will.
Hamlet V, 2
Hamlet to Horatio

3 Here burns my candle out; ay, here it dies,
Which, whiles it lasted, gave King Henry light.
3 Henry VI II, 6
Lord Clifford as he lies dying

4 I have touch'd the highest point of all my greatness:
And, from that full meridian of all my glory,
I haste now to my setting.
Henry VIII III, 2
Cardinal Wolsey, after having offended the king

5 Think you I bear the shears of destiny?
Have I commandment on the pulse of life?
King John IV, 3
John, repudiating responsibility for Prince Arthur's death

6 The ancient saying is no heresy,
Hanging and wiving goes by destiny.
The Merchant of Venice II, 9
Nerissa to Portia

7 They say there's a divinity in odd numbers, either in nativity,
chance, or death.
The Merry Wives of Windsor V, 1
Falstaff to Mistress Quickly

8 A man whom both the waters and the wind,
In that vast tennis-court, have made the ball
For them to play upon.
Pericles II, 1
Pericles, about himself

9 They that stand high have many blasts to shake them;
And if they fall, they dash themselves to pieces.
Richard III I, 3
Queen Margaret to nobles

---

36   DEVIL

1   The spirit I have seen
May be the devil; and the devil hath power
To assume a pleasing shape.
Hamlet II, 2
Hamlet, soliloquizing

2   'Tis too much proved, that with devotion's visage
And pious action we do sugar o'er
The devil himself.
Hamlet III, 1
Polonius to King Claudius

3   How agrees the devil and thee about thy soul, that thou soldest him on Good Friday.
1 Henry IV I, 2
Poins to Falstaff

4   He was never yet a breaker of proverbs; he will give the devil his due.
1 Henry IV I, 2
Prince Hal to Poins, concerning Falstaff

5   I can teach thee, coz, to shame the devil
By telling truth: tell truth and shame the devil.
1 Henry IV III, 1
Hotspur to Owen Glendower

6   What! Can the devil speak true?
Macbeth I, 3
Banquo, when a witch's prophecy is confirmed

7   'Tis the eye of childhood
That fears a painted devil.
Macbeth II, 2
Lady Macbeth to her husband, who is unwilling to re-enter the room in which he has slain Duncan

8   The devil damn thee black, thou cream-faced loon!
Macbeth V, 3
Macbeth to a servant bringing bad news

9   The devil can quote Scripture for his purpose.
The Merchant of Venice I, 3
Antonio to Bassanio, concerning Shylock

10   (He) sees more devils than vast hell can hold.
A Midsummer Night's Dream V, 1
Theseus, referring to a lunatic

11   And thus I clothe my naked villany . . .
And seem a saint when most I play the devil.
Richard III I, 3
Richard to himself

12   Why, he's a devil, a devil, a very fiend.
The Taming of the Shrew III, 2
Gremio, describing Petruchio's wedding behaviour in church

37 DOGS

1 Thy words are too precious to be cast away upon curs; throw
some of them at me.
As You Like It I, 3
Celia to Rosalind

2 Let Hercules himself do what he may,
The cat will mew, and dog will have his day.
Hamlet V, 1
Wild words from Hamlet to Laertes

3 I had rather be a dog and bay the moon
Than such a Roman.
Julius Caesar IV, 3
Brutus to Cassius, on the accepting of bribes

4 Thou hast seen a farmer's dog bark at a beggar?
King Lear IV, 6
Lear to Earl of Gloucester

5   Mine enemy's dog
Though he had bit me, should have stood that night
Against my fire.
King Lear IV, 7
Cordelia, stressing the horror of a stormy night

6   I am Sir Oracle,
And, when I ope my lips, let no dog bark!

The Merchant of Venice I, 1
Gratiano, imitating pompous pretenders to wisdom

7   Dogs bark at me as I halt by them.

Richard III I, 1
Richard, complaining of his ugliness

8 One that I brought up of a puppy . . . I'll be sworn,
I have sat in the stocks for puddings he hath stolen, otherwise
he had been executed.

The Two Gentlemen of Verona IV, 4
Launce on his dog, Crab

---

38 DREAMS

---

1 I dream'd there was an emperor Antony,
O, such another sleep, that I might see
But such another man!

Antony and Cleopatra V, 2
Cleopatra, after Antony's death

2 I could be bounded in a nutshell, and count myself a king of
infinite space, were it not that I have bad dreams.

Hamlet II, 2
Hamlet to Rosencrantz

3 A dream itself is but a shadow.

Hamlet II, 2
Hamlet to Rosencrantz

4   To die, to sleep;
To sleep! perchance to dream: ay, there's the rub;
For in that sleep of death what dreams may come,
When we have shuffled off this mortal coil,
Must give us pause.

Hamlet III, 1
Hamlet, soliloquizing

5   *Soothsayer:* Beware the ides of March.
    Caesar: He is a dreamer; let us leave him.
    Julius Caesar I, 2

6   Between the acting of a dreadful thing
    And the first motion, all the interim is
    Like a phantasma, or a hideous dream.
    Julius Caesar II, 1
    Brutus to himself

7   There is some ill a-brewing towards my nest,
    For I did dream of money-bags tonight.
    The Merchant of Venice II, 5
    Shylock to Jessica

8   And, gentle Puck, take this transformed scalp
    From off the head of this Athenian swain;
    That he . . .
    May all to Athens back again repair,
    And think no more of this night's accidents
    But as the fierce vexation of a dream.
    A Midsummer Night's Dream IV, 1
    Oberon concerning Bottom

9 I have had a dream past the wit of man to say what dream it was.
  A Midsummer Night's Dream IV, 1
  Bottom to himself

10   Swift as a shadow, short as any dream.
     A Midsummer Night's Dream I, 1
     Lysander to Hermia, on the course of true love

11   This is the rarest dream that e'er dull sleep
     Did mock sad fools withal.
     Pericles V, 1
     Pericles to himself

12   O, I have passed a miserable night,
So full of ugly sights, of ghastly dreams.
Richard III I, 4
Duke of Clarence, shortly before being murdered

13   For never yet one hour in his bed
Did I enjoy the golden dew of sleep,
But with his timorous dreams was still awak'd.
Richard III IV, 1
Anne concerning Richard

14   I talk of dreams;
Which are the children of an idle brain,
Begot of nothing but vain fantasy.
Romeo and Juliet I, 4
Mercutio to Romeo

15   If I may trust the flattering truth of sleep,
My dreams presage some joyful news at hand.
Romeo and Juliet V, 1
Romeo to himself

16   I dreamt my lady came and found me dead —
Strange dream that gives a dead man leave to think! —
And breath'd such life with kisses in my lips,
That I revived and was an emperor.
Romeo and Juliet V, 1
Romeo to himself

17   We are such stuff
As dreams are made on; and our little life
Is rounded with a sleep.
The Tempest IV, 1
Prospero to Ferdinand

18   All days are nights to see till I see thee,
And nights bright days when dreams do show thee
me.
Sonnet 43

39   DRESS

1   The soul of this man is his clothes.
All's Well That Ends Well II, 5
Lafeu to Bertram, concerning Parolles

2   Winter garments must be lined,
So must slender Rosalind.
As You Like It III, 2
Touchstone, making fun of Orlando's poetic tributes to Rosalind

3   Thou villain base,
Knowst me not by my clothes?
Cymbeline IV, 2
Self-important Cloten to Guiderius

4   Costly thy habit as thy purse can buy,
But not express'd in fancy; rich, not gaudy:
For the apparel oft proclaims the man.
Hamlet I, 3
Polonius, giving advice to Laertes

5   Lord Hamlet, with his doublet all unbrac'd;
No hat upon his head, his stockings foul'd,
Ungartered, and down-gyved to his ankle.
Hamlet II, 1
Ophelia to Polonius, indicating Hamlet's apparent mental
disturbance

6   I have cases of buckram for the nonce, to mask our noted outer
garments.
1 Henry IV I, 2
Poins, planning with Prince Hal a mock robbery

7   It yearns me not if men my garments wear;
Such outward things dwell not in my desires.
Henry V IV, 3
Henry to Earl of Westmoreland

8 Their clothes are after such a pagan cut too,
That, sure, they've worn out Christendom.
Henry VIII I, 3
Lord Chamberlain to Lord Sandys, concerning the French

9 Give me your gloves, I'll wear them for your sake.
The Merchant of Venice IV, 1
Balthasar to Bassanio, after successfully defeating Shylock

10 Fashion wears out more apparel than the man.
Much Ado About Nothing III, 3
Conrade to Borachio

11 Thy garments are not spotted with our blood.
Richard III I, 3
Queen Margaret to Duke of Buckingham

12 Petruchio is coming in a new hat and an old jerkin, a pair of old
breeches thrice turned, a pair of boots that have been candle-
cases, one buckled, the other laced.
The Taming of the Shrew III, 2
Baptista's servant to his master

13   Now, my honey love,
We will return unto thy father's house . . .
With silken coats and caps and golden rings,
With ruffs and cuffs and fardingales and things.
The Taming of the Shrew IV, 3
Petruchio to Katherina

14   So tedious is this day
As is the night before some festival
To an impatient child that hath new robes
And may not wear them.
Romeo and Juliet III, 2
Juliet to herself

15 Thy gown? Why, ay; come, tailor, let us see't . . .
What's this? a sleeve? 'tis like a demi-cannon:
What, up and down, carved like an apple-tart?
Here's snip and nip and cut and slish and slash.
The Taming of the Shrew IV, 3
Petruchio being deliberately hard to please

16 A silken doublet! a velvet hose! a scarlet cloak!
The Taming of the Shrew V, 1
Vincentio, shocked at the finery apparently worn by his son's
servant

17 Our garments, being as they were, drenched in the sea, hold
notwithstanding, their freshness and glosses, being rather
new-dyed than stained with salt water.
The Tempest II, 1
Gonzalo, wrecked on Prospero's island, to his companions

18 He will come to her in yellow stockings, and 'tis a colour she
abhors, and cross-gartered, a fashion she detests.
Twelfth Night II, 5
Maria, having tricked Malvolio into believing that Olivia will admire him

40 DRINKING

1 I am one that loves a cup of hot wine.
Coriolanus II, 1
Menenius to the tribunes

2 Drunkenness is his best virtue.
All's Well That Ends Well IV, 3
Parolles concerning an acquaintance

3 We'll teach you to drink deep ere you depart.
Hamlet I, 2
Hamlet to Horatio

4   O monstrous! one halfpenny-worth of bread to this intolerable deal of sack.
1 Henry IV II, 4
Prince Hal to Peto, concerning a bill in Falstaff's pocket

5   A man cannot make him laugh, but that's no marvel; he drinks no wine.
2 Henry IV IV, 3
Falstaff concerning Prince John of Lancaster

6   If I had a thousand sons, the first humane principle I would teach them should be, to forswear thin potations, and to addict themselves to sack.
2 Henry IV IV, 3
Falstaff to himself

7   A cup of wine that's brisk and fine,
And drink unto the leman mine.
2 Henry IV V, 3
Song by Silence to Falstaff and others

8   I have half a dozen healths
To drink to these fair ladies.
Henry VIII I, 4
King at a party in York Palace

9   Give me some wine. Fill full.
I drink to the general joy of the whole table.
Macbeth III, 4
Macbeth at a banquet just before Banquo's ghost appears

10   Drunk many times a day, if not many days entirely drunk.
Measure for Measure IV, 2
Provost to Duke, concerning one of the prisoners

11   If I be drunk, I'll be drunk with those that have the fear of God, and not with drunken knaves.
The Merry Wives of Windsor I, 1
Slender, who has had his pocket picked while drunk

12   Come gentlemen, I hope we shall drink down all unkindness.
The Merry Wives of Windsor I, 1
Page to disputing acquaintances

13   O God, that men should put an enemy in their mouths to steal away their brains!
Othello II, 1
Cassio to Iago

14   Trinculo is reeling ripe: where should they
Find this grand liquor that hath gilded them?
The Tempest V, 1
Alonso to Sebastian

15   I'll drink to her as long as there is a passage in my throat and drink in Illyria.
Twelfth Night I, 3
Sir Toby Belch, concerning his niece, Countess Olivia

41 DUELLING

1   I dare him
To lay his gay comparisons apart
And answer me declined, sword to sword,
Ourselves alone.
Antony and Cleopatra III, 13
Antony, with a most improbable challenge to Octavius Caesar

2   He gave you such a masterly report
For art and exercise in your defence,
And for your rapier most especially.
Hamlet IV, 7
Claudius passing on to Laertes an expert's tribute to his fencing skill

3 He is every man in no man . . . he will fence with his own shadow.
The Merchant of Venice I, 2
Portia on her suitor, M. Le Bon

4 Why man, he's a very devil . . . I had a pass with him, rapier, scabbard and all, and he gives me the stuck in with such a mortal motion, that it is inevitable.
Twelfth Night III, 4
Sir Toby Belch to Sir Andrew Aguecheek, concerning a pretended opponent

5 An I thought he had been so valiant and cunning in fence, I'd have seen him damned ere I'd have challenged him.
Twelfth Night III, 4
Sir Andrew to Sir Toby

6 He fights as you sing prick-song, keeps time, distance and proportion . . . the very butcher of a silk button, a duellist, a duellist.
Romeo and Juliet II, 4
Mercutio on Tybalt

---

42 DUTY

---

1 My duty, then, shall pay me for my pains.
All's Well That Ends Well II, 1
Helena to King of France

2 Where is our daughter? She hath not appeared . . .
Nor to us hath tender'd
The duty of the day.
Cymbeline III, 5
Cymbeline to Queen, concerning Imogen

3 Every subject's duty is the king's; but every subject's soul is his own.
Henry V IV, 1
Henry, chatting incognito with some soldiers before the battle of Agincourt

4 Though all the world should crack their duty to you,
  And throw it from their soul . . . yet my duty,
  As doth a rock against the chiding flood,
  Should the approach of this wild river break.
  Henry VIII III, 2
  Cardinal Wolsey to the king

5 I should not urge thy duty past thy might.
  Julius Caesar IV, 3
  Brutus to his weary servant boy

6 Thinkst thou that duty shall have dread to speak,
  When power to flattery bows?
  King Lear I, 1
  Earl of Kent, not afraid to speak his mind to Lear

7 Never anything can be amiss,
  When simpleness and duty tender it.
  A Midsummer Night's Dream V, 1
  Theseus, asking to be shown Quince's unsophisticated play

8   My noble father,
  I do perceive here a divided duty.
  Othello I, 3
  Desdemona's duty is divided between her father and her newly-
  married husband

9 My duty pricks me on to utter that
  Which else no worldly good should draw from me.
  The Two Gentlemen of Verona III, 1
  Proteus about to betray his great friend, Valentine, to Duke of
  Milan

10 Fleet-wing'd duty with thought's feathers flies.
   The Rape of Lucrece Stanza 174

11 Lord of my love, to whom in vassalage
   Thy merit hath my duty strongly knit,
   To thee I send this written ambassage,
   To witness duty, not to show my wit.
   Sonnet 26

43   EARTH

1   Where is this young gallant that is so desirous to lie with his mother earth?
As You Like It I, 2
Charles the wrestler, concerning Orlando's wish to accept the strong man's challenge

2   This goodly frame, the earth, seems to me a sterile promontory.
Hamlet II, 2
Hamlet to Rosencrantz and Guildenstern

3   Hold off the earth awhile,
Till I have caught her once more in mine arms.
Hamlet V, 1
Laertes at Ophelia's funeral

4   He made me mad . . . telling me . . .
That it was a great pity, so it was,
That villainous salt-petre should be digg'd
Out of the bowels of the harmless earth.
1 Henry IV I, 3
Hotspur, enraged because an unwarlike lord objected to gunpowder

5   Thy brother's blood the thirsty earth hath drunk,
Broach'd with the steely point of Clifford's lance.
3 Henry VI II, 3
Richard of Gloucester to Earl of Warwick, on the death of the young Earl of Rutland

6   O, pardon me, thou bleeding piece of earth,
That I am meek and gentle with these butchers!
Julius Caesar III, 1
Antony to Caesar's body, after his assassination

7   The earth hath bubbles as the water has,
And these are of them.
Macbeth I, 3
Banquo to Macbeth, concerning the sudden vanishing of the witches they had met

8 I'll put a girdle round about the earth
   In forty minutes.
   A Midsummer Night's Dream II, 1
   Puck to Oberon

9 And nothing can we call our own but death
   And that small model of the barren earth
   Which serves as paste and cover to our bones.
   Richard II III, 2
   Richard has been made unhappy by bad news

10 O mickle is the powerful grace that lies
    In herbs, plants, stones, and their true qualities:
    For nought so vile that on the earth doth live
    But to the earth some special good doth give.
    Romeo and Juliet II, 3
    Friar Laurence, soliloquizing

44 EATING

1 Sit down and feed, and welcome to our table.
   As You Like It II, 7
   Duke Senior to Orlando

2 Perhaps some merchant hath invited him,
   And from the mart he's somewhere gone to dinner.
   Good sister, let us dine.
   The Comedy of Errors II, 1
   Luciana, persuading Adriana not to wait for her husband

3 He has eaten me out of house and home; he hath put all my
   substance into that fat belly of his.
   2 Henry IV II, 1
   Mistress Quickly, concerning Falstaff

4   They are as sick that surfeit with too much, as they that starve with nothing.
    The Merchant of Venice I, 2
    Nerissa to Portia

5   I will make an end of my dinner; there's pippins and cheese to follow.
    The Merry Wives of Windsor I, 2
    Sir Hugh Evans

6   About the sixth hour, when beasts most graze, birds best peck, and men sit down to that nourishment which is called supper.
    Love's Labour's Lost I, 1
    Don Armado, in a letter

7   A surfeit of the sweetest things
        The deepest loathing to the stomach brings.
        A Midsummer Night's Dream II, 2
        Lysander to Hermia, asleep

8   With eager feeding food doth choke the feeder.
    Richard II II, 1
    John of Gaunt, on Richard's excesses

9   'Tis an ill cook that cannot lick his own fingers.
    Romeo and Juliet IV, 2
    Capulet serving-man

10   There's small choice in rotten apples.
    The Taming of the Shrew I, 1
    Hortensio to Gremio

11   I prithee go and get me some repast;
    I care not what, so it be wholesome food.
    The Taming of the Shrew IV, 3
    Kate to Gremio

12   How say you to a fat tripe finely broil'd?
    The Taming of the Shrew IV, 3
    Gremio to Kate

45   ENEMY

1   Sir, you have wrestled well and overthrown
More than your enemies.
As You Like It I, 2
Rosalind to Orlando, after his victory over Charles the Wrestler

2   In cases of defence 'tis best to weigh
The enemy more mighty than he seems.
Henry V II, 4
Dauphin to Constable of France

3   You have many enemies that know not
Why they are so, but, like to village curs,
Bark when their fellows do.
Henry VIII II, 4
King to Cardinal Wolsey

4   I do believe . . .
You are mine enemy, and therefore make my
   challenge
You shall not be my judge.
Henry VIII II, 4
Queen Katherine, accusing Cardinal Wolsey, though mistakenly

5   'Tis better that the enemy seek us:
So shall he waste his means, weary his soldiers.
Julius Caesar IV, 3
Cassius to Brutus

6   We are at the stake,
And bay'd about with many enemies.
Julius Caesar IV, 1
Octavius Caesar to Antony

7   'Tis death to me to be at enmity;
I hate it, and desire all good men's love.
Richard III II, 1
Richard, hypocritically, to assembled lords

8 I do defy him, and spit at him;
   Call him a slanderous coward and a villain.
   Richard II I, 1
   Thomas Mowbray, at enmity with Henry Bolingbroke

46 ENGLAND

1 It was always the trick of our English nation, if they have a
   good thing, to make it too common.
   2 Henry IV I, 3
   Falstaff, complaining of being over-used

2 O noble English, that could entertain
   With half their forces the full pride of France.
   Henry V I, 2
   Archbishop of Canterbury

3 Now all the youth of England are on fire,
   And silken dalliance in the wardrobe lies.
   Henry V Prologue II
   Chorus

4 I thought upon one pair of English legs
   Did march three Frenchmen. Yet forgive me, God,
   That I do brag thus.
   Henry V III, 6
   Henry to French herald

5 O England! model to thy inward greatness,
   Like little body with a mighty heart,
   What might'st thou do, that honour would thee do,
   Were all thy children kind and natural.
   Henry V Prologue II
   Chorus

6   O that we now had here
But one ten thousand of those men in England
That do no work today!
Henry V IV, 3
Earl of Westmoreland to Henry at Agincourt

7   No, faith, my coz, wish not a man from England . . .
Rather proclaim it, Westmoreland, through my host,
That he which hath no stomach to this fight,
Let him depart.
Henry V IV, 3
Henry's reply to Westmoreland

8   England is safe, if true within itself.
3 Henry VI IV, 1
Hastings to other lords

9   England, hedged in with the main,
That water-walled bulwark, still secure
And confident from foreign purposes.
King John II, 1
Duke of Austria to Arthur

10   This blessed plot, this earth, this realm, this England,
This nurse, this teeming womb of royal kings.
Richard II II, 1
John of Gaunt to other nobles

11   England, that was wont to conquer others,
Hath made a shameful conquest of itself.
Richard II II, 1
John of Gaunt to other nobles

12   This England never did, nor ever shall,
Lie at the proud foot of a conqueror.
King John V, 7
Philip the Bastard

47   EYES

1   Lie not, to say mine eyes are murderers!
Now show the wound mine eye hath made in thee.
As You Like It III, 5
Phebe to Silvius

2   For there is none of you so mean and base,
That hath not noble lustre in your eyes.
Henry V II, 1
Henry to troops before Harfleur

3   I have not from your eyes that gentleness
And show of love as I was wont to have.
Julius Caesar I, 2
Cassius to Brutus

4   By heaven, the wonder in a mortal eye!
Love's Labour's Lost IV, 3
Dumain to himself

5   Is this a dagger which I see before me
The handle toward my hand? Come, let me clutch
thee.
I have thee not, and yet I see thee still.
Macbeth II, 1
Macbeth, deceived by an imaginary dagger

6   Mine eyes are made the fool o' the other senses,
Or else worth all the rest.
Macbeth II, 1
Macbeth, still deceived

7   In her eye there hath appeared a fire,
To burn the error that these princes hold
Against her maiden truth.
Much Ado About Nothing IV, 1
Friar Francis to Leonato and others, concerning Hero

8   O, how mine eyes do loathe his visage now!
A Midsummer Night's Dream IV, 1
Titania, recovering from her passion for donkey-headed Bottom

9   If these be true spies which I wear in my head, here's a goodly sight.
The Tempest V, 1
Trinculo to Stephano, seeing the wrecked courtiers on Prospero's island

10   An you had any eye behind, you might see more detraction at your heels than fortune before you.
Twelfth Night II, 5
Fabian, aside, concerning Malvolio

11   He's drunk an hour agone; his eyes were set at eight i' the morning.
Twelfth Night V, 1
Feste to Sir Toby, concerning the surgeon

12   Like a virtuous monument she lies,
To be admired of lewd unhallow'd eyes.
The Rape of Lucrece Stanza 56

48   FACE

1   The whining schoolboy, with his satchel
And shining morning face.
As You Like It II, 7
Jaques, moralizing on the seven ages of man

2   So loving to my mother
That he might not beteem the winds of heaven
Visit her face too roughly.
Hamlet I, 2
Hamlet, thinking of his father
beteem 'permit'

3 I never see thy face but I think upon hell-fire, and Dives that
lived in purple, for there he is in his robes, burning, burning.
1 Henry IV III, 3
Falstaff to his red-faced follower, Bardolph

4 That face of his the hungry cannibals
Would not have touched, would not have stained with
blood
But you are more inhuman, more inexorable.
3 Henry VI I, 4
Duke of York to Queen Margaret, concerning his murdered
child

5 Thou hast the sweetest face I ever looked on.
Sir, as I have a soul, she is an angel.
Henry VIII IV, 1
A gentleman to himself and to a friend, watching Anne Bullen in
a procession

6 I have seen better faces in my time
Than stands on any shoulder that I see
Before me at this instant.
King Lear II, 2
Earl of Kent to Duke of Cornwall

7 Your face, my thane, is as a book where men
May read strange matters.
Macbeth I, 5
Lady Macbeth to Macbeth

8 Was this the face
That like the sun did make beholders wink?
Richard II IV, 1
Richard, looking sadly in a mirrror

9 It cannot be, I find,
But such a face should bear a wicked mind.
The Rape of Lucrece Stanza 220

10 A woman's face with Nature's own hand painted
Hast thou, the master-mistress of my passion.
Sonnet 20

11 Look in your glass, and there appears a face
That over-goes my blunt invention quite.
Sonnet 103

---

49 FAREWELL

1 Farewell! a long farewell to all my greatness!
Henry VIII III, 2
Cardinal Wolsey to himself

2 For ever, and for ever, farewell, Cassius!
If we do meet again, why, we shall smile;
If not, why then this parting was well made.
Julius Caesar V, 1
Brutus to Cassius

3 Farewell the tranquil mind! farewell content!
Farewell the plumed troop and the big wars
That make ambition virtue. O farewell,
Farewell the neighing steed and the shrill trump . . .
Farewell! Othello's occupation's gone!
Othello III, 3
Othello to Iago, who has gulled him into believing Desdemona
unfaithful

4 Would the word 'Farewell' have lengthen'd hours
And added years to his short banishment,
He should have had a volume of farewells.
Richard II I, 4
Duke of Aumerle to Richard, concerning Bolingbroke

5 As many farewells as be stars in heaven.
Troilus and Cressida IV, 4
Troilus to Cressida

6   Welcome ever smiles
And farewell goes out sighing.
Troilus and Cressida III, 3
Ulysses to Achilles

7   Farewell, fair cruelty.
Twelfth Night I, 5
Viola, wooing Olivia on behalf of Orsino

8   If you can separate yourself and your misdemeanours you are
welcome to the house; if not, and it would please you to take
leave of her, she is very willing to bid you farewell.
Twelfth Night II, 3
Malvolio to Sir Toby Belch on behalf of Countess Olivia

9   Farewell! thou art too dear for my possessing,
And like enough, thou know'st thy estimate.
Sonnet 87

50   FATE
see also **Destiny** 35

1   My fate cries out
And makes each petty artery in this body
As hardy as the Nemean lion's nerve.
Hamlet I, 4
Hamlet, determined to follow the ghost of his father
The Nemean lion was noted for its tough skin

2   Our wills and fates do so contrary run
That our devices still are overthrown.
Hamlet III, 2
Player King to Player Queen in the 'Mousetrap' play

3   O God! that one might read the book of fate,
And see the revolution of the times
Make mountains level, and the continent —
Weary of solid firmness — melt itself
Into the sea.
2 Henry IV III, 1
Henry to the Earl of Warwick

4   What fates impose, that men must needs abide;
It boots not to resist both wind and tide.
3 Henry VI IV, 3
Edward IV to Earl of Warwick, who has just forced him to give
up kingship

5   Men at some time are masters of their fates:
The fault, dear Brutus, is not in our stars,
But in ourselves, that we are underlings.
Julius Caesar I, 2
Cassius, anxious to involve Brutus in a conspiracy against Caesar

6   If thou read this, O Caesar, thou mayst live;
If not, the Fates with traitors do contrive.
Julius Caesar II, 3
A supporter of Caesar, vainly offering a warning of conspiracy
against him

7   Fates, we will know your pleasures;
That we shall die, we know; 'tis but the time
And drawing days out, that men stand upon.
Julius Caesar III, 1
Brutus, after the assassination

8   It is the stars,
The stars above us, govern our conditions.
King Lear IV, 3
Earl of Kent to a gentleman

9   What should be spoken here, where our fate,
Hid in an auger-hole, may rush and seize us?
Let's away.
Macbeth II, 3
Donalbain, one of Duncan's two sons, who, immediately after
the discovery of Duncan's murder, fear danger for themselves

10   Fate, show thy force; ourselves we do not owe;
     What is decreed must be, and be this so.
     Twelfth Night I, 5
     Olivia, attracted to Viola, supposing her a youth

---

51   FATHER

1   Good Hamlet, cast thy nighted colour off . . .
    Do not for ever with thy vailed lids
    Seek for thy noble father in the dust.
    Hamlet I, 2
    Gertrude to her son, regarding the death of her late husband

2   If by chance I talk a little wild, forgive me;
    I had it from my father.
    Henry VIII I, 4
    Lord Sands, humorously excusing his lively conversation

3   The dear father
    Would with his daughter speak, commands her
        service;
    Are they inform'd of this?
    King Lear II, 4
    Lear, finding a cool reception at the home of his daughter Regan
    and her husband

4   I laid their daggers ready;
    He could not miss 'em. Had he not resembled
    My father as he slept, I had done't.
    Macbeth II, 2
    Lady Macbeth, waiting for Macbeth to murder Duncan

5   It is a wise father that knows his own child.
    The Merchant of Venice II, 2
    Launcelot Gobbo to his blind father

6   To you your father should be as a god.
    A Midsummer Night's Dream I, 1
    Theseus to Hermia

7   You have her father's love, Demetrius;
  Let me have Hermia's: do you marry him!
    A Midsummer Night's Dream I, 1
    Lysander

8   My father had no less
  Than three great argosies; besides two galliasses,
  And twelve tight galleys.
    The Taming of the Shrew II, 1
    Tranio, countering Gremio's boasts about his property

9   Full fathom five thy father lies;
  Of his bones are coral made.
    The Tempest I, 2
    Song by Ariel

10   O, that our fathers would applaud our loves,
  To seal our happiness with their consents!
    The Two Gentlemen of Verona I, 3
    Proteus to himself

11   As a decrepit father takes delight
  To see his active child do deeds of youth,
  So I, made lame by fortune's dearest spite,
  Take all my comfort of thy worth and truth.
    Sonnet 37

---

52   FEAR

1   It is the part of men to fear and tremble
  When the most mighty gods by tokens send
  Such dreadful heralds to astonish us.
    Julius Caesar I, 3
    Casca to Cassius, on strange events preceding Caesar's murder

2   Of all the wonders that I yet have heard,
It seems to me most strange that men should fear;
Seeing that death, a necessary end,
Will come when it will come.
Julius Caesar II, 2
Caesar to Calpurnia

3   For I am sick and capable of fears,
Oppress'd with wrongs, and therefore full of fears,
A widow, husbandless, subject to fears.
King John III, 1
Constance to Earl of Shrewsbury

4   You make me strange . . .
When now I think you can behold such sights,
And keep the natural ruby of your cheeks,
When mine is blanch'd with fear.
Macbeth III, 4
Macbeth to supper guests who fail to see the ghost of Banquo

5   Our fears do make us traitors.
Macbeth IV, 2
Lady Macduff to Ross

6   Or in the night, imagining some fear,
How easy is a bush supposed a bear.
A Midsummer Night's Dream V, 1
Theseus to Hippolyta

7   'Tis time to fear when tyrants seem to kiss.
Which fear so grew in me, I hither fled.
Pericles I, 2
Pericles is fleeing from an overlord

8   To fear the foe, since fear oppresseth strength,
Gives, in your weakness, strength unto your foe,
And so your follies fight against yourself.
Richard II III, 2
Bishop of Carlisle to Richard

9　I have a faint cold fear thrills through my veins,
　　That almost freezes up the heat of life.
　　Romeo and Juliet IV, 3
　　Juliet, about to swallow a powerful drug

10　To do a thing, where I the issue doubted,
　　Whereof the execution did cry out
　　Against the non-performance, 'twas a fear
　　Which oft infects the wisest.
　　The Winter's Tale I, 2
　　Camillo to Leontes

53　FLOWERS

1　There's rosemary, that's for remembrance . . . and there is
　pansies, that's for thoughts.
　Hamlet IV, 5
　Ophelia, distributing flowers in her madness

2　　　　　　　Hoary-headed frosts
　　Fall in the fresh lap of the crimson rose.
　　A Midsummer Night's Dream II, 1
　　Titania to Oberon

3　In the wood, where often you and I
　　Upon faint primrose beds were wont to lie.
　　A Midsummer Night's Dream I, 1
　　Hermia to Lysander

4　I know a bank where the wild thyme blows;
　　Where oxslips and the nodding violet grows,
　　Quite over-canopied with luscious woodbine.
　　A Midsummer Night's Dream II, 1
　　Oberon to Puck

5   Yet mark'd I where the bolt of Cupid fell:
It fell upon a little western flower,
Before milk-white, now purple, with love's wound,
And maidens call it love-in-idleness.
A Midsummer Night's Dream II, 1
Oberon, on the flower whose juice caused love at sight

6   Honeysuckles, ripen'd by the sun,
Forbid the sun to enter.
Much Ado About Nothing III, 1
Hero to Margaret

7   The marigold, that goes to bed wi' the sun
And with him rises weeping.
The Winter's Tale IV, 4
Perdita to Camillo and others

8   Daffodils
That come before the swallow dares, and take
The winds of March with beauty.
The Winter's Tale IV, 4
Perdita to Camillo and others

9   The fairest flowers o' the season
Are our carnations and streak'd gillyvors.
The Winter's Tale IV, 4
Perdita to Camillo and others

10   The rose looks fair, but fairer we it deem
For that sweet odour which doth in it live.
Sonnet 54

11   Lilies that fester smell far worse than weeds.
Sonnet 94

54 FOLLY

1   I had rather a fool to make me merry than experience to make
me sad.
As You Like It IV, 1
Rosalind to Jaques

2   Now I am in Arden, the more fool I; when I was at home I was
in a better place.
As You Like It II, 4
Touchstone to Rosalind

3   I do now remember a saying, 'The fool doth think he is wise,
but the wise man knows himself to be a fool'.
As You Like It V, 1
Touchstone to William

4   Here comes a pair of very strange beasts, which in all tongues
are called fools.
As You Like It V, 4
Jaques, concerning Touchstone and Audrey

5   Let the doors be shut upon him, that he may play the fool
nowhere but in his own house.
Hamlet III, 1
Hamlet to Ophelia, concerning her father

6   Thus we play the fools with the time, and the spirits of the wise
sit in the clouds and mock us.
2 Henry IV II, 2
Prince Hal to Poins

7   When we are born, we cry that we are come
To this great stage of fools.
King Lear IV, 6
Lear to Gloucester

8   But love is blind, and lovers cannot see
The pretty follies that themselves commit.
The Merchant of Venice II, 6
Jessica to Lorenzo

9 Lord, what fools these mortals be!
A Midsummer Night's Dream III, 2
Puck to Oberon

10 O murderous coxcomb! what should such a fool
Do with so good a wife?
Othello V, 2
Emilia to Othello after he has killed Desdemona

11 To wisdom he's a fool that will not yield.
Pericles II, 4
First Lord, yielding to Helicanus's wise opinions

12 The common curse of mankind, folly and ignorance.
Troilus and Cressida II, 3
Thersites to Patroclus

13 I hold him but a fool that will endanger
His body for a girl that loves him not.
The Two Gentlemen of Verona V, 4
Thurio to Valentine, renouncing his claim to Silvia

14 (My friends) praise me and make an ass of me; now my foes tell
me plainly that I am an ass: so that by my foes, sir, I profit in
the knowledge of myself; and by my friends I am abused.
Twelfth Night V, 1
Clown Feste to Duke Orsino

15 This fellow is wise enough to play the fool;
And to do that well craves a kind of wit.
Twelfth Night III, 1
Viola, concerning Feste

16 Sometimes nature will betray its folly.
The Winter's Tale I, 2
Leontes to Hermione

17   You may as well
Forbid the sea for to obey the moon,
As or by oath remove or counsel shake
The fabric of his folly.
The Winter's Tale I, 2
Camillo to Polixenes, on the insane jealousy of Leontes

55   FORTUNE

1   Fortune knows
We scorn her most when most she offers blows.
Antony and Cleopatra III, 11
Antony to Cleopatra

2   Let us sit and mock the good housewife Fortune from her
wheel, that her gifts may henceforth be bestowed equally.
As You Like It I, 2
Celia to Rosalind

3   Wear this for me, one out of suits with fortune,
That could give more but that her hand lacks means.
As You Like It I, 2
Rosalind, giving Orlando a chain from her neck

4   (He) rail'd on Lady Fortune in good terms
As You Like It I, 2
Jaques, concerning Touchstone

5   Fortune brings in some boats that are not steer'd.
Cymbeline IV, 12
Pisanio to himself

6   Blest are those
Whose blood and judgement are so well commingled
That they are not a pipe for fortune's finger
To sound what stop she please.
Hamlet III, 2
Hamlet, paying tribute to Horatio

7   Thou hast been . . .
A man that fortune's buffets and rewards
Hath ta'en with equal thanks.
Hamlet III, 2
Hamlet to Horatio

8   Will fortune never come with both hands full,
But write her fair words still in foulest letters?
2 Henry IV IV, 4
King Henry to courtiers

9 Fortune is painted blind with a muffler afore her eyes.
Henry V III, 6
Fluellen to Pistol

10   Fortune is merry.
And in this mood will give us anything.
Julius Caesar III, 2
Antony, having roused the crowd against Caesar's killers

11 There is a tide in the affairs of men
Which taken at the flood, leads on to fortune;
Omitted, all the voyage of their life
Is bound in shallows and in miseries.
Julius Caesar IV, 3
Brutus to Cassius

12 When Fortune means to men most good,
She looks upon them with a threatening eye.
King John III, 4
Cardinal Pandulph to Dauphin

13 A good man's fortune may grow out at heels.
King Lear II, 2
Earl of Kent, on being placed in the stocks by the Duke of
Cornwall

14 Fortune, that arrant whore,
Ne'er turns the key to the poor.
King Lear II, 4
Fool, chanting a verse

15 O, fortune, fortune! all men call thee fickle.
    Romeo and Juliet III, 5
    Juliet, after a sad parting from Romeo

16 Some men creep in skittish Fortune's hall
    Whiles others play the idiots in her eyes.
    Troilus and Cressida III, 3
    Ulysses to Achilles

56   FREEDOM

1 In a dark and dankish vault at home
   (They) left me and my man, both bound together;
   Till, gnawing with my teeth my bonds in sunder,
   I gained my freedom.
   The Comedy of Errors V, 1
   Antipholus of Ephesus, telling the Duke of his escape from
   incarceration for madness

2   This twenty years
   The rock and these demesnes have been my world,
   Where I have liv'd at honest freedom.
   Cymbeline III, 3
   Belarius to his two 'sons'

3 I had as lief have the foppery of freedom as the morality of
   imprisonment.
   Measure for Measure I, 2
   Lucio to Claudio

4   Thou shalt be as free
   As mountain winds.
   The Tempest I, 2
   Prospero to Ariel

5   Are not the streets as free
For me as for you?
The Taming of the Shrew I, 2
Tranio to Gremio, who openly resents Tranio's presence as a
rival suitor

6 Steal thine own freedom, and complain on theft.
Venus and Adonis Stanza 27

7 Among the many that mine eyes have seen . . .
Harm have I done to them but ne'er was harmed;
Kept hearts in liveries, but mine own was free.
A Lover's Complaint Stanza 28

---

57 FRIENDSHIP

---

1   Keep thy friend
Under thy own life's key.
All's Well That Ends Well I, 1
Countess of Rousillon to Bertram

2   We still have slept together,
Rose at an instant, learn'd, play'd, eat together,
And wheresoe'er we went, like Juno's swans,
Still we went coupled and inseparable.
As You Like It I, 3
Celia to her father, concerning Rosalind

3 Most friendship is feigning, most loving mere folly.
As You Like It II, 7
Song by Amiens

4 He that wants money, means, and content is without three
good friends.
As You Like It III, 2
Corin to Touchstone

5   Those friends thou hast, and their adoption tried,
    Grapple them to thy soul with hoops of steel.
    Hamlet I, 3
    Polonius to Laertes

6   For who not needs shall never lack a friend,
    And who in want a hollow friend doth try
    Directly seasons him his enemy.
    Hamlet III, 2
    Player King to Player Queen

7   Those you make friends
    And give your hearts to, when they once perceive
    The least rub in your fortunes, fall away
    Like water from ye.
    Henry VIII II, 1
    Duke of Buckingham before his execution

8   A friend should bear his friend's infirmities,
    But Brutus makes mine greater than they are.
    Julius Caesar IV, 3
    Cassius to Brutus

9   To wail friends lost
    Is not by much so wholesome-profitable
    As to rejoice at friends but newly-found.
    Love's Labour's Lost V, 2
    King of Navarre to Princess of France

10 If thou wilt lend this money, lend it not
    As to thy friends; for when did friendship take
    A breed for barren metal of his friend.
    The Merchant of Venice I, 3
    Antonio to Shylock

58 GENTLEMAN

1 An absolute gentleman, full of most excellent differences, of
very soft society and great showing.
Hamlet V, 2
Osric to Hamlet, on Laertes

2 In faith, he is a worthy gentleman,
Exceedingly well read . . . valiant as a lion,
And wondrous affable.
1 Henry IV III, 1
Mortimer to Hotspur, concerning Owen Glendower

3 I do not think a braver gentleman,
More active-valiant or more valiant-young,
More daring or more bold, is now alive.
1 Henry IV V, 1
Prince Hal to his father, on Hotspur

4 Spoke like a sprightful noble gentleman.
King John IV, 2
King to Philip the Bastard, who has agreed to carry a swift
message

5 He was a gentleman on whom I built
An absolute trust.
Macbeth I, 4
King Duncan concerning the traitorous Thane of Cawdor

6   We are gentlemen
That neither in our hearts nor outward eyes
Envy the great nor do the low despise.
Pericles II, 3
A knight at the court of Simonides to Pericles

7 Since every Jack became a gentleman,
There's many a gentle person made a Jack.
Richard III I, 3
Richard of Gloucester

8   Of all the fair resort of gentlemen
    That every day with parle encounter me,
    In thy opinion which is worthiest love?
    The Two Gentlemen of Verona I, 2
    Julia to her servant, Lucetta

9   A gentleman of noble parentage,
    Of fair demesnes, youthful, and nobly train'd,
    Stuff'd, as they say, with honourable parts.
    Romeo and Juliet III, 5
    Capulet, praising Count Paris to Juliet

10 *Olivia:* What is your parentage?
    Viola: Above my fortunes, yet my state is well:
               I am a gentleman.
    Twelfth Night I, 5
    Viola, acting as a youth, has aroused Olivia's interest

11 What a fool Honesty is! and Trust, his sworn brother, a very
    simple gentleman!
    The Winter's Tale IV, 4
    Autolycus to himself

59   GIFTS

1   To the noble mind
    Rich gifts wax poor when givers prove unkind.
    Hamlet III, 1
    Ophelia to Hamlet

2   And humbly now upon my bended knee . . .
    Deliver up my title in the queen . . .
    The happiest gift that ever marquess gave,
    The fairest queen that ever king received.
    2 Henry VI I, 1
    Earl of Suffolk, who escorted Margaret from France to marry
    Henry

3 If I be served such another trick I'll have my brains ta'en out and buttered, and give them to a dog for a new year's gift.
The Merry Wives of Windsor III, 5
Falstaff, to himself

4 I here do give thee that with all my heart
Which, but thou hast already, with all my heart,
I would keep from thee.
Othello I, 3
Brabantio reluctantly gives Desdemona to Othello after their marriage

5 Men may take women's gifts for impudence.
Pericles II, 3
Thaisa to her father, Simonides

6   What will this come to?
He commands us to provide and give great gifts,
And all out of an empty coffer.
Timon of Athens IV, 3
Complaint by Timon's steward, Flavius

7   Rich men deal gifts,
Expecting in return twenty for one.
Timon of Athens IV, 3
Timon to Flavius

8 Win her with gifts, if she respects not words:
Dumb jewels often in their silent kind
More than quick words do move a woman's mind.
The Two Gentlemen of Verona III, 1
Valentine, giving advice to the Duke of Milan

9 She prizes not such trifles as these are:
The gifts she looks from me are pack'd and lock'd
Up in my heart; which I have given already.
The Winter's Tale IV, 4
Florizel to Polixenes, concerning Perdita

60   GOD

1   God has given you one face, and you make yourselves another.
Hamlet III, 1
Hamlet to Ophelia, on women

2   This might be the pate of a politician . . . one that would circumvent God, might it not?
Hamlet V, 1
Hamlet, observing gravedigger turning up a skull

3   If sack and sugar be a fault, God help the wicked.
1 Henry IV II, 4
Falstaff to Prince Hal

4   God shall be my hope
My stay, my guide and lantern to my feet.
2 Henry VI II, 3
King Henry, deciding to rule England without a Protector

5   Had I but served my God with half the zeal
I served my king, he would not in mine age
Have left me naked to mine enemies.
Henry VIII III, 2
Wolsey to Cromwell

6   (We'll) take upon's the mystery of things
As if we were God's spies.
King Lear V, 3
Lear, reconciled with Cordelia

7   Mercy is above this sceptr'd sway . . .
It is an attribute to God himself,
And earthly power doth then show likest God's
When mercy seasons justice.
The Merchant of Venice IV, 1
Portia as Balthasar to Shylock

8   God made him, and therefore let him pass for a man.
The Merchant of Venice I, 2
Portia to Nerissa, concerning a French lord

9   Here will be an old abusing of God's patience and the King's English.

The Merry Wives of Windsor I, 4
Mistress Quickly, concerning the Frenchman, Dr Caius

10   Write down that they hope they serve God; and write God first; for God defend but God should go before such villains.

Much Ado About Nothing IV, 2
Dogberry, attempting to charge two arrested men

61   GODS

1   If the great gods be just, they shall assist
The deeds of justest men.

Antony and Cleopatra II, 1
Pompey to Menecrates

2   Since Cleopatra died
I have liv'd in such dishonour, that the gods
Detest my baseness.

Antony and Cleopatra IV, 14
Antony to Eros; the report of Cleopatra's death was, in fact, incorrect

3   I would the gods had made thee poetical.

As You Like It III, 3
Touchstone to Audrey

4   Behold, the heavens do ope,
The gods look down, and this unnatural scene
They laugh at.

Coriolanus V, 3
Coriolanus, successfully leading an attack on the Rome that has banished him, suddenly spares it

5   To your protection I commend me, gods!
From fairies and the tempters of the night
Guard me, beseech ye!
Cymbeline II, 2
Imogen, retiring to bed

6   Let's carve him as a dish fit for the gods,
Not hew him as a carcass fit for hounds.
Julius Caesar II, 1
Brutus to the other conspirators against Caesar

7   When Marcus Brutus grows so covetous . . .
Be ready, gods, with all your thunderbolts;
Dash him to pieces.
Julius Caesar IV, 2
Brutus, reproving Cassius for greed over money

8   As flies to wanton boys, are we to the gods;
They kill us for their sport.
King Lear IV, 1
Earl of Gloucester to an Old Man

9   The gods are just, and of our pleasant vices
Make instruments to plague us.
King Lear V, 3
Edgar to Edmund and Albany

10 Wilt thou draw near the nature of the gods?
Draw near them, then, in being merciful.
Titus Andronicus I, 1
Tamora pleads that her first-born son should not be sacrificed

---

62 GOLD
see also **Money** 111

---

1   All gold and silver rather turn to dirt.
Cymbeline III, 6
Arviragus to Imogen

2 How quickly nature falls into revolt
   When gold becomes her object!
   2 Henry IV IV, 5
   King Henry to his sons

3 By Jove, I am not covetous for gold.
   Henry V IV, 3
   Henry to Earl of Westmoreland

4   I did send to you
   For certain sums of gold, which you denied me . . .
   Was that done like Cassius?
   Julius Caesar IV, 3
   Brutus to Cassius

5 Let's see once more this saying graved in gold:
   'Who chooseth me shall gain what many men desire'.
   The Merchant of Venice II, 7
   Prince of Morocco, choosing the gold casket

6   Thou gaudy gold,
   Hard food for Midas, I will none of thee.
   The Merchant of Venice III, 2
   Bassanio, rejecting the gold casket

7 I know a discontented gentleman
   Whose humble means match not his haughty mind:
   Gold were as good as twenty orators,
   And will, no doubt, tempt him to anything.
   Richard III IV, 2
   Richard, receiving information from a page about a potential
   murderer for the two princes

8 There is thy gold, worse poison to men's souls,
   Doing more murder in this loathsome world
   Than these poor compounds that thou mayst not sell.
   Romeo and Juliet V, 1
   Romeo, buying poison from a poor apothecary

9   Plutus, the god of Gold,
Is but his steward: no meed, but he repays
Sevenfold above itself.
Timon of Athens I, 1
A Lord speaking of Timon's generosity with his money

10   What is here?
Gold? yellow, glittering precious gold . . .
This yellow slave
Will knit and break religions; bless the accursed.
Timon of Athens IV, 3
Timon to Alcibiades

11   He that had wit would think that I had none
To bury so much gold under a tree,
And never after to inherit it.
Titus Andronicus II, 3
Aaron, using the gold as part of a plot against Andronicus and
his sons

63   GOODNESS

1   There's no goodness in thy face.
Antony and Cleopatra II, 5
Cleopatra unfairly blames a messenger for bringing unwelcome
news

2   Down on your knees
And thank heaven, fasting, for a good man's love.
As You Like It III, 5
Rosalind to Phebe

3   And this our life . . .
Finds tongues in trees, books in the running brooks,
Sermons in stones, and good in everything.
As You Like It II, 1
Duke Senior to his companions in the Forest of Arden

4　There is some soul of goodness in things evil,
　　Would men observingly distil it out.
　　Henry V IV, 1
　　Henry V to his companions

5　The evil that men do lives after them;
　　The good is oft interred with their bones.
　　Julius Caesar III, 2
　　Antony's speech over Caesar's body

6　Wisdom and goodness to the vile seem vile.
　　King Lear IV, 2
　　Duke of Albany to Goneril

7　　　　　　　Our doubts are traitors,
　　And make us lose the good we oft might win,
　　By fearing to attempt.
　　Measure for Measure I, 4
　　Lucio to Isabella

8　The hand that hath made you fair hath made you good.
　　Measure for Measure III, 1
　　Duke to Isabella

9　Virtue is bold, and goodness never fearful.
　　Measure for Measure III, 1
　　Duke to Isabella

10　How far that little candle throws his beams!
　　So shines a good deed in a naughty world.
　　The Merchant of Venice V, 1
　　Portia to Nerissa

11　　　　　　　The kindest man,
　　The best-condition'd and unwearied spirit
　　In doing courtesies.
　　The Merchant of Venice III, 3
　　Bassanio, describing Antonio to Portia

12   (There's) nought so vile that on the earth doth live
But to the earth some special good doth give.
Romeo and Juliet II, 3
Friar Laurence, soliloquizing

64 GRIEF
see also **Sorrow** 162

1 A heavier task could not have been imposed
Than I to speak my griefs unspeakable.
The Comedy of Errors I, 1
Aegeon to Duke of Ephesus

2 Great griefs, I see, medicine the less.
Cymbeline IV, 2
Belarius to his sons

3 But I have that within which passeth show;
These but the trappings and the suits of woe.
Hamlet I, 2
Hamlet to his mother

4 The bravery of his grief did put me
Into a towering passion.
Hamlet V, 2
Hamlet, excusing his behaviour to Laertes at Ophelia's funeral

5   'Tis better to be lowly born,
And range with humble livers in content
Than to be perk'd up in a glistering grief.
Henry VIII II, 3
Anne Bullen to an old lady

6 Grief fills the room up of my absent child,
Lies in his bed, walks up and down with me,
Puts on his pretty looks, repeats his words . . .
Then have I reason to be fond of grief.
King John III, 4
Constance to King Philip of France, on young Arthur's
imprisonment

7   I am not mad: I would to heaven I were!
For then 'tis like I should forget myself.
O, if I could, what grief should I forget!
King John III, 4
Constance to Cardinal Pandulph

8   Everyone can master a grief but he that hath it.
Much Ado About Nothing III, 2
Benedick to friends

9   Each substance of a grief hath twenty shadows,
Which shows like grief itself.
Richard II II, 2
Bushy to Queen

10   My grief lies all within;
And these external manners of laments
Are merely shadows to the unseen grief
That swells with silence in the tortur'd soul.
Richard II IV, 1
Richard to Bolingbroke

11   Alas, poor man! grief has so wrought on him,
He takes false shadows for true substances.
Titus Andronicus III, 2
Marcus Andronicus, concerning his brother Titus

65 HAIR

1   My very hairs do mutiny, for the white
Reprove the brown for rashness.
Antony and Cleopatra III, 11
Antony to attendants

2   Spread o'er the silver waves thy golden hairs,
And as a bed I'll take them and there lie.
The Comedy of Errors III, 2
Antipholus of Syracuse to Luciana

3   These grey locks, the pursuivants of death,
     Nestor-like aged in an age of care,
     Argue the end of Edmund Mortimer.
     1 Henry VI II, 5
     Mortimer to gaolers

4   Comb down his hair; look, look! it stands upright,
     Like lime-twigs set to catch my winged soul.
     2 Henry VI III, 3
     Cardinal Beaufort, raving on his death-bed

5   Let but the commons hear this testament . . .
     And they would go and kiss dead Caesar's wounds
     And dip their napkins in his sacred blood,
     Yea, beg a hair of him for memory.
     Julius Caesar III, 2
     Antony to citizens, over Caesar's dead body

6   Thou canst not say I did it: never shake
     Thy gory locks at me.
     Macbeth III, 4
     Macbeth to Banquo's ghost

7   Her sunny locks
     Hang on her temples like a golden fleece.
     The Merchant of Venice I, 1
     Bassanio to Antonio, describing Portia

8   Here in her hairs
     The painter plays the spider, and hath woven
     A golden mesh to entrap the hearts of men.
     The Merchant of Venice III, 2
     Bassanio to himself, on Portia's portrait

9 I will . . . fetch you a hair off the great Cham's beard.
   Much Ado About Nothing II, 1
   Benedick to Don Pedro

10   His browny locks did hang in crooked curls:
     And every light occasion of the wind
     Upon his lips their silken parcels hurls.
     A Lover's Complaint Stanza 13

66   HAND

1   These hands do lack nobility, that they strike
A meaner than myself.
Antony and Cleopatra II, 5
Cleopatra, who has attacked a messenger for informing her that
Antony is married to Octavia

2   This hand, whose touch,
Whose every touch, would force the feeler's soul
To the oath of loyalty.
Cymbeline I, 6
Iachimo to Imogen

3   For thou shalt know this strong right hand of mine
Can pluck the diadem from faint Henry's head.
3 Henry VI II, 1
Earl of Warwick to Lords

4   This is the hand that stabb'd thy father York;
And this is the hand that slew thy brother Rutland.
3 Henry VI II, 4
Lord Clifford to Richard of Gloucester

5   Warwick and Clarence, give me both your hands;
Now join your hands, and with your hands your
          hearts.
3 Henry VI IV, 6
Henry, offering them both the protectorship of the throne

6   A common slave — you know him well by sight —
Held up his left hand, which did flame and burn
Like twenty torches join'd, and yet his hand
Not sensible of fire remain'd unscorch'd.
Julius Caesar I, 3
Casca, telling Cicero of strange events

7   Let each man render me his bloody hand:
First Marcus Brutus, will I shake with you;
Next Caius Cassius, do I take your hand.
Julius Caesar III, 1
Antony, hiding his feelings towards Caesar's killers

8 (With) your hands in your pocket, like a man after the old painting.
Love's Labour's Lost III, 1
Moth to Armado

9 A giving hand, though foul, shall have fair praise.
Love's Labour's Lost IV, 1
Princess of France to a forester

10 Here's the smell of the blood still: all the perfumes of Arabia will not sweeten this little hand.
Macbeth V, 1
Lady Macbeth, sleep-walking with Duncan's murder on her conscience

11 She took me kindly by the hand
And gazed for tidings in my eager eyes.
The Rape of Lucrece Stanza 37

67 HAPPINESS

1 How bitter a thing it is to look into happiness through another man's eyes.
As You Like It V, 2
Orlando to Rosalind in the Forest of Arden

2 I earn that I eat, get that I wear, owe no man hate, envy no man's happiness.
As You Like It III, 2
Corin to Touchstone

3 (We are) happy in that we are not over-happy;
On Fortune's cap we are not the very button.
Hamlet II, 2
Guildenstern to Hamlet

4 O God! methinks it were a happy life
To be no better than a homely swain;
To sit upon the hills, as I do now.
3 Henry VI II, 5
King Henry, musing

5 Saw you not even now a blessed troop
Invite me to a banquet, whose bright faces
Cast beams upon me, like the sun?
They promised me eternal happiness.
Henry VIII IV, 2
Queen Katherine, very ill, relating a dream

6 Fair thoughts and happy hours attend on you.
The Merchant of Venice III, 4
Lorenzo to Portia

7 Silence is the perfect herald of joy; I were but little happy if I
could say how much.
Much Ado About Nothing II, 1
Claudio, engaged to marry Hero

8   If it were now to die,
'Twere now to be most happy; for I fear
My soul hath her content so absolute
That not another comfort like to this
Succeeds.
Othello II, 1
Othello to Desdemona

9 O happiness enjoy'd but of a few!
And, if possess'd, as soon decay'd and done
As is the morning's silver-melting dew.
The Rape of Lucrece Stanza 4

10 Then happy I, that love and am beloved
Where I may not remove nor be removed.
Sonnet 25

68   HARM

1   Ten thousand harms, more than the ills I know,
My idleness doth hatch.
Antony and Cleopatra I, 2
Antony to himself, on the time spent with Cleopatra

2   Good masters, harm me not.
Cymbeline III, 6
Imogen as a youth, to Belarius and sons, whose cave she has
entered uninvited

3   Thou hast done much harm upon me, Hal; God forgive thee
for it. Before I knew thee, Hal, I knew nothing.
1 Henry IV I, 2
Falstaff to Prince Henry

4   To do them good I would sustain some harm.
3 Henry VI III, 2
Lady Grey to King Edward IV, speaking of her children; the
king later marries her

5   *Portia:*   Know'st thou any harm's intended
towards him?
Soothsayer: None that I know will be; much that I
fear may chance.
Julius Caesar II, 4
Brutus's wife believes her husband is engaged in some plot
against Caesar

6   Publius, good cheer;
There is no harm intended to thy person,
Nor to no Roman else.
Julius Caesar III, 1
Brutus reassures an elderly senator after Caesar's murder

7   Lo, by my troth, the instrument is cold
And would not harm me.
King John IV, 1
Young Arthur refers to the hot iron meant to blind him

8   Laugh to scorn
The power of man, for none of woman born
Shall harm Macbeth.
Macbeth IV, 1
An apparition conjured up by witches is addressing Macbeth

9   None can cure their harms by wailing them.
Richard III II, 2
Duke of Gloucester, later Richard III

10   I am a great eater of beef, and I believe that does harm to my wit.
Twelfth Night I, 3
Sir Andrew Aguecheek to Sir Toby Belch

69   HASTE

1   Celerity is never more admired
Than by the negligent.
Antony and Cleopatra III, 7
Cleopatra to Antony

2   Farewell, and let your haste commend your duty.
Hamlet I, 2
Claudius, sending messengers to Norway

3   Nay, but make haste; the better foot before . . .
Be Mercury, set feathers to thy heels,
And fly like thought from them to me again.
King John IV, 2
John, asking Philip the Bastard to contradict dangerous rumours

4   That spirit's possessed with haste
That wounds the unsisting postern with these strokes.
Measure for Measure IV, 2
Duke to himself, concerning a loud knocking at the prison door

5 I'll take my leave of the Jew in the twinkling of an eye.
   The Merchant of Venice II, 2
   Launcelot Gobbo, leaving Shylock's service for Bassanio's

6   Haste away,
   For we must measure twenty miles today.
   The Merchant of Venice III, 4
   Portia to Nerissa

7   I go, I go; look how I go,
   Swifter than arrow from the Tartar's bow.
   A Midsummer Night's Dream III, 2
   Puck to Oberon

8 He tires betimes that spurs too fast betimes.
   Richard II II, 1
   John of Gaunt to Duke of York

9 Wisely and slow; they stumble that run fast.
   Romeo and Juliet II, 3
   Friar Laurence, on Romeo's sudden love for Juliet

10 Be gone! I will not hear thy vain excuse;
   But, as thou lovest thy life, make speed from hence.
   The Two Gentlemen of Verona III, 1
   Duke, banishing Valentine

11 Like as the waves make towards the pebbled shore,
   So do our minutes hasten to their end.
   Sonnet 60

70 HATE

1 In time we hate that which we often fear.
   Antony and Cleopatra I, 3
   Charmian to Cleopatra

2   My soul, yet I know not why, hates nothing more than he.
   As You Like It I, 1
   Oliver on his brother Orlando

3   He seeks their hate with greater devotion than they can render
   it him.
   Coriolanus II, 2
   First Officer, on the attitude of Coriolanus to the people

4   By the very truth of it, I care not for you . . .
                   I hate you; which I had rather
        You felt than make my boast.
        Cymbeline II, 3
        Imogen to Cloten

5   I am bid forth to supper, Jessica . . .
        I am not bid for love; they flatter me;
        But yet I'll go in hate, to feed upon
        The prodigal Christian.
        The Merchant of Venice II, 5
        Shylock to his daughter

6   The love of wicked friends converts to fear;
        That fear to hate.
        Richard II V, 1
        Richard to a nobleman, who has helped Bolingbroke to usurp
        the throne

7   Can you not hate me, as I know you do,
        But you must join in souls to mock me too.
        A Midsummer Night's Dream III, 2
        Helena to Demetrius, not realizing that he has been affected by a
        love charm applied by Puck

8   Were you snarling all before I came,
        Ready to catch each other by the throat,
        And turn you all your hatred now on me?
        Richard III I, 3
        Queen Margaret to nobles

9   Ah, sirs, consider he that set you on
    To do this deed will hate you for the deed.
    Richard III I, 4
    Duke of Clarence to murderers hired by Richard III

10 I say thou liest, Camillo, and I hate thee.
    The Winter's Tale I, 2
    Leontes, angry that Camillo will not support his unjustified
    charges against Hermione's honour

11 Thou art so possessed with murderous hate
    That 'gainst thyself thou stick'st not to conspire.
    Sonnet 10

71   HEART

1   His captain's heart . . .
    In the scuffles of great fights hath burst
    The buckles on his breast.
    Antony and Cleopatra I, 1
    Philo, discussing Antony with a friend

2   Thou knew'st too well
    My heart was to thy rudder tied by th' strings,
    And thou should'st tow me after.
    Antony and Cleopatra III, 11
    Antony to Cleopatra

3   It is young Orlando that tripped up the wrestler's heels and
    your heart both in an instant.
    As You Like It III, 2
    Celia to Rosalind

4   You'll question this gentlewoman about me; and I know, Kate,
    you will to her dispraise those parts in me that you love with
    your heart.
    Henry V V, 2
    Henry to French princess, to whom he is suitor

5   O tiger's heart wrapped in a woman's hide!
3 Henry VI I, 4
Richard Duke of York to Margaret

6   In sweet music is such art,
Killing care and grief of heart.
Henry VIII III, 1
Song, *Orpheus with his lute*

7   Bear with me;
My heart is in the coffin there with Caesar,
And I must pause till it come back to me.
Julius Caesar III, 2
Antony in his speech to the citizens

8   There is my dagger,
And here my naked breast; within, a heart
Dearer than Plutus' mine, richer than gold . . .
Strike, as thou didst at Caesar.
Julius Caesar IV, 3
Cassius during a quarrel with Brutus

9   I cannot heave
My heart into my mouth: I love your majesty
According to my bond; nor more, nor less.
King Lear I, 1
Cordelia to Lear

10   A light heart lives long.
Love's Labour's Lost V, 2
Katherine to Rosaline

11 By heart you love her, because your heart cannot come by her.
Love's Labour's Lost III, 1
Moth to Armado

12 What a sigh is there! the heart is sorely charged.
Macbeth V, 1
Doctor watching Lady Macbeth uneasily sleep-walking

13 A woman would run through fire and water for such a kind heart.
The Merry Wives of Windsor III, 4
Mistress Quickly, concerning Anne Page's lover, Fenton

14 I mean, that my heart unto yours is knit,
So that but one heart we can make of it.
A Midsummer Night's Dream II, 2
Lysander to Hermia

15 I love you with so much of my heart that none is left to protest.
Much Ado About Nothing IV, 1
Beatrice to Benedick

16 My heart
Leaps to be gone into my mother's bosom.
Pericles V, 3
Marina to Thaisa, her mother

17 Even in the glasses (mirrors) of thine eyes
I see thy grieved heart.
Richard II I, 3
Richard to John of Gaunt, whose son, Bolingbroke, has been banished

18 Farewell: if heart's presages be not vain,
We three here part that ne'er shall meet again.
Richard II II, 2
Bagot to Bushy and Green

19 Had not God, for some strong purpose, steel'd
The hearts of men, they must perforce have melted.
Richard II V, 2
Duke of York to Duchess, concerning Richard's downfall

20 We know each other's faces,
But for our hearts, he knows no more of mine
Than I of yours; nor I, no more of his.
Richard III III, 4
Duke of Buckingham to Bishop of Ely and others, concerning Richard III

21 My heart, all mad with misery,
Beats in the hollow prison of my flesh.
Titus Andronicus III, 2
Titus to Marcus, his brother

22 My heart beats thicker than a feverous pulse.
Troilus and Cressida III, 1
Troilus to Pandarus, concerning Cressida

23 His tears pure messengers sent from his heart;
His heart as far from fraud as heaven from earth.
The Two Gentlemen of Verona II, 7
Julia to Lucetta, concerning Proteus

24 I saw his heart in's face.
The Winter's Tale I, 2
Polixenes to Camillo, concerning Leontes

25 Love thrives not in the heart that shadows dreadeth.
The Rape of Lucrece Stanza 39

26 Dismiss your vows, your feigned tears, your flattery;
For where a heart is hard they make no battery.
Venus and Adonis Stanza 71

72 HEAT

1 I am as hot as molten lead, and as heavy too.
1 Henry IV V, 3
Falstaff during a battle

2 Heat not a furnace for your foe so hot
That it do singe yourself.
Henry VIII I, 1
Duke of Norfolk to Duke of Buckingham, on the latter's attack
on Wolsey

3   Lords, I am hot with haste in seeking you.
   King John IV, 3
   Hubert de Burgh with a message from the king.

4   O, who can hold a fire in his hand
   By thinking on the frosty Caucasus? . . .
   Or wallow naked in December snow
   By thinking on fantastic summer's heat?
   Richard II I, 3
   Bolingbroke after being banished

5   For she's not forward, but modest as the dove;
   She is not hot, but temperate as the morn.
   The Taming of the Shrew II, 1
   Petruchio, pretending that Kate is not really hot-tempered

6   One draught above heat makes him a fool.
   Twelfth Night I, 5
   Clown Feste to Countess Olivia, defining a drunkard

7   She, red and hot as coals of glowing fire.
   Venus and Adonis Stanza 6
   Venus has just pulled Adonis from his horse

8   I'll sigh celestial breath, whose gentle wind
   Shall cool the heat of the descending sun.
   Venus and Adonis Stanza 32

73   HEAVEN

1   Our remedies oft in ourselves do lie,
   Which we ascribe to heaven.
   All's Well That Ends Well I, 1
   Helena to herself

2 Do not, as some ungracious pastors do,
Show me the steep and thorny way to heaven,
Whiles, like a puff'd and reckless libertine,
Himself the primrose path of dalliance treads.
Hamlet I, 3
Ophelia to Laertes

3 There are more things in heaven and earth, Horatio,
Than are dreamt of in your philosophy.
Hamlet I, 5
Hamlet, after his meeting with the ghost of his father

4 Be thou a spirit of health or goblin damn'd,
Bring with thee airs from heaven or blasts from hell . . .
(Yet) I will speak to thee.
Hamlet I, 4
Hamlet to Ghost

5 Thy heaven is on earth; thine eyes and thoughts
Bear on a crown, the treasure of thy heart.
2 Henry VI II, 1
Cardinal Beaufort to Richard of Gloucester

6 Then, heaven, set ope thy everlasting gates,
To entertain my vows of thanks and praise.
2 Henry VI IV, 9
Henry, after the defeat of Cade's revolt

7 Methought I stood not in the smile of heaven.
Henry VIII II, 4
King Henry, deciding that he ought not to have married his
brother's widow, Katherine

8 Dread sovereign, how much are we bound to heaven
In daily thanks that gave us such a prince.
Henry VIII V, 3
Bishop Gardiner to Henry

9   When the cross blue lightning seem'd to open
The breast of heaven, I did present myself
Even in the aim and very flash of it.
Julius Caesar I, 3
Cassius to Casca

10   There's husbandry in heaven,
Their candles are all out.
Macbeth II, 1
Banquo, returning from a ride on a starless night

11   Heaven doth with us as we with torches do,
Not light them for themselves.
Measure for Measure I, 1
Duke to Angelo

12   I do think that you might pardon him,
And neither heaven nor man grieve at the mercy.
Measure for Measure II, 2
Isabella to Angelo, pleading for her brother Claudio

13   She wished
That heaven had made her such a man.
Othello I, 3
Othello, telling the Senators of Desdemona's response to his
stories

14   My comfort is that heaven will take our souls
And plague injustice with the pains of hell.
Richard II III, 1
Green, sentenced to death by Bolingbroke

15   If angels fight,
Weak men must fall, for heaven still guards the right.
Richard II III, 2
Richard, hoping for an army of angels to support him

16   Now he delivers thee
From this world's thraldom to the joys of heaven.
Richard III I, 4
Murderer, indicating ironically that Richard has ordered the
Duke of Clarence to be killed

17 So smile the heavens upon this holy act.
Romeo and Juliet II, 6
Friar Laurence, about to marry the young couple

18 Alack, alack, that heaven should practise stratagems
Upon so soft a subject as myself!
Romeo and Juliet III, 5
Juliet, after Romeo's banishment

19 Weep ye now, seeing she is advanced
Above the clouds, as high as heaven itself?
Romeo and Juliet IV, 5
Friar Laurence to Capulet, concerning Juliet's supposed death

20 When heaven doth weep, doth not the earth o'erflow?
Titus Andronicus III, 1
Titus to his brother Marcus

21 Here comes the countess; now heaven walks on earth.
Twelfth Night V, 1
Duke Orsino, on seeing Olivia

74 HELL

1 My ancient incantations are too weak,
And hell too strong for me to buckle with.
1 Henry VI V, 3
Joan of Arc conjures up spirits, which fail her

2 Break thou in pieces and consume to ashes,
Thou foul accursed minister of hell.
1 Henry VI V, 4
Duke of York to Joan of Arc

3 The sight of any of the house of York
Is as a fury to torment my soul;
And till I root out their accursed line
And leave not one alive, I live in hell.
3 Henry VI I, 3
Lord Clifford, about to murder the young Earl of Rutland

4 Down, down to hell; and say I sent thee thither!
3 Henry VI V, 6
Richard of Gloucester, stabbing Henry

5 There's hell, there's darkness, there's the sulphurous pit.
King Lear IV, 6
Lear, raving

6   You, mistress,
That have the office opposite to Saint Peter,
And keep the gate of hell!
Othello IV, 2
Othello to Desdemona, giving vent to his insane jealousy

7 O, I were damn'd beneath all depth in hell,
But that I did proceed upon just grounds
To this extremity.
Othello V, 2
Othello to Emilia, after the murder of his wife

8 Hie thee to hell for shame, and leave the world,
Thou cacodemon! there thy kingdom is.
Richard III I, 3
Queen Margaret to Richard Duke of Gloucester

9   Terrible hell make war
Upon their spotted souls for this offence.
Richard II III, 2
Richard, unjustly cursing three dead followers

10 Thinkest thou, Hortensio, though her father be very rich, any
man is so very a fool to be married to hell?
The Taming of the Shrew I, 1
Gremio on Kate the Shrew

75 HOME

1 He hath eaten me out of house and home.
2 Henry IV II, 1
Mistress Quickly concerning Falstaff

2 'Tis ever common
Men are merriest when they are from home.
Henry V I, 2
Henry to French Ambassadors

3 He hath no home, no place to fly to,
Nor knows he how to live but by the spoil.
2 Henry VI IV, 8
Lord Clifford talking to a mob about their leader, Jack Cade

4 Rebellious hinds . . .
Mark'd for the gallows, lay your weapons down;
Home to your cottages.
2 Henry VI IV, 2
Sir Humphrey Stafford to Cade's rebel mob

5 Hence! home, you idle creatures, get you home!
Julius Caesar I, 1
A tribune, opposed to Caesar, admonishing the crowd for
welcoming him

6 He wondered that your lordship
Would suffer him to spend his youth at home,
While other men, of slender reputation,
Put forth their sons to seek preferment out.
The Two Gentlemen of Verona I, 3
Panthino to Antonio. 'Him' refers to Antonio's son, Proteus,
who is without travel experience

7 I had rather than forty pound I were at home.
Twelfth Night V, 1
Sir Andrew Aguecheek, complaining that Cesario has assaulted
him

8   Home-keeping youth have ever homely wits.
The Two Gentlemen of Verona I, 1
Valentine to Proteus

9   As easy might I from myself depart
As from my soul, which in thy breast doth lie:
That is my home of love.
Sonnet 109

---

76   HONESTY

1   Though honesty be no puritan, yet it will do no hurt.
All's Well That Ends Well I, 3
Clown to Countess of Rousillon

2   No legacy is so rich as honesty.
All's Well That Ends Well III, 5
Mariana to Diana

3   He has everything that an honest man should not have; what an honest man should have, he has nothing.
All's Well That Ends Well IV, 3
Parolles, describing a fellow officer

4   Mine honesty
Shall not make poor my greatness.
Antony and Cleopatra II, 2
Antony to Octavius

5   Honesty coupled to beauty is to have honey a sauce to sugar.
As You Like It III, 3
Touchstone to Audrey

6   To be honest, as this world goes, is to be one man picked out of ten thousand.
Hamlet II, 2
Hamlet, feigning madness to Polonius

7   The power of beauty will sooner transform honesty from what
it is than the force of honesty can translate beauty into his
likeness.
Hamlet III, 1
Hamlet to Ophelia

8   I thank God I am as honest as any man living that is an old man
and no honester than I.
Much Ado About Nothing III, 5
Verges to Leonato

9   This fellow's of exceeding honesty.
Othello III, 3
Othello concerning the exceedingly dishonest Iago

10   Though he be merry, yet withal he's honest.
The Taming of the Shrew III, 2
Tranio to Baptista and Kate, concerning Petruchio

11   Every man has his fault, and honesty is his.
Timon of Athens III, 1
Lucullus, happy to praise Timon but not to lend him money

12   Though I am not naturally honest, I am so sometimes by
chance.
The Winter's Tale IV, 4
Autolycus to Clown and Shepherd

77   HONOUR

1   If I lose mine honour I lose myself.
Antony and Cleopatra III, 4
Antony to Cleopatra

2   A scar nobly got, or a noble scar, is a good livery of honour.
All's Well That Ends Well IV, 5
Lafeu to Clown

3   Rightly to be great
        Is not to stir without great argument,
        But greatly to find quarrel in a straw
        When honour's at the stake.
        Hamlet IV, 4
        Hamlet, soliloquizing

4   By heaven, methinks it were an easy leap,
        To pluck bright honour from the pale-faced moon,
        Or dive into the bottom of the deep,
        Where fathom-line could never touch the ground,
        And pluck up drowned honour by the locks.
        1 Henry IV I, 3
        Hotspur to nobles

5   Honour pricks me on. Yea, but how if honour pricks me off
    when I come on? how then?
    1 Henry IV V, 1
    Falstaff, musing on honour

6   What is honour? a word.
        1 Henry IV V, 1
        Falstaff, musing on honour

7   If it be a sin to covet honour,
        I am the most offending soul alive.
        Henry V IV, 3
        Henry to Earl of Westmoreland at Agincourt

8   Set honour in one eye and death i' the other,
        And I will look on both indifferently.
        Julius Caesar I, 2
        Brutus to Cassius

9   For Brutus is an honourable man;
        So are they all, all honourable men.
        Julius Caesar III, 2
        Antony to citizens, with hidden irony regarding Caesar's killers

10   O, that estates, degrees and offices
Were not derived corruptly, and that clear honour
Were purchased by the merit of the wearer.
The Merchant of Venice II, 9
Prince of Arragon, while choosing a casket

11   Honour we love;
For who hates honour hates the gods above.
Pericles II, 3
Simonides, at a banquet following a tournament which Pericles wins

12   Mine honour is my life; both grow in one;
Take honour from me, and my life is done.
Richard II II, 1
Thomas Mowbray to Richard

---

78   HOPE

1   (He) lined himself with hopes
Eating the air on promise of supply.
2 Henry IV I, 3
Lord Bardolph on Hotspur

2   The miserable have no other medicine
But only hope.
Measure for Measure III, 1
Claudio to Duke

3   How shall I be revenged on him? I think the best way were to
entertain him with hope, till the wicked fire of lust have melted
him in his own grease.
The Merry Wives of Windsor II, 1
Mrs Ford to Mrs Page, concerning Falstaff

4   I will despair, and be at enmity
With cozening hope; he is a flatterer.
Richard II II, 2
Queen to Bushy

5 Hope to joy is little less in joy
   Than hope enjoy'd.
   Richard II II, 3
   Earl of Northumberland to Bolingbroke

6 True hope is swift, and flies with swallow's wings.
   Richard III V, 2
   Earl of Richmond to a follower

7 Nothing that can be can come between me and the full
   prospect of my hopes.
   Twelfth Night III, 4
   Malvolio to himself

8 Hope is a lover's staff; walk hence with that,
   And manage it against despairing thoughts.
   The Two Gentlemen of Verona III, 1
   Proteus to Valentine, banished from Verona and his love, Silvia

9 When in disgrace with Fortune and men's eyes,
   I all alone beweep my outcast state . . .
   Wishing me like to one more rich in hope.
   Sonnet 29

79 HORSE

1   Is he on his horse?
   O happy horse, to bear the weight of Antony!
   Antony and Cleopatra I, 5
   Cleopatra to Charmian

2 O for a horse with wings!
   Cymbeline III, 2
   Imogen to Pisanio

3   A gentleman of Normandy . . .
                             grew into his seat,
And to such wondrous doing brought his horse
As had he been incorpsed and demi-natured
With the brave beast.
Hamlet IV, 7
Claudius to Laertes

4   When I am o'horseback, I will swear
     I love thee infinitely.
     1 Henry IV II, 3
     Hotspur, eager for battle, to his wife

5   Think, when we talk of horses, that you see them
     Printing their proud hoofs i'the receiving earth.
     Henry V Prologue 1
     Chorus to audience

6   I will not change my horse with any that treads but on four
pasterns . . . When I bestride him, I soar, I am a hawk. He trots
the air.
Henry V III, 7
Dauphin to French nobles

7   It is the prince of palfreys; his neigh is like the bidding of a
monarch, and his countenance enforces homage.
Henry V III, 7
Dauphin to French nobles

8   Mount thou my horse and hide my spurs in him,
     Till he have brought thee up to yonder troops
     And here again; that I may rest assured
     Whether yond troops are friend or enemy.
     Julius Caesar V, 3
     Cassius to Titinius

9   And Duncan's horses — a thing most strange and
        certain —
    Beauteous and swift, the minions of their race,
    Turn'd wild in nature, broke their stalls, flung out,
    Contending 'gainst obedience as they would make
    War with mankind.
    Macbeth II, 4
    Ross, describing events on the night of Duncan's murder

10 A horse! A horse! My kingdom for a horse!
    Richard III V, 7
    King Richard, after his horse is slain

11   I was not made a horse
    And yet I bear a burden like an ass.
    Richard II V, 5
    Richard in prison

80   HOURS
see also **Time** 176

1   Twice before, and jump at this dead hour,
    With martial stalk hath he gone by our watch.
    Hamlet I, 1
    Marcellus to Horatio, concerning the ghost of Hamlet's father

2   O let the hours be short
    Till fields and blows and groans applaud our sport.
    1 Henry IV I, 3
    Hotspur, on the coming battle

3   What a devil hast thou to do with the time of the day? Unless
    hours were cups of sack, and minutes capons ... I see no
    reason why thou shouldst be so superfluous to demand the
    time of the day.
    1 Henry IV I, 2
    Prince Hal to Falstaff

4   Talbot, farewell; thy hour is not yet come:
    I must go victual Orleans forthwith.
    1 Henry VI I, 5
    Joan of Arc, breaking off combat with Lord Talbot

5   I know not, gentlemen, what you intend,
    Who else must be let blood, who else is rank:
    If I myself, there is no hour so fit
    As Caesar's death's hour.
    Julius Caesar III, 1
    Antony to Caesar's killers

6   A merrier hour was never wasted there.
    A Midsummer Night's Dream II, 1
    Puck, telling a fairy of his practical jokes

7   Let Romeo hence in haste,
    Else, when he's found, that hour is his last.
    Romeo and Juliet III, 1
    Prince of Verona, announcing Romeo's banishment

8   Most miserable hour that e'er time saw.
    Romeo and Juliet IV, 5
    Lady Capulet, on Juliet's supposed death

9   Acquaint the princess
    With the sweet silent hours of marriage joys.
    Richard III IV, 4
    Richard to the mother of Princess Elizabeth

10 My watch has told me, toward my grave
    I have travelled but two hours.
    Twelfth Night V, 1
    A priest to Countess Olivia

11 Those hours that with gentle work did frame
    The lovely gaze where every eye doth dwell.
    Sonnet 5

81   HUSBAND
see also **Marriage** 106

1   Get thee a good husband, and use him as he uses thee.
All's Well That Ends Well I, 1
Parolles to Helena

2   Then shalt thou give me with thy kingly hand
What husband in thy power I will command.
All's Well That Ends Well II, 1
Helena to the King of France, on the reward for curing a deadly
illness

3   Thy jealous fits
Have scared thy husband from the use of wits.
The Comedy of Errors V, 1
Abbess to Adriana

4   I will remain
The loyal'st husband that did e'er plight troth.
Cymbeline I, 1
Posthumus to Imogen

5   What shall I do the while? where abide? how live?
Or in my life what comfort when I am
Dead to my husband?
Cymbeline III, 4
Her husband's unjustified jealousy has left Imogen distraught

6   A second time I kill my husband dead,
When second husband kisses me in bed.
Hamlet III, 2
Player Queen to Player King in the 'Mousetrap' play

7   I have a daughter;
Would any of the stock of Barrabas
Had been her husband rather than a Christian.
The Merchant of Venice IV, 1
Shylock to himself

8 By my troth, niece, thou wilt never get a husband if thou be so
   shrewd of thy tongue.
   Much Ado About Nothing II, 1
   Leonato to Beatrice

9 Thy husband is thy lord, thy life, thy keeper,
   Thy head, thy sovereign.
   The Taming of the Shrew V, 2
   Katherina, after being tamed, gives a lecture on how wives
   should behave

10   Let still the woman take
   An elder than herself: so wears she to him,
   So sways she level in her husband's heart.
   Twelfth Night II, 4
   Orsino to Viola/Cesario

11 So shall I live, supposing thou art true,
   Like a deceived husband; so love's face
   May still seem true to me, though alter'd new.
   Sonnet 93

82 HYPOCRISY

1 My tables — meet it is I set it down,
   That one may smile and smile, and be a villain.
   Hamlet I, 5
   Hamlet concerning his uncle

2   With devotion's visage
   And pious action we do sugar o'er
   The devil himself.
   Hamlet III, 1
   Polonius to Ophelia

3 I will speak daggers to her, but use none;
   My tongue and soul in this be hypocrites.
   Hamlet III, 2
   Hamlet concerning his mother

4　Away, and mock the time with fairest show:
　　False face must hide what the false heart doth know.
　　Macbeth I, 7
　　Macbeth to Lady Macbeth

5　To show an unfelt sorrow is an office
　　Which the false man does easy.
　　Macbeth II, 3
　　Malcolm to Donalbain, suspicious of Macbeth, after the
　　discovery of Duncan's murder

6　O, what may man within him hide
　　Though angel on the outward side.
　　Measure for Measure III, 2
　　Duke to himself

7　Look you get a prayer-book in your hand,
　　And stand between two churchmen, good my lord.
　　Richard III III, 7
　　Buckingham advising Richard to simulate piety to increase his
　　popularity

8　Gloucester's show
　　Beguiles him, as the mournful crocodile
　　With sorrow snares relenting passengers.
　　2 Henry VI III, 1
　　Margaret on how Henry VI is deceived by Duke of Gloucester,
　　later Richard III

83　IGNORANCE

1　　　　　　We, ignorant of ourselves,
　　Beg often our own harms, which the wise powers
　　Deny us for our good.
　　Antony and Cleopatra II, 1
　　Menecrates to Pompey

2   Let me not burst in ignorance; but tell
Why thy canonized bones, hearsed in death
Have burst their cerements.
Hamlet I, 4
Hamlet, on first meeting his father's ghost

3   Ignorance is the curse of God,
Knowledge the wing wherewith we fly to heaven.
2 Henry VI IV, 7
Lord Say to Cade, leader of a rebel mob

4   O thou monster Ignorance, how deform'd dost thou look!
Love's Labour's Lost IV, 2
The pedant, Holofernes, has been airing his knowledge at the expense of a foolish constable

5   Man, proud man,
Drest in a little brief authority,
Most ignorant of what he's most assured,
Plays such fantastic tricks before high heaven
As make the angels weep.
Measure for Measure II, 2
Isabella to Angelo

6   Dull, unfeeling, barren ignorance
Is made my gaoler to attend on me.
Richard II I, 3
Mowbray, on being banished from England

7   The common curse of mankind, folly and ignorance, be thine.
Troilus and Cressida II, 3
Thersites to Patroclus

8   There is no darkness but ignorance.
Twelfth Night IV, 2
Feste, baiting Malvolio

9   Well learned is that tongue that well can thee commend:
All ignorant that soul that sees without wonder.
The Passionate Pilgrim Stanza 5

84   INCONSTANCY

1   Too unruly deer, he breaks the pale,
    And feeds from home; poor I am but his stale.
    The Comedy of Errors II, 1
    Adriana of Ephesus to her sister, referring to her husband

2   Hath not his eye
    Stray'd his affection in unlawful love?
    A sin prevailing much in youthful men.
    The Comedy of Errors V, 1
    Abbess to Adriana

3   You see how full of changes his age is . . . He always loved our
    sister most, and with what poor judgement he hath now cast
    her off.
    King Lear I, 1
    Goneril to Regan, on their father's wayward treatment of Cordelia

4   I have suffered more for their sakes, more than the villainous
    inconstancy of man's disposition is able to bear.
    The Merry Wives of Windsor IV, 5
    Falstaff to Mrs Quickly, on Mrs Ford and Mrs Page

5   Men were deceivers ever,
    One foot in sea and one on shore,
    To one thing constant never.
    Much Ado About Nothing II, 3
    Singer to Don Pedro

6   More inconstant than the wind, who wooes
    Even now the frozen bosom of the north,
    And, being anger'd, puffs away from thence,
    Turning his face to the dew-dropping south.
    Romeo and Juliet I, 4
    Mercutio to Romeo, concerning dreams

7   O swear not by the moon, th'inconstant moon,
    That monthly changes in her circled orb,
    Lest that thy love prove likewise variable.
    Romeo and Juliet II, 2
    Juliet to Romeo

8 Thou canst not vex me with inconstant mind,
Since that my life on thy revolt doth lie . . .
But what's so blessed-fair that fears no blot?
Thou mayst be false, but yet I know it not.
Sonnet 92

85 INGRATITUDE

1 Blow, blow, thou winter wind,
Thou art not so unkind
As man's ingratitude.
As You Like It II, 7
Song by Amiens to Duke Senior and his companions

2 Ingratitude is monstrous; and for the multitude to be
ingrateful were to make a monster of the multitude.
Coriolanus II, 3
Third Citizen to others

3 This was the most unkindest cut of all;
For when the noble Caesar saw him stab,
Ingratitude, more strong than traitors' arms,
Quite vanquish'd him.
Julius Caesar III, 2
Antony's speech to the citizens, here referring to Brutus

4 How sharper than a serpent's tooth it is
To have a thankless child.
King Lear I, 4
Lear concerning Goneril

5 Ingratitude, thou marble-hearted fiend,
More hideous when thou show'st thee in a child
Than the sea-monster.
King Lear I, 4
Lear concerning Goneril

6   All the stor'd vengeances of heaven fall
     On her ingrateful top!
     King Lear II, 2
     Lear concerning Regan

7   Filial ingratitude!
     Is it not as this mouth should tear this hand
     For lifting food to't?
     King Lear III, 4
     Lear to Earl of Kent

8   O worthiest cousin!
     The sin of my ingratitude even now
     Was heavy on me.
     Macbeth I, 4
     King Duncan chiding himself, needlessly, for tardiness in
     thanking Macbeth

9   O see the monstrousness of man
     When he looks out in an ungrateful shape.
     Timon of Athens III, 2
     Timon's supposed friends criticized, by a stranger, for their
     treatment of him

86   INJURY

1   The record of what injuries you did us,
     Though written in our flesh, we shall remember
     As things but done by chance.
     Antony and Cleopatra V, 2
     Octavius Caesar, trying to reassure Cleopatra after her capture

2   Justice, sweet prince, against that woman there!
     She whom thou gavest to me to be my wife,
     That hath abused and dishonour'd me
     Even in the strength and height of injury.
     The Comedy of Errors V, 1
     Antipholus of Ephesus and his wife in an identity mix-up with
     his twin

3 Tell him we could have rebuked him at Harfleur, but that we thought not good to bruise an injury till it were full ripe.
Henry V III, 6
French herald with message from Dauphin

4   O, sir, to wilful men
The injuries that they themselves procure
Must be their schoolmasters.
King Lear II, 4
Regan to Lear

5 Will you rent our ancient love asunder,
To join with men in scorning your poor friend? . . .
Our sex, as well as I, may chide you for it,
Though I alone do feel the injury.
A Midsummer Night's Dream III, 2
Helena to Hermia

6 Go, girl; I cannot blame thee now to weep;
For such an injury would vex a very saint.
The Taming of the Shrew III, 2
Baptista sympathizes with Kate over Petruchio's seeming failure
to attend his wedding

7   It is a greater grief
To bear love's wrong, than hate's known injury.
Sonnet 40

87 INNOCENCE

1 Thou knowest in the state of innocency Adam fell; and what should poor Jack Falstaff do in the days of villainy?
1 Henry IV III, 3
Falstaff to Prince Hal

2   You, lord Archbishop . . .
Whose learning and good letters peace hath tutor'd,
Whose white investments figure innocence.
2 Henry IV IV, 1
Earl of Westmoreland to Archbishop of York

3   It will help me nothing
To plead my innocence; for that dye is on me
Which makes my whitest part black.
Henry VIII I, 1
Duke of Buckingham, charged with high treason

4   How innocent I was
From any private malice in his end,
His noble jury and foul cause can witness.
Henry VIII III, 2
Wolsey, concerning the execution of Buckingham

5   Our kinsman Gloucester is as innocent
From meaning treason to our royal person
As is the sucking lamb or harmless dove.
2 Henry VI III, 1
Henry innocently praises his future murderer

6   Are you call'd forth from out a world of men
To slay the innocent?
Richard III I, 4
Duke of Clarence to two murderers

7   God and our innocency defend and guard us.
Richard III III, 5
Buckingham to Gloucester

8   Prompt me, plain and holy innocence!
I am your wife, if you will marry me.
The Tempest III, 1
Miranda to Ferdinand

9   We were as twinn'd lambs that did frisk i'the sun,
And bleat the one at the other; what we chang'd
Was innocence for innocence; we knew not
The doctrine of ill-doing.
The Winter's Tale I, 2
Polixenes on his childhood with Leontes.

10   If powers divine
Behold our human actions, as they do,
I doubt not then but innocence shall make
False accusation blush.
The Winter's Tale III, 2
Hermione, defending herself against Leonte's wild jealousy

---

88   JEALOUSY

---

1   The venom clamours of a jealous woman
Poisons more deadly than a mad dog's tooth.
The Comedy of Errors V, 1
Abbess to Adriana

2   So full of artless jealousy is guilt
It spills itself in fearing to be spilt.
Hamlet IV, 5
Gertrude, troubled by a guilty conscience

3   Page is an ass, a secure ass; he will trust his wife; he
will not be jealous . . . God be praised for my jealousy!
The Merry Wives of Windsor II, 2
Ford to himself

4   O beware, my lord, of jealousy;
It is the green-eyed monster, which doth mock
The meat it feeds on.
Othello III, 3
Iago, ironically warning Othello against the vice he is
encouraging

5   Jealous souls will not be answer'd so;
    They are not ever jealous for the cause
    But jealous for they are jealous.
    Othello III, 4
    Emilia to Desdemona

6   Why should I not, had I the heart to do it,
    Like to the Egyptian thief at point of death,
    Kill what I love? – a savage jealousy
    That sometimes savours nobly.
    Twelfth Night V, 1
    Orsino is jealous of his apparent 'rival' – actually Viola

7   Love, thou know'st, is full of jealousy.
    The Two Gentlemen of Verona II, 4
    Valentine, formerly a mocker of love, is now captivated by Silvia

8   This jealousy
    Is for a precious creature: as she's rare,
    Must it be great; and, as his person's mighty,
    Must it be violent.
    The Winter's Tale I, 2
    Polixenes on Leonato's jealousy over Hermione

89 JEWELS

1   Let's away,
    And get our jewels and our wealth together,
    Devise the fittest time and safest way
    To hide us from pursuit.
    As You Like It I, 3
    Celia to Rosalind

2   The toad, ugly and venomous,
    Wears yet a precious jewel in his head.
    As You Like It II, 1
    Duke Senior to his followers

3 From the east to western Ind,
   No jewel is like Rosalind.
   As You Like It III, 2
   Rhyme fastened by Orlando to a tree

4 I took a costly jewel from my neck –
   A heart it was, bound in with diamonds –
   And threw it towards the land.
   2 Henry VI III, 2
   Queen Margaret, recalling an incident when she first sailed to
   England from France

5 The jewel that we find, we stoop and take it
   Because we see it; but what we do not see
   We tread upon.
   Measure for Measure II, 1
   Angelo to Escalus

6 As jewels lose their glory if neglected,
   So princes their renowns if not respected.
   Pericles II, 2
   Simonides to jousting knights

7 I'll give my jewels for a set of beads,
   My gorgeous palace for a hermitage.
   Richard II III, 3
   Richard, anticipating his coming downfall

8 It seems she hangs upon the cheek of night
   Like a rich jewel in an Ethiop's ear.
   Romeo and Juliet I, 5
   Romeo on first seeing Juliet

9 Dumb jewels often in their silent kind
   More than quick words do move a woman's mind.
   The Two Gentlemen of Verona III, 1
   Valentine to Duke of Milan

10 Look here, what tributes wounded fancies sent me
   Of paled pearls and rubies red as blood.
   A Lover's Complaint Stanza 29

90 JOY

1 If this be so, the gods do mean to strike me
    To death with immortal joy.
    Cymbeline V, 5
    Cymbeline learns that his daughter Imogen, believed dead, is
    alive

2 Where joy most revels, grief doth most lament;
    Grief joys, joy grieves, on slender accident.
    Hamlet III, 2
    Player King to Player Queen

3 If he be sick with joy, he'll recover without physic.
    2 Henry IV IV, 5
    Prince Henry about his father

4   My plenteous joys
    Wanton in fullness, seek to hide themselves
    In drops of sorrow.
    Macbeth I, 4
    King Duncan, after victory in battle

5 My lord Bassanio and my gentle lady,
    I wish you all the joy that you can wish.
    The Merchant of Venice III, 2
    Gratiano, after Bassanio has chosen the right casket

6 How much better is it to weep at joy than to joy at weeping.
    Much Ado About Nothing I, 1
    Leonato to a messenger bringing news of military success

7   I weep for joy
    To stand upon my kingdom once again.
    Richard II III, 2
    Richard, after returning from Ireland

8   Come what sorrow can,
    It cannot countervail the exchange of joy.
    Romeo and Juliet II, 6
    Romeo to Friar Laurence

9   A joy past joy calls out on me.
Romeo and Juliet III, 3
Romeo, about to spend the night secretly with Juliet

10   Sweets with sweets war not, joy delights in joy,
Why lovest thou that which thou receivest not gladly.
Sonnet 8

11   Some glory in their birth, some in their skill,
Some in their wealth, some in their body's force . . .
And every humour has his adjunct pleasure,
Wherein it finds a joy above the rest.
Sonnet 91

---

91   JUDGEMENT

1   My salad days,
When I was green in judgement.
Antony and Cleopatra I, 5
Cleopatra to Charmian, on her love for Caesar before that for
Antony

2   Give every man thine ear, but few thy voice;
Take each man's censure, but reserve thy judgement.
Hamlet I, 3
Polonius's advice to Laertes

3   Forbear to judge, for we are sinners all.
2 Henry VI III, 3
Henry at Cardinal Beaufort's death

4   O judgement! thou art fled to brutish beasts,
And men have lost their reason
Julius Caesar III, 2
Antony to citizens over Caesar's body

5   I not deny
The jury, passing on the prisoner's life
May in the sworn twelve have a thief or two
Guiltier than him they try.
Measure for Measure II, 1
Angelo to Escalus

6   How would you be
If He, which is the top of judgement, should
But judge you as you are? O, think on that.
Measure for Measure II, 2
Isabella to Angelo

7 I stand for judgement: answer; shall I have it?
The Merchant of Venice IV, 1
Shylock, insisting on the terms of his bond with Antonio

8 A Daniel come to judgement! yea, a Daniel!
O wise young judge, how I do honour thee!
The Merchant of Venice IV, 1
Shylock, when 'Balthasar' appears to support his case

9 The urging of that word 'judgement' hath bred a kind of remorse in me.
Richard III I, 4
Second Murderer, concerning the Duke of Clarence, whom he none the less helps to murder

92 JUSTICE

1 Use every man after his desert, and who shall 'scape whipping.
Hamlet II, 2
Hamlet to Polonius

2 In the corrupted currents of this world
Offence's gilded hand may shove by justice.
And oft 'tis seen the wicked prize itself
Buys out the law: but 'tis not so above.
Hamlet III, 3
Claudius, suffering from an attack of conscience

3   Thrice is he arm'd that hath his quarrel just,
     And he but naked, though lock'd up in steel,
     Whose conscience with injustice is corrupted.
     2 Henry VI III, 2
     Henry to quarrelling lords

4   See how yond justice rails upon yond simple thief . . . Change
     places, and, handy-dandy, which is the justice, which is the
     thief?
     King Lear IV, 6
     Lear to Earl of Gloucester

5   The gods are just, and of our pleasant vices
     Make instruments to plague us.
     King Lear V, 3
     Edgar to his bastard brother, Edmund

6   This even-handed justice
     Commends the ingredients of our Poison'd chalice
     To our own lips.
     Macbeth I, 7
     Macbeth, considering the reasons against murdering King
     Duncan

7   *Isabella:* Yet show some pity
     Angelo: I show it most of all when I show justice,
                 For then I pity those I do not know.
     Measure for Measure II, 2
     Concerning the death sentence on Claudio

8   Though justice be thy plea, consider this,
     That, in the course of justice, none of us
     Should see salvation.
     The Merchant of Venice IV, 1
     Portia, as Balthasar, to Shylock

9   As thou urgest justice, be assured
     Thou shalt have justice, more than thou desirest.
     The Merchant of Venice IV, 1
     Portia, as Balthasar, to Shylock

93 KING

1 There's such divinity doth hedge a king
That treason can but peep to what it would.
Hamlet IV, 5
King Claudius to Laertes

2 Uneasy lies the head that wears a crown.
2 Henry IV III, 1
Henry, soliloquizing

3 Upon the king! let us, our lives, our souls,
Our debts, our careful wives,
Our children and our sins lay on the kings!
Henry V IV, 1
King Henry to himself

4 The king is but a man, as I am.
Henry V IV, 1
Henry, incognito, to Bates

5 Thou wouldst find me such a plain king that thou wouldst
think I had sold my farm to buy my crown.
Henry V V, 2
Henry to Princess Katherine

6 The king himself is to be feared as the lion.
1 Henry IV III, 3
Falstaff to Prince Hal

7 The presence of a king engenders love
Amongst his subjects and his loyal friends.
1 Henry VI III, 1
Duke of Gloucester to Henry

8 I see no reason why a king of years
Should be protected like a child.
2 Henry VI II, 3
Queen Margaret to Humphrey of Gloucester, who for a while
ruled as Protector

9 I am far better born than is the king,
   More like a king, more kingly in my thoughts.
   2 Henry VI V, 1
   Duke of York to himself

10 Farewell, faint-hearted and degenerate king,
    In whose cold blood no spark of honour bides,
    3 Henry VI I, 1
    Earl of Westmoreland to Henry

11 And now to London with triumphant march,
    There to be crowned England's royal king.
    3 Henry VI II, 6
    Earl of Warwick to Edward IV

12 Gives not the hawthorn bush a sweeter shade
    To shepherds looking on their silly sheep,
    Than doth a rich embroider'd canopy
    To kings that fear their subjects' treachery?
    3 Henry VI II, 5
    Henry to himself

13 *Gloucester:* The trick of that voice I do well remember:
                  Is't not the King?
    Lear: Ay, every inch a king.
    King Lear IV, 6
    Lear, meeting the blinded Gloucester

14   To be king
    Stands not within the prospect of belief.
    Macbeth I, 3
    Macbeth to the witches

15 A substitute shines brightly as a king
    Until a king be by.
    The Merchant of Venice V, 1
    Portia to Nerissa

16 Kings are earth's gods; in vice their law's their will;
    And if Jove stray, who dares say Jove doth ill?
    Pericles I, 1
    Pericles to Antiochus

17 They do abuse the king that flatter him:
    For flattery is the bellows blows up sin.
    Pericles I, 2
    Helicanus to Pericles

18 Not all the water in the rough rude sea
    Can wash the balm from an anointed king.
    Richard II III, 2
    Richard to Aumerle, trying to be confident

19 For God's sake, let us sit upon the ground
    And tell sad stories of the death of kings.
    Richard II III, 2
    Richard, bitterly, after receiving increasingly bad news

20 What must the king do now? Must he submit?
    The king shall do it: must he be deposed?
    The king shall be contented: must he lose
    The name of king? o'God's name let it go.
    Richard II III, 3
    Richard, sadly accepting his downfall

21 God save the king! Will no man say amen?
    Am I both priest and clerk? well then, amen.
    Richard II IV, 1
    Richard, preparing to resign his kingship

22 This royal throne of kings, this sceptr'd isle.
    Richard II II, 1
    John of Gaunt in his praise of England

23 Weigh you the worth and honour of a king,
    So great as our dread father, in a scale
    Of common ounces?
    Troilus and Cressida II, 2
    Troilus to Hector, concerning Priam

24 Kings' misdeeds cannot be hid in clay.
    The Rape of Lucrece Stanza 87

94 KISSES
see also **Lips** 100

1   There is gold, and here
My bluest veins to kiss: a hand that kings
Have lipp'd, and trembled kissing.
Antony and Cleopatra II, 5
Cleopatra to messenger

2   We have kiss'd away
Kingdoms and provinces.
Antony and Cleopatra III, 10
Scarus to Enobarbus

3   Of many thousand kisses the poor last
I lay upon thy lips.
Antony and Cleopatra IV, 15
Antony, dying, to Cleopatra

4   His kissing is as full of sanctity as the touch of holy bread.
As You Like It III, 4
Rosalind to Celia, concerning Orlando

5   A kiss
Long as my exile, sweet as my revenge! . . .
              That kiss
I carried from thee, dear, and my true lip
Hath virgin'd it e'er since.
Coriolanus V, 3
Coriolanus to Virgilia

6   Ere I could
Give him that parting kiss, which I had set
Betwixt two charming words, comes in my father . . .
Shakes all our buds from growing.
Cymbeline I, 3
Imogen to Pisanio, concerning her banished husband,
Posthumus

7   I understand thy kisses and thou mine,
    And that's a feeling disputation.
    1 Henry IV III, 1
    Mortimer to Glendower's daughter

8   By my troth, I kiss thee with a most constant heart.
    2 Henry IV II, 4
    Doll Tearsheet to Falstaff

9   It is not a fashion for the maids in France to kiss before they are
    married, would she say?
    Henry V V, 2
    Henry to Princess's interpreter

10   I can express no kinder sign of love
     Than this kind kiss.
     2 Henry VI I, 1
     Henry first meeting Margaret

11   Take, O, take thy lips away,
     That so sweetly were forsworn . . .
     But my kisses bring again, bring again;
     Seals of love, but seal'd in vain, seal'd in vain.
     Measure for Measure IV, 1
     Boy's song to Mariana

12   Speak, cousin; or, if you cannot, stop his mouth with a kiss,
     and let not him speak neither.
     Much Ado About Nothing II, 1
     Beatrice to Hero, concerning Claudio

13   'Tis time to fear when tyrants seem to kiss.
     Pericles I, 2
     Pericles to Helicanus, concerning Antiochus

14   Teach not thy lips such scorn, for they were made
     For kissing, lady, not for such contempt.
     Richard III I, 2
     Richard to Lady Anne, whose husband he had recently
     murdered

15 And steal immortal blessing from her lips.
    Romeo and Juliet III, 3
    Romeo concerning Juliet

16 He took the bride about the neck
    And kiss'd her lips with such a clamorous smack
    That at the parting all the church did echo.
    The Taming of the Shrew III, 2
    Gremio to Tranio, on Petruchio's wedding

17 In kissing, do you render or receive? . . .
    The kiss you take is better than you give.
    Troilus and Cressida IV, 5
    Cressida to Patroclus

18 In delay there lies no plenty;
    Then come kiss me, sweet and twenty.
    Twelfth Night II, 3
    Clown's song

19 Seal the bargain with a holy kiss.
    The Two Gentlemen of Verona II, 2
    Julia to Proteus: the bargain is an exchange of rings

20   Is whispering nothing?
    Is leaning cheek to cheek? is meeting noses?
    Kissing with inside lip . . . is this nothing?
    The Winter's Tale I, 2
    Leontes, revealing his wild jealousy of Polixenes to Camillo

95 KNIGHTHOOD

1 Arise my knights o' the battle: I create you
   Companion to our person.
   Cymbeline V, 5
   Cymbeline to Belarius and his two 'sons'

2   Great is the rumour of this dreadful knight,
    And his achievement of no less account.
    1 Henry VI II, 3
    Countess of Auvergne concerning Lord Talbot

3   When first this order was ordain'd, my lords,
    Knights of the Garter were of noble birth,
    Valiant and virtuous, full of haughty courage . . .
    He then that is not furnish'd in this sort
    Doth but usurp the sacred name of knight.
    1 Henry VI IV, 1
    Lord Talbot, referring to the cowardice of Sir John Fastolf

4   You promised knighthood to our forward son:
    Unsheath your sword and dub him presently.
    3 Henry VI II, 2
    Queen Margaret to Henry, concerning Prince Edward

5   Robert Faulconbridge,
    A soldier, by the honour-giving hand
    Of Coeur-de-lion, knighted in the field.
    King John I, 1
    Philip the Bastard, referring to his father

6   His knights grow riotous.
    King Lear I, 3
    Goneril on Lear's retainers

7   Marshal, ask yonder knight in arms
    Both who he is, and why he cometh hither.
    Richard II I, 3
    Richard's formal words as Bolingbroke approaches to joust
    against Mowbray

8   For 'tis a meritorious fair design
    To chase injustice with revengeful arms:
    Knights, by their oaths, should right poor ladies'
        harms.
    The Rape of Lucrece Stanza 242

96 KNOWLEDGE

1 He was skilful enough to have lived still, if knowledge could be set up against mortality.
All's Well That Ends Well I, 1
Lafeu on Helena's father, a great physician

2 We know what we are, but not what we may be.
Hamlet IV, 5
Ophelia, offering a flash of sanity during her madness

3 Ignorance is the curse of God,
Knowledge the wing wherewith we fly to heaven.
2 Henry VI IV, 7
Lord Say, attempting to defend himself against an ignorant and violent mob

4 Be govern'd by your knowledge, and proceed
I' the sway of your own will.
King Lear IV, 7
Cordelia to the doctor attending Lear

5 Too much to know, is to know nought but fame.
Love's Labour's Lost I, 1
Biron to King of Navarre and others

6 The full sum of me . . .
Is an unlesson'd girl, unschool'd, unpractised;
Happy in this, she is not yet so old
But she may learn.
The Merchant of Venice III, 2
Portia to Bassanio

7 Beguile the time and feed your knowledge
With viewing of the town.
Twelfth Night III, 3
Antonio to Sebastian

8 Thou art as fair in knowledge as in hue,
Finding thy worth a limit past my praise.
Sonnet 82

97 LADY
see also **Woman** 193

1 'Twas a good lady, 'twas a good lady: we may pick a thousand
salads ere we light on such another herb.
All's Well That Ends Well IV, 5
Lafeu to Countess de Rousillon, concerning the supposed death of Helena

2 If ladies be but young and fair,
They have the gift to know it.
As You Like It II, 7
Jaques, quoting Touchstone

3 Your lady
Is one of the fairest that I have look'd upon.
Cymbeline II, 4
Iachimo to Posthumus, concerning Imogen

4 Constant you are,
But yet a woman: and for secrecy,
No lady closer; for I well believe
Thou wilt not utter what thou dost not know.
1 Henry IV II, 3
Hotspur to his wife

5 Swear at me, Kate, like a lady as thou art,
A good mouth-filling oath.
1 Henry IV III, 1
Hotspur to his wife

6 So good a lady that no tongue could ever
Pronounce dishonour of her.
Henry VIII II, 3
Anne Bullen, talking of Queen Katherine

7 *Chamberlain:* It seems the marriage with his
brother's wife
Has crept too near his conscience.
Lord Say: No, his conscience
Has crept too near another lady.
Henry VIII II, 2
Say is referring to Anne Bullen

8   Your own ladies and pale-visaged maids
Like Amazons come tripping after drums,
Their thimbles into armed gauntlets change,
Their needles to lances.
King John V, 2
Philip the Bastard, on feminine militarism

9 In mine eye she is the sweetest lady that ever I looked on.
Much Ado About Nothing I, 1
Claudio to Benedick about Hero

10   Full many a lady
I have eyed with best regard . . . but you, O you,
So perfect and so peerless are created
Of every creature's best!
The Tempest III, 1
Ferdinand to Miranda

---

98 LAW

---

1 Faith, I have been a truant in the law,
And never yet could frame my will to it.
1 Henry VI II, 4
Earl of Suffolk to other lords

2 Shall there be gallows standing when thou art king? and resolution thus fobbed as it is with the rusty curb of old father antic the law?
1 Henry IV I, 2
Falstaff to Prince Hal

3 The first thing we do, let's kill all the lawyers.
2 Henry VI IV, 2
Dick to Jack Cade, leaders of a rebel mob

4 Press not a falling man too far! 'tis virtue:
His faults lie open to the laws; let them,
Not you, correct them.
Henry VIII III, 2
Lord Chamberlain to Earl to Surrey

5 Law cannot give my child his kingdom here,
For he that holds his kingdom holds the law.
King John III, 1
Constance, concerning Prince Arthur and his uncle, King John

6 We must not make a scarecrow of the law,
Setting it up to fear the birds of prey,
And let it keep one shape, till custom make it
Their perch, and not their terror.
Measure for Measure II, 1
Angelo to Escalus

7 The law hath not been dead, though it hath slept.
Measure for Measure II, 2
Angelo to Isabella, on the law for which Claudio has been
sentenced to death

8 The brain may devise laws for the blood, but a hot temper
leaps o'er a cold decree.
The Merchant of Venice I, 2
Portia to Nerissa

9 The world is still deceiv'd with ornament:
In law, what plea so tainted and corrupt
But, being season'd with a gracious voice,
Obscures the show of evil?
The Merchant of Venice III, 2
Bassanio, considering the golden casket

10   I crave the law,
The penalty and forfeit of my bond.
The Merchant of Venice IV, 1
Shylock in his law suit against Antonio

11   I beseech you,
Wrest once the law to your authority:
To do a great right, do a little wrong.
The Merchant of Venice IV, 1
Bassanio to Balthasar/Portia

12   There is no power in Venice
Can alter a decree established;
'Twill be recorded as a precedent.
The Merchant of Venice IV, 1
Balthasar/Portia to Bassanio

13   It is enacted in the laws of Venice,
If it be proved against an alien
That by direct or indirect attempts
He seek the life of any citizen . . .
     the offender's life lies in the mercy
Of the Duke only.
The Merchant of Venice IV, 1
Balthasar/Portia to the court

14   What would you have me do? I am a subject,
And I challenge law: attorneys are denied me;
And therefore personally I lay my claim
To my inheritance of free descent.
Richard II II, 3
Bolingbroke to Duke of York

15   Before I be convict by course of law,
To threaten me with death is most unlawful.
Richard III I, 4
Duke of Clarence, hoping, desperately, to put off his two
murderers

16   Please ye we may contrive this afternoon . . .
And do as adversaries do in law,
Strive mightily, but eat and drink as friends.
The Taming of the Shrew I, 2
Tranio to Gremio and Hortensio – all three being rival suitors to
Bianca

17 Still you keep o' the windy side of the law.
Twelfth Night III, 4
Fabian, making fun of Sir Andrew's absurd challenge to
Cesario/Viola

99 LIFE

1 The web of our life is of mingled yarn, good and ill together.
All's Well That Ends Well IV, 3
One French lord to another

2 I love long life better than figs.
Antony and Cleopatra I, 2
Charmian to Soothsayer

3 This our life exempt from public haunt
Finds tongues in trees, books in the running brooks,
Sermons in stones and good in everything.
As You Like It II, 1
Duke Senior to his companions in the Forest of Arden

4 O gentlemen, the time of life is short!
To spend that shortness basely were too long
1 Henry IV V, 2
Hotspur, eager for battle

5 Let life be short; else shame will be too long.
Henry V IV, 5
Duke of Bourbon to other Frenchmen at Agincourt

6 The sands are number'd that make up my life;
Here must I stay, and here my life must end.
3 Henry VI I, 4
Duke of York, shortly before he is stabbed by his opponents

7   I cannot tell what you and other men
    Think of this life; but for my single self,
    I had as lief not be as live to be
    In awe of such a thing as I myself.
    I was born free as Caesar; so were you.
    Julius Caesar I, 2
    Cassius to Brutus

8   Life is as tedious as a twice-told tale
    Vexing the dull ear of a drowsy man.
    King John III, 4
    Dauphin to Cardinal Pandulph

9   Life's but a walking shadow, a poor player
    That struts and frets his hour upon the stage
    And then is heard no more.
    Macbeth V, 5
    Macbeth, soliloquizing after the death of his wife

10   From this instant
    There's nothing serious in mortality . . .
    The wine of life is drawn.
    Macbeth II, 3
    Macbeth shams distress when Duncan's murder is revealed

11   Reason thus with life:
    If I do lose thee, I do lose a thing
    That none but fools would keep.
    Measure for Measure III, 1
    Duke gives cheerless advice to Claudio

100   LIPS
see also **Kisses** 94

1   There was a pretty redness in his lip,
A little riper and more hasty red
Than that mix'd in his cheek.
As You Like It III, 5
Phebe to Silvius, about Ganymede/Rosalind

2   You have witchcraft in your lips, Kate: there is more eloquence
in a sugar touch of them than in the tongues of the French
council.
Henry V V, 2
Henry to Katherine, the French King's daughter

3   Here could I breathe my soul into the air . . .
To have thee with thy lips to stop my mouth.
2 Henry VI III, 2
Earl of Suffolk, lover to Margaret, Henry's queen

4   Take, O, take thy lips away,
That so sweetly were forsworn.
Measure for Measure IV, 1
Song by a boy to Mariana

5   O, how ripe in show
Those lips, those kissing cherries, tempting grow.
A Midsummer Night's Dream III, 2
Demetrius to Helena, who thinks he is mocking her

6   The king is angry: see, he bites the lip.
Richard III IV, 2
Catesby to a stander-by

7   I'll take that winter from your lips, fair lady:
Achilles bids you welcome.
Troilus and Cressida IV, 5
Several Greek officers give a similar welcome

8 O! what a deal of scorn looks beautiful
In the contempt and anger of his lip.
Twelfth Night III, 1
Olivia to herself, observing Cesario/Viola

9 Diana's lip is not more rubious.
Twelfth Night I, 4
Orsino, considering the feminine appearance of his page,
Cesario

10 'Even then,' quoth she 'he seized upon my lips,'
And with her lips on his did act the seizure.
The Passionate Pilgrim Stanza 11

101 LOVE

1 There's beggary in the love that can be reckoned.
Antony and Cleopatra I, 5
Antony to Cleopatra

2 Love is merely a madness, and, I tell you, deserves as well a
dark house and a whip as madmen do.
As You Like It III, 2
Rosalind as Ganymede to Orlando

3 We that are true lovers run into strange capers.
As You Like It II, 4
Touchstone, looking back to his youth

4 Mistress, know yourself; down on your knees,
And thank heaven, fasting, for a good man's love.
As You Like It III, 5
Rosalind/Ganymede, scolding Phebe for scorning Silvius

5   (My) love was of that dignity
That it went hand in hand even with the vow
I made to her in marriage.
Hamlet I, 5
Ghost of his father to Hamlet

6 This is the very ecstasy of love,
Whose violent property fordoes itself
And leads the will to desperate undertaking.
Hamlet II, 1
Polonius to Ophelia, on Hamlet's behaviour

7 When Love speaks, the voice of all the Gods
Makes heaven drowsy with the harmony.
Love's Labour's Lost IV, 3
Biron to King of Navarre and others

8 By heaven, I do love; and it hath taught me to rhyme, and to be
melancholy.
Love's Labour's Lost IV, 3
Biron to himself

9 O love, be moderate; allay thy ecstasy;
In measure rain thy joy . . . make it less,
For fear I surfeit!
The Merchant of Venice III, 2
Portia, aside, as Bassanio chooses the right casket

10 The course of true love never did run smooth.
A Midsummer Night's Dream I, 1
Lysander to Hermia

11 Love looks not with the eyes but with the mind;
And therefore is wing'd Cupid painted blind.
A Midsummer Night's Dream I, 1
Helena to herself

12 O Helen, goddess, nymph, perfect, divine!
   To what, my love, shall I compare thine eyne?
   A Midsummer Night's Dream III, 2
   Demetrius, waking with magic love-juice in his eyes, falls madly
   in love with disbelieving Helena

13 Lovers and madmen have such seething brains,
   Such shaping fantasies, that apprehend
   More than cool reason ever comprehends.
   A Midsummer Night's Dream V, 1
   Theseus to Hippolyta

14 She will die, if he love her not; and she will die, ere she makes
her love known.
   Much Ado About Nothing II, 3
   Claudio to Don Pedro, concerning Beatrice and Benedick

15 Speak . . .
   Of one who loved not wisely but too well.
   Othello V, 2
   Othello, after murdering his wife

16 Love is a smoke raised with the fume of sighs.
   Romeo and Juliet I, 1
   Romeo to Benvolio

17 Alas, that love, so gentle in his view,
   Should be so tyrannous and rough in proof.
   Romeo and Juliet I, 1
   Benvolio to Romeo

18 These violent delights have violent ends . . .
   Therefore, love moderately.
   Romeo and Juliet II, 6
   Friar Laurence to Romeo

19 Is love a tender thing? it is too rough,
   Too rude, too boisterous, and it pricks like thorn.
   Romeo and Juliet I, 4
   Romeo to Mercutio

20 O spirit of love, how quick and fresh art thou!
Twelfth Night I, 1
Duke Orsino to followers and friends

21 Away before me to sweet beds of flowers:
Love-thoughts lie rich when canopied with bowers.
Twelfth Night I, 1
Duke Orsino to followers and friends

22 Love sought is good, but given unsought is better.
Twelfth Night III, 1
Olivia to Viola/Cesario

23   She never told her love,
But let concealment, like a worm i' the bud,
Feed on her damask cheek.
Twelfth Night II, 4
Viola/Cesario to Orsino, telling of a supposed sister

24 O, they love least that let men know their love.
The Two Gentlemen of Verona I, 2
Lucetta to Julia

25   How wayward is this foolish love,
That, like a testy babe, will scratch the nurse,
And presently, all humbled, kiss the rod.
The Two Gentlemen of Verona I, 2
Julia to Lucetta

26 Didst thou but know the inly touch of love,
Thou wouldst as soon go kindle fire with snow
As seek to quench the fire of love with words.
The Two Gentlemen of Verona II, 7
Julia to Lucetta

27   Love is like a child
That longs for everything that he can come by.
The Two Gentlemen of Verona III, 1
Duke of Milan to Valentine

28   He says he loves my daughter:
I think so too, for never gazed the moon
Upon the water, as he'll stand and read
As 'twere my daughter's eyes.
The Winter's Tale IV, 4
Shepherd to Polixenes on Florizel's love for Perdita

29 For thy sweet love remember'd such wealth brings,
That then I scorn to change my state with kings.
Sonnet 29

30 O know sweet love I always write of you,
And you and love are still my argument.
Sonnet 76

31   Love is not love
Which alters when it alteration finds.
Sonnet 116

32 Love is a spirit all compact of fire,
Not gross to sink, but light, and will aspire.
Venus and Adonis Stanza 25

33 Love comforteth like sunshine after rain.
Venus and Adonis Stanza 134

---

102 MADNESS

---

1 O, how comes it now, my husband, O, how comes it,
That thou art estranged from thyself?
The Comedy of Errors II, 2
Adriana, unaware that she is talking to her husband's twin

2 Mistress, both man and master is possess'd;
   I know it by their pale and deadly looks:
   They must be bound, and laid in some dark room.
   The Comedy of Errors IV, 4
   Pinch, a not very reputable schoolmaster, offers his advice to
   Adriana on her husband and his servant

3 What if it tempt you toward the flood, my lord . . .
   And there assume some other horrible form,
   Which might deprive your sovereignty of reason
   And draw you into madness?
   Hamlet I, 4
   Horatio to Hamlet

4 O, what a noble mind is here o'erthrown!
   Hamlet III, 1
   Ophelia, after Hamlet has assumed madness

5 Though this be madness, yet there is method in't.
   Hamlet II, 2
   Polonius in conversation with Hamlet, supposedly mad

6 Madness in great ones must not unwatch'd go.
   Hamlet III, 1
   Claudius to Polonius, after the 'Mousetrap' play

7 Can you . . .
   Get from him why he puts on this confusion,
   Grating so harshly all his days of quiet
   With turbulent and dangerous lunacy?
   Hamlet III, 1
   Claudius to Rosencrantz and Guildenstern

8 *1st Gravedigger:* A' shall recover his wits there (England); or if
                      a' do not, 'tis no great matter . . . 'Twill not be
                      seen in him there; there the men are as mad
                      as he.
                      Hamlet V, 1
                      In conversation with Hamlet, incognito

9   Thou art essentially mad, without seeming so.
1 Henry IV II, 4
Falstaff to Prince Hal

10   Good lord, what madness rules in brainsick men!
1 Henry VI IV, 1
King Henry to quarrelling members of his court

11   Shall I be frighted when a madman speaks?
Julius Caesar IV, 3
Brutus to Cassius, during a quarrel

12   I am not mad; I would to heaven I were!
For then, 'tis like, I should forget myself.
King John III, 4
Constance, whose son Arthur has been taken from her

13   O let me not be mad, not mad, sweet heaven!
Keep me in temper; I would not be mad!
King Lear I, 5
Lear, upset by his daughters

14   I am a very foolish fond old man,
Fourscore and upward, not an hour more nor less;
And to deal plainly,
I fear I am not in my perfect mind.
King Lear IV, 7
Lear to Cordelia

15   Have we eaten on the insane root
That takes the reason prisoner?
Macbeth I, 3
Banquo to Macbeth, after meeting the witches

16   Some say he's mad, others, that lesser hate him,
Do call it valiant fury.
Macbeth V, 2
Caithness, discussing Macbeth with other Scottish noblemen

17   If she be mad — as I believe no other —
     Her madness hath the oddest frame of sense.
     Measure for Measure V, 1
     Duke of Vienna concerning Isabella

18 Any madness I ever yet beheld seemed but tameness, civility,
    and patience, to this his distemper he is in now.
    The Merry Wives of Windsor IV, 2
    Mrs Page on Ford's angry jealousy

    19   I have heard my grandsire say full oft
         Extremity of grief would make men mad.
         Titus Andronicus IV, 1
         Boy to Marcus Andronicus

20 With too much blood and too little brain, these two may run
    mad.
    Troilus and Cressida V, 1
    Thersites, on Achilles and Patroclus

21 As a madman's epistles are no gospels, so it skills not much
    when they are delivered.
    Twelfth Night V, 1
    Feste to Olivia, excusing his tardy delivery of a letter from Malvolio

    22   Why, this is very midsummer madness.
         Twelfth Night III, 4
         Countess Olivia, concerning strange behaviour by Malvolio

    23   For if I should despair, I should grow mad,
         And in my madness might speak ill of thee.
         Sonnet 140

103   MAGIC

1   I have, since I was three year old, conversed with a magician,
    most profound in his art.
    As You Like It V, 2
    Rosalind to Orlando

2   They say this town is full of cozenage;
    As, nimble jugglers that deceive the eye,
    Dark-working sorcerers that change the mind,
    Soul-killing witches that deform the body.
    The Comedy of Errors I, 2
    Antipholus of Syracuse in Ephesus

3   Thou art, as you all are, a sorceress;
    I conjure you to leave me and be gone.
    The Comedy of Errors IV, 3
    Antipholus of Syracuse to Courtesan who confuses him with his
    twin

4   Henry is dead and never shall revive . . .
    (and) shall we think the subtle-witted French
    Conjurers and sorcerers, that, afraid of him,
    By magic verses have contrived his end?
    1 Henry VI I, 1
    Duke of Exeter, at funeral of King Henry V

5   Upon the corner of the moon
    There hangs a vaporous drop profound;
    I'll catch it ere it come to ground;
    And that distill'd by magic sleights . . .
    Shall draw him on to his confusion.
    Macbeth III, 5
    Hecate, concerning Macbeth

6   By some illusion see thou bring her here:
    I'll charm his eyes against she do appear.
    A Midsummer Night's Dream III, 2
    Oberon, kindly wishing to bring Helena and Demetrius together

7   That handkerchief
Did an Egyptian to my mother give . . .
          There's magic in the web of it.
Othello III, 4
Othello to Desdemona

8   This rough magic
I here abjure.
The Tempest V, 1
Prospero to himself

9   I'll break my staff,
Bury it certain fathoms in the earth.
And deeper than did ever plummet sound
I'll drown my book.
The Tempest V, 1
Prospero to himself

10   Pluck my magic garment from me.
The Tempest I, 2
Prospero to Mirando

---

104   MALICE

---

1   I can tell you that of late this duke
Hath ta'en displeasure 'gainst his gentle niece . . .
And, on my life, his malice 'gainst the lady
Will suddenly break forth.
As You Like It I, 2
Le Beau to Orlando about Rosalind

2   I fear me, if thy thoughts were sifted,
The king thy sovereign is not quite exempt
From envious malice of thy swelling heart.
1 Henry VI III, 1
The Bishop of Winchester is being accused by the Duke of
Gloucester

3   We must not stint
Our necessary actions in the fear
To cope malicious censurers.
Henry VIII I, 2
Wolsey to the king, on the subject of taxation

4   Men that make
Envy and crooked malice nourishment
Dare bite the best.
Henry VIII V, 3
Archbishop Cranmer, whom the nobles wish to try for heresy

5 I hate him for he is a Christian . . .
If I can catch him once upon the hip.
I will feed fat the ancient grudge I bear him.
The Merchant of Venice I, 3
Shylock against Antonio

6 Speak of me as I am; nothing extenuate,
Nor set down aught in malice: then must you speak
Of one that loved not wisely but too well.
Othello V, 2
Othello, preparing to kill himself

7 Some devil whisper curses in mine ear,
And prompt me, that my tongue may utter forth
The venomous malice of my swelling heart.
Titus Andronicus V, 3
Aaron the Moor after his arrest

105 MAN

1 You are a thousand times a properer man
Than she a woman.
As You Like It III, 5
Rosalind/Ganymede to Silvius regarding Phebe

2   Give me that man
That is not passion's slave, and I will wear him
In my heart's core.
Hamlet III, 2
Hamlet to Horatio.

3   What is a man
If his chief good and market of his time
Is but to sleep and feed?
Hamlet IV, 4
Hamlet, soliloquizing

4 What a piece of work is man! How noble in reason, how infinite in faculty, in form and moving how express and admirable . . . And yet to me what is this quintessence of dust?
Hamlet II, 2
Hamlet to Rosencrantz and Guildenstern

5 I am no orator, as Brutus is;
But, as you know me all, a plain blunt man.
Julius Caesar III, 2
Antony to the crowd, after Caesar's assassination

6   Shall one of us
That struck the foremost man of all this world . . .
Contaminate our fingers with base bribes?
Julius Caesar IV, 3
Brutus is referring to Julius Caesar

7 You can play no part but Pyramus; for Pyramus is a sweet-faced man; a proper man, as one shall see in a summer's day.
A Midsummer Night's Dream I, 2
Quince, coaxing Bottom with a little flattery

8 He that hath no beard is less than a man.
Much Ado About Nothing II, 1
Beatrice to Leonato

9 I wonder men dare trust themselves with men.
Timon of Athens I, 2
Apemantus to Timon

10   For men, like butterflies,
Show not their mealy wings but to the summer,
Troilus and Cressida III, 3
Achilles to fellow Greeks

---

106 MARRIAGE
see also **Husband** 81, **Wife** 191

---

1 Let me be married to three kings in a forenoon, and widow them all.
Antony and Cleopatra I, 2
Charmian to a Soothsayer

  2   By this marriage
All little jealousies which now seem great,
And all great fears which now import their dangers,
Would then be nothing.
Antony and Cleopatra II, 2
Agrippa on the proposed marriage between Antony and Octavia Caesar

  3 A young man married is a man that's marred.
All's Well That Ends Well II, 3
Parolles on Bertram, forced into marriage against his will

  4 Come, I will fasten on this sleeve of thine:
Thou art an elm, my husband, I a vine,
Whose weakness, married to thy stronger state,
Makes me with thy strength to communicate.
The Comedy of Errors II, 2
Adriana to her supposed husband, though in fact his twin

5 I say we will have no more marriages; those that are married already, all but one, shall live; the rest shall keep as they are.
Hamlet III, 1
Hamlet feigning madness, to Ophelia

6   The instances that second marriage move
     Are base respects of thrift, but none of love.
     Hamlet III, 2
     Player Queen to Player King

7   God, the best maker of all marriages,
     Combine your hearts in one, your realms in one.
     Henry V V, 2
     Queen Isabel of France to Henry and her daughter

8   Marriage is a matter of more worth
     Than to be dealt with by attorneyship.
     1 Henry VI V, 5
     Earl of Suffolk, discussing a suitable bride for Henry

9   Hasty marriage seldom proveth well.
     3 Henry VI IV, 1
     Duke of Gloucester – a sly reference to King Edward IV's
     marriage

10   You are my true and honourable wife,
     As dear to me as are the ruddy drops
     That visit my sad heart.
     Julius Caesar II, 1
     Brutus to Portia

11 I will do anything, Nerissa, ere I'll be married to a sponge.
    The Merchant of Venice I, 2
    Portia on an alcoholic German suitor

12 The ancient saying is no heresy,
     Hanging and wiving go by destiny.
     The Merchant of Venice II, 9
     Nerissa to Portia

13 Those dulcet sounds in break of day
     That creep into the dreaming bridegroom's ear,
     And summon him to marriage.
     The Merchant of Venice III, 2
     Portia to Bassanio

14 I will marry her, sir, at your request: but if there be no great love in the beginning, yet heaven may decrease it upon better acquaintance, when we are married.
The Merry Wives of Windsor I, 1
Slender to Justice Shallow, concerning Anne Page

15 If they were but a week married they would talk themselves mad.
Much Ado About Nothing II, 1
Leonato, concerning Beatrice and Benedick

16 Since I do purpose to marry, I will think nothing to any purpose that the world can say against it.
Much Ado About Nothing V, 4
Benedick to Don Pedro

17 Think of marriage now; younger than you,
Here in Verona, ladies of esteem
Are made already mothers.
Romeo and Juliet I, 3
Lady Capulet to Juliet

18 She's not well married that lives married long,
But she's best married that dies married young.
Romeo and Juliet IV, 5
Friar Laurence to Capulet

19 I come to wive it wealthily in Padua;
If wealthily, then happily in Padua.
The Taming of the Shrew I, 2
Petruchio to Hortensio

20 To me she's married, not unto my clothes.
The Taming of the Shrew III, 2
Petruchio, preparing to be married in very eccentric garb

21   Your father has consented
That you should be my wife; your dowry 'greed on;
And, will you, nill you, I will marry you.
The Taming of the Shrew II, 1
Petruchio to Kate

22   Hence, bashful cunning!
And prompt me, plain and holy innocence!
I am your wife if you will marry me;
If not, I'll die your maid.
The Tempest III, 1
Miranda to Ferdinand

---

107   MEDICINE

---

1   He and his physicians
Are of a mind; he, that they cannot help him,
They, that they cannot help.
All's Well That Ends Well I, 3
Countess Rousillon to Helena, concerning the king's illness

2   I have seen a medicine
That's able to breathe life into a stone.
All's Well That Ends Well II, 1
Lafeu to the sick king of France

3 By medicine life may be prolong'd, but death
Will seize the doctor too.
Cymbeline V, 5
Cymbeline to Cornelius

4 'Twixt his finger and his thumb he held
A pouncet box . . .
Telling me the sovereign'st thing on earth
Was parmaceti for an inward bruise.
1 Henry IV I, 3
Hotspur, annoyed during a battle by a 'popinjay'

5 If the rascal have not given me medicines to make me love him,
I'll be hanged; it could not be else; I have drunk medicines.
1 Henry IV II, 2
Falstaff concerning Poins

6   In poison there is physic; and these news,
    Having been well, that would have made me sick,
    Being sick, have in some measure made me well.
    2 Henry IV I, 1
    Earl of Northumberland, receiving bad news

7   Before the curing of a strong disease,
    Even in the instant of repair and health,
    The fit is strongest; evils that take leave,
    On their departure most of all show evil.
    King John III, 4
    Cardinal Pandulph to the Dauphin

8   Canst thou not minister to a mind diseased,
    Pluck from the memory a rooted sorrow . . .
    And with some sweet oblivious antidote
    Cleanse the stuff'd bosom?
    Macbeth V, 3
    Macbeth to doctor

9   Throw physic to the dogs, I'll none of it.
    Macbeth V, 3
    Macbeth to doctor

10 What rhubarb, senna, or what purgative drug
    Would scour these English hence?
    Macbeth V, 3
    Macbeth to doctor

11 The miserable have no other medicine
    But only hope.
    Measure for Measure III, 1
    Claudio to Duke

12   In such a night
    Medea gather'd the enchanted herbs
    That did renew old Aeson.
    The Merchant of Venice V, 1
    Jessica to Lorenzo

13   Not poppy, nor mandragora
Nor all the drowsy syrups of the world
Shall ever medicine thee to that sweet sleep
Which thou owed'st yesterday.
Othello III, 3
Iago, aside, having aroused Othello's jealous feelings

14 It is silliness to live when to live is torment; and then have we
a prescription to die when death is our physician.
Othello I, 3
Roderigo, suffering hopeless love for Desdemona

  15 Our doctors say this is no month to bleed.
    Richard II I, 1
    Richard to Mowbray and Bolingbroke

  16 I do remember an apothecary,
    And hereabouts he dwells, which late I noted
    In tatter'd weeds, with overwhelming brows,
    Culling of simples.
    Romeo and Juliet V, 1
    Romeo, desiring a poison for suicide

  17 O mickle is the powerful grace that lies
    In herbs, plants, stones, and their true qualities.
    Romeo and Juliet II, 3
    Friar Laurence

  18   Trust not the physician;
    His antidotes are poison, and he slays
    More than you rob.
    Timon of Athens IV, 3
    Timon to bandits

  19 When I was sick, you gave me bitter pills;
    And I must minister the like to you.
    The Two Gentlemen of Verona II, 4
    Proteus to Valentine

108   MEMORY

1   Praising what is lost
Makes the remembrance dear.
All's Well That Ends Well V, 3
King of France to members of his court

2   Though yet of Hamlet our dear brother's death
The memory be green . . .
We with wisest sorrow think on him,
Together with remembrance of ourselves.
Hamlet I, 2
King Claudius to his court

3   Die two months ago, and not forgotten yet? Then there's hope
a great man's memory may outlive his life half a year.
Hamlet III, 2
Hamlet's ironical comments on his mother's too-early second marriage

4   Then shall our names
Familiar in his mouth as household words . . .
Be in their flowing cups freshly remembered.
Henry V IV, 3
Henry, forecasting the lasting fame of English soldiers at
Agincourt

5   His two chamberlains
Will I with wine and wassail so convince,
That memory, the warder of the brain,
Shall be a fume.
Macbeth I, 7
Lady Macbeth, preparing for Duncan's murder

6   I cannot but remember such things were,
That were most precious to me.
Macbeth IV, 3
Macduff is referring to his slaughtered wife and children

7   Pluck from the memory a rooted sorrow.
Macbeth V, 3
Macbeth to doctor

8   If a man do not erect in this age his own tomb ere he dies, he shall live no longer in monument than the bell rings and the widow weeps.
Much Ado About Nothing V, 2
Benedick to Beatrice

9   I count myself in nothing else so happy
As in a soul remembering my good friends.
Richard II II, 3
Bolingbroke, returning to England during his banishment

10   When to the sessions of sweet silent thought
I summon up remembrance of things past,
I sigh the lack of many a thing I sought.
Sonnet 30

109   MIRTH

1   A jest's prosperity lies in the ear
Of him that hears it, never in the tongue
Of him that makes it.
Love's Labour's Lost V, 2
Rosaline to Biron

2   A merrier man
Within the limit of becoming mirth,
I never spent an hour's talk withal.
Love's Labour's Lost II, 1
Rosaline to Princess, concerning Biron

3   Mirth cannot move a soul in agony.
Love's Labour's Lost V, 2
Biron to Rosaline

4   Nature hath framed strange fellows in her time:
     Some that will evermore peep through their eyes,
     And laugh like parrots at a bag-piper.
     The Merchant of Venice I, 1
     Salarino to Antonio

5   Let me play the fool:
     With mirth and laughter let old wrinkles come.
     The Merchant of Venice I, 1
     Gratiano to Antonio

6   From the crown of his head to the sole of his foot he is all
     mirth.
     Much Ado About Nothing III, 2
     Don Pedro on Benedick

7   He shows me where the bachelors sit, and there live we as
     merry as the day is long.
     Much Ado About Nothing II, 1
     Beatrice with St Peter in heaven

8   Frame your mind to mirth and merriment,
     Which bars a thousand harms, and lengthens life.
     The Taming of the Shrew Induction 2
     Messenger, announcing the performance of a play

9   See, your guests approach,
     Address yourself to entertain them sprightly,
     And let's be red with mirth.
     The Winter's Tale IV, 4
     Florizel to Perdita

10   A merry heart goes all the day
     Your sad tires in a mile-a.
     The Winter's Tale IV, 3
     Song by Autolycus

110   MISFORTUNE

1   By misfortunes was my life prolong'd,
To tell sad stories of my own mishaps.
The Comedy of Errors I, 1
Aegeon to Duke of Ephesus

2   The worst is not
So long as we can say 'This is the worst'.
King Lear IV, 1
Edgar, in the company of his blinded father

3   Every object that might make me fear
Misfortune to my ventures, out of doubt,
Would make me sad.
The Merchant of Venice I, 1
Salanio, sympathizing with Antonio, whose wealth is locked up
in shipping

4   A gentleman of Tyre
Who only by misfortune of the seas,
Bereft of ships and men, cast on this shore.
Pericles II, 3
Pericles's description of himself

5   Shall we sit here
And by relating tales of others' griefs
See if 'twill teach us to forget our own.
Pericles I, 4
Cleon, governor of Tarsus, which is suffering a famine

6   Give me thy hand,
One writ with me in sour misfortune's book.
Romeo and Juliet V, 3
Romeo to Paris, whom he has been forced to kill

7   Need and oppression starveth in thy eyes,
Contempt and beggary hangs upon thy back,
The world is not thy friend.
Romeo and Juliet V, 1
Romeo to a poor and unfortunate apothecary

8   Never was a story of more woe
Than this of Juliet and her Romeo.
Romeo and Juliet V, 3
Prince Escalus, closing the play

9   Misery acquaints a man with strange bedfellows.
The Tempest II, 2
Trinculo, sharing a coverlet with Caliban

10   In me more woes than words are now depending;
And my laments would be drawn out too long
To tell them all with one poor tired tongue.
The Rape of Lucrece Stanza 231

---

111 MONEY
see also **Gold** 62

---

1   I think you have no money in your purse.
As You Like It II, 4
Touchstone to Celia

2   He that wants money, means and content is without three good
friends.
As You Like It III, 2
Corin to Touchstone

3   'Tis gold
Which makes the true man kill'd and saves the thief.
Cymbeline II, 3
Cloten to himself

4   How quickly nature falls into revolt
When gold becomes her object.
2 Henry IV IV, 5
Henry to his sons

5   I can get no remedy against this consumption of the purse . . .
the disease is incurable.
2 Henry IV I, 2
Falstaff in financial trouble

6   There is money; spend it, spend it; spend more.
The Merry Wives of Windsor II, 2
Ford to Falstaff, eager to get evidence of his wife's supposed
unfaithfulness

7   If money go before, all ways do lie open.
The Merry Wives of Windsor II, 2
Ford to Falstaff

8   Money is a good soldier, sir, and will go.
The Merry Wives of Windsor II, 2
Falstaff to Ford

9   This is my father's choice.
O what a world of vile illfavour'd faults
Looks handsome in three hundred pounds a year!
The Merry Wives of Windsor III, 4
Anne Page, on her father's choice of husband

10   Put money in thy purse.
Othello I, 3
Iago to Roderigo

11   I see that thou art poor;
Hold, there is forty ducats: let me have
A dram of poison.
Romeo and Juliet V, 1
Romeo to apothecary

12   Give him gold enough and marry him to a puppet . . . or an old
trot with ne'er a tooth in her head . . . nothing comes amiss, so
money comes withal.
The Taming of the Shrew I, 2
Grumio to Hortensio, on Petruchio's intention to marry for money

112 MONTHS

1   Men are April when they woo, December when they wed;
maids are May when they are maids, but the sky changes when
they are wives.
As You Like It IV, 1
Rosalind to Orlando

2   A soothsayer bids you beware the Ides of March.
Julius Caesar I, 2
Brutus to Caesar

3   A day in April never came so sweet,
To show how costly summer was at hand.
The Merchant of Venice II, 9
Servant to Portia

4   Her cousin . . . exceeds her as much in beauty as the first of
May doth the last of December.
Much Ado About Nothing I, 1
Benedick praises Beatrice to Claudio at Hero's expense

5   Such comfort as do lusty young men feel
When well-apparell'd April on the heel
Of limping winter treads.
Romeo and Juliet I, 2
Capulet to Paris

6   Blasts of January
Would blow you through and through.
The Winter's Tale IV, 4
Perdita to Camillo

7   He makes a July's day short as December.
The Winter's Tale I, 2
Polixenes, describing his young son

8   Rough winds do shake the darling buds of May,
And summer's lease hath all too short a date.
Sonnet 18

9   Proud-pied April (dress'd in all his trim)
Hath put a spirit of youth in everything.
Sonnet 98

10   Thou art thy mother's glass, and she in thee
Calls back the lovely April of her prime.
Sonnet 3

---

113 MOON

---

1   There is nothing left remarkable
Beneath the visiting moon.
Antony and Cleopatra IV, 15
Cleopatra at Antony's death

2 Let us be Diana's foresters, gentlemen of the shade, minions of
the moon.
1 Henry IV I, 2
Falstaff to Prince Hal, objecting to be called 'thief'

3 The moon shines bright; in such a night as this
When the sweet wind did gently kiss the trees
And they did make no noise, in such a night
Troilus methinks mounted the Troyan walls.
The Merchant of Venice V, 1
Lorenzo to Jessica

4 How sweet the moonlight sleeps upon this bank!
Here will we sit, and let the sounds of music
Creep in our ears.
The Merchant of Venice V, 1
Lorenzo to Jessica

5   Our nuptial hour
Draws on apace; four happy days bring in
Another moon: but O, methinks, how slow
This old moon wanes.
A Midsummer Night's Dream I, 1
Duke Theseus to Hippolyta

6 This man, with lanthorn, dog, and bush of thorn,
Presenteth Moonshine; for, if you will know,
By moonshine did these lovers think no scorn
To meet.
A Midsummer Night's Dream V, 1
Quince as Prologue to the 'Pyramus and Thisbe' play

7 Let us listen to the moon.
A Midsummer Night's Dream V, 1
Theseus at the play

8 Sweet Moon, I thank thee for they sunny beams,
I thank thee, Moon, for shining now so bright.
A Midsummer Night's Dream V, 1
Bottom as Pyramus in the play

9 Think'st thou I'd make a life of jealousy,
To follow still the changes of the moon.
Othello III, 3
Othello to Iago

10 It is the very error of the moon;
She comes more nearer earth than she was wont,
And makes men mad.
Othello V, 2
Othello to Emilia

11 O swear not by the moon, th'inconstant moon,
That monthly changes in her circled orb,
Lest that thy love prove likewise variable.
Romeo and Juliet II, 2
Juliet to Romeo

114 MORNING
see also **Day 31**

1   But soft! methinks I scent the morning air.
Hamlet I, 5
Ghost to Hamlet

2   But look, the morn, in russet mantle clad,
Walks o'er the dew of yon high eastward hill.
Hamlet I, 1
Horatio to Marcellus

3   The day begins to break, and night is fled,
Whose pitchy mantle over-veil'd the earth.
1 Henry VI II, 2
Duke of Bedford at Orleans

4   See how the morning opes her golden gates,
And takes her farewell of the glorious sun.
3 Henry VI II, 1
Duke of Gloucester

5   Many a morning hath he there been seen,
With tears augmenting the fresh morning dew.
Romeo and Juliet I, 1
Romeo's father on his son's rejected passion for his first love,
Rosaline

6   The grey-eyed morn smiles on the frowning night,
Chequering the eastern clouds with streaks of light.
Romeo and Juliet II, 3
Friar Laurence to himself

7   Night's candles are burnt out, and jocund day
Stands tiptoe on the misty mountain-tops.
I must be gone.
Romeo and Juliet III, 5
Romeo, after a night with Juliet

8   As when the golden sun salutes the morn,
    And, having gilt the ocean with his beams,
    Gallops the zodiac in his glistering coach
    And overlooks the highest-peering hills.
    Titus Andronicus II, 1
    Aaron to himself

9   The busy day
    Wak'd by the lark, hath roused the ribald crows,
    And dreaming night will hide our joys no longer.
    Troilus and Cressida IV, 2
    Troilus to Cressida

10 Full many a glorious morning have I seen
    Flatter the mountain-tops with sovereign eye,
    Kissing with golden face the meadows green.
    Sonnet 33

---

115   MURDER

1   Murder most foul, as in the best it is,
    But this most foul, strange, and unnatural.
    Hamlet I, 5
    Ghost to Hamlet

2   Sleeping within my orchard . . .
    Upon my secure hour thy uncle stole,
    With juice of cursed hebenon in a vial,
    And in the porches of my ear did pour
    The leperous distilment.
    Hamlet I, 5
    Ghost to Hamlet

3   Murder, though it have no tongue, will speak
    With most miraculous organ.
    Hamlet II, 2
    Hamlet, soliloquizing

4   O, my offence is rank, it smells to heaven;
It hath the primal eldest curse upon it;
A brother's murder.
Hamlet III, 3
Claudius to himself

5   When your vile daggers
Hack'd one another in the sides of Caesar,
You show'd your teeth like apes.
Julius Caesar V, 1
Antony to Cassius and Brutus

6   Blood hath been shed ere now, i' the olden time . . .
Ay, and since too, murders have been perform'd
Too terrible for the ear.
Macbeth III, 4
Macbeth to Banquo's ghost

7   Here lay Duncan,
His silver skin laced with his golden blood . . .
There, the murderers,
Steep'd in the colours of their trade, their daggers
Unmannerly breach'd with gore.
Macbeth II, 3
Macbeth, pretending the two grooms were guilty

8   Methought I heard a voice cry, 'Sleep no more!
Macbeth does murder sleep'.
Macbeth II, 2
Macbeth to Lady Macbeth

9   Exton, thy fierce hand
Hath with the king's blood stain'd the king's own land.
Richard II V, 5
Richard to his murderer

10   The great king of kings
Hath in the tables of his law commanded
That thou shalt do no murder.
Richard III I, 4
Duke of Clarence to his murderers

116 MUSIC

1   Give me some music; music, moody food
     Of us that trade in love.
     Antony and Cleopatra II, 5
     Cleopatra to attendants

2   I am advised to give her music o' mornings; they say it will
     penetrate.
     Cymbeline II, 3
     Cloten, trying vainly to gain Imogen's love

3   Govern these ventages with your finger and thumb, give it
     breath with your mouth, and it will discourse most eloquent
     music.
     Hamlet III, 2
     Hamlet to Guildenstern, showing him a recorder

4   How irksome is this music to my heart!
     When such strings jar, what hope of harmony?
     2 Henry VI II, 1
     Henry to Lords

5   In sweet music is such art,
     Killing care and grief of heart
     Fall asleep, or hearing die.
     Henry VIII III, 1
     Song to Queen Katherine

6   Orpheus with his lute made trees,
     And the mountain tops that freeze,
     Bow themselves when he did sing.
     Henry VIII III, 1
     Song to Queen Katherine

7   The choir
     With all the choicest music of the kingdom,
     Sang the 'Te Deum'.
     Henry VIII IV, 1
     Gentleman, describing the coronation of Anne Bullen

8   A man in all the world's new fashion planted . . .
    One whom the music of his own vain tongue
    Doth ravish with enchanting harmony.
    Love's Labour's Lost I, 1
    King of Navarre, describing Armado

9   Music oft hath such a charm
    To make bad good, and good provoke to harm.
    Measure for Measure IV, 1
    Duke to Mariana

10 Let music sound while he doth make his choice:
    Then, if he lose, he makes a swan-like end,
    Fading in music.
    The Merchant of Venice III, 2
    Portia, as Bassanio chooses his casket

11 I am never merry when I hear sweet music.
    The Merchant of Venice V, 1
    Jessica to Lorenzo

12 Here will we sit and let the sounds of music
    Creep in our ears.
    The Merchant of Venice V, 1
    Lorenzo to Jessica

13 The man that hath no music in himself
    Nor is not moved with concord of sweet sounds,
    Is fit for treasons, stratagems, and spoils.
    The Merchant of Venice V, 1
    Lorenzo to Jessica

14   How sour sweet music is
    When time is broke and no proportion kept!
    So is it in the music of men's lives.
    Richard II V, 5
    Richard, soliloquizing in prison

15   Preposterous ass, that never read so far
To know the cause why music was ordain'd!
Was it not to refresh the mind of man
After his studies or his usual pain?
The Taming of the Shrew III, 1
Lucentio, addressing Hortensio

16   Wilt thou have music? hark! Apollo plays,
And twenty caged nightingales do sing.
The Taming of the Shrew Induction II
Christopher Sly being hoaxed that he is a lord

17   The isle is full of noises,
Sounds and sweet airs, that give delight and hurt not.
Sometimes a thousand twangling instruments
Will hum about mine ears, and sometimes voices.
The Tempest III, 2
Caliban to Stephano

18   This music crept by me upon the waters,
Allaying both their fury and my passion
With its sweet air.
The Tempest I, 2
Ferdinand finding himself alone on the island where he was
wrecked

19   If music be the food of love, play on;
Give me excess of it, that, surfeiting,
The appetite may sicken and so die.
That strain again! it had a dying fall:
O, it came o'er my ear like the sweet sound
That breathes upon a bank of violets.
Twelfth Night I, 1
Duke Orsino, with his mind on Olivia

117 NAME

1   The last she spake
Was 'Antony! most noble Antony!'
Then in the midst a tearing groan did break
The name of Antony.
Antony and Cleopatra IV, 14
Mardian, telling Antony of Cleopatra's supposed death

2 I'll have no worse a name than Jove's own page;
And therefore look you call me Ganymede.
As You Like It I, 3
Rosalind, adopting male identity for travelling in the Forest of
Arden

3   She became
A joyful mother of two goodly sons;
And, which was strange, the one so like the other
As could not be distinguished but by name.
The Comedy of Errors I, 1
Aegeon to Duke

4   Renowned Douglas! whose high deeds,
Whose hot incursions and great name in arms
Holds from all soldiers chief majority.
1 Henry IV III, 2
Henry, praising a notable enemy

5 So great fear of my name 'mongst them was spread,
That they supposed I could bend bars of steel,
And spurn in pieces posts of adamant.
1 Henry VI I, 4
Lord Talbot on the French

6 Wherever the bright sun of heaven shall shine,
His honour and the greatness of his name
Shall be, and make new nations.
Henry VIII V, 5
Prophetic flattery of James I from Archbishop Cranmer

7   If his name be George, I'll call him Peter;
For new-made honour does forget men's names.
King John I, 1
Philip the Bastard, humorously to himself

8   I cannot tell what the dickens his name is.
The Merry Wives of Windsor III, 2
Mrs Page to Ford, concerning Falstaff

9   As imagination bodies forth
The form of things unknown, the poet's pen
Turns them to shapes, and gives to airy nothing
A local habitation and a name.
A Midsummer Night's Dream V, 1
Theseus to Hippolyta

10   He that filches from me my good name
Robs me of that which not enriches him
And makes me poor indeed.
Othello III, 3
Iago to Othello

11   I had forgot myself. Am I not king? . . .
Is not the king's name twenty thousand names?
Richard II III, 2
Richard, trying to boost his confidence

12   I have no name, no title,
No, not that name was given me at the font,
But 'tis usurp'd.
Richard II IV, 1
Richard, after abdicating

13   The king's name is a tower of strength,
Which they upon the adverse party want.
Up with my tent there!
Richard III V, 3
Richard, before the battle of Bosworth Field

14   O Romeo, Romeo! wherefore art thou Romeo?
     Deny thy father and refuse thy name.
     Romeo and Juliet II, 2
     Juliet to herself

15   What's in a name? that which we call a rose
     By any other name would smell as sweet.
     Romeo and Juliet II, 2
     Juliet to herself

16   O you gods divine!
     Make Cressid's name the very crown of falsehood,
     If ever she leave Troilus.
     Troilus and Cressida IV, 3
     Cressida to Pandarus

17   (I would) halloo your name to the reverberate hills,
     And make the babbling gossip of the air
     Cry out 'Olivia!'
     Twelfth Night I, 5
     Viola, as Cesario, telling Olivia how, if she were suitor, he/she
     would make love

18   Here is writ 'love-wounded Proteus'.
     Poor wounded name! my bosom, as a bed,
     Shall lodge thee.
     The Two Gentlemen of Verona I, 2
     Julia to herself

19   Your name from hence immortal life shall have . . .
     Your monument shall be my gentle verse,
     Which eyes not yet created shall o'er-read.
     Sonnet 81

20   Naming thy name blesses an ill report.
     Sonnet 95

118 NATURE

1 His nature is too noble for the world:
He would not flatter Neptune for his trident,
Or Jove for's power to thunder.
Coriolanus III, 1
Menenius concerning Coriolanus

2 How hard it is to hide the sparks of nature.
Cymbeline III, 3
Belarius, whose supposed sons are really royal princes

3 The purpose of playing . . . is to hold, as 'twere, the mirror up
to Nature; to show virtue her own feature, scorn her own
image.
Hamlet III, 2
Hamlet to First Player

4 Diseased nature oftentimes breaks forth
In strange eruptions; oft the teeming earth
Is with a kind of colic pinched.
1 Henry IV III, 1
Hotspur to Owen Glendower

5 Nature does require
Her times of preservation.
Henry VIII III, 2
Wolsey to the king

6 (If you) allow not nature more than nature needs,
Man's life's as cheap as beast's.
King Lear II, 4
Lear to Regan

7 Nature in you stands on the very verge
Of her confine.
King Lear II, 4
Regan to Lear, referring to his age

8   We are not ourselves
When nature being oppress'd commands the mind
To suffer with the body.
King Lear II, 4
Lear to Earl of Gloucester

9   Yet do I fear thy nature;
It is too full of the milk of human kindness
To catch the nearest way.
Macbeth I, 5
Lady Macbeth concerning her husband

10   One touch of nature makes the whole world kin.
Troilus and Cressida III, 3
Ulysses to Achilles

11   This fortress built by Nature for herself
Against infection and the hand of war.
Richard II II, 1
John of Gaunt, speaking of England

119   NECESSITY

1   The strong necessity of time commands
Our services awhile: but my full heart
Remains in use with you.
Antony and Cleopatra I, 3
Antony to Cleopatra

2   Now sit we close about this taper here,
And call in question our necessities.
Julius Caesar IV, 3
Brutus to colleagues

3 The deep of night is crept upon our talk,
And nature must obey necessity,
Which we will niggard with a little rest.
Julius Caesar IV, 3
Brutus to colleagues

4 Return to her? . . .
No, rather I abjure all roofs, and choose
To wage against the enmity of the air,
To be a comrade with the wolf and owl –
Necessity's sharp pinch!
King Lear II, 4
Lear to Regan, who has advised him to go back to stay with
Goneril

5   How dost, my boy? art cold?
I am cold myself. Where is this straw, my fellow?
The art of our necessities is strange,
That can make vile things precious.
King Lear III, 2
Seeking shelter in a hovel

6 Teach thy necessity to reason thus:
There is no virtue like necessity.
Think not the king did banish thee,
But thou the king.
Richard II I, 3
John of Gaunt to Bolingbroke, banished for six years

7   I am sworn brother, sweet,
To grim Necessity, and he and I
Will keep a league till death.
Richard II V, 1
Richard to his queen

120   NIGHT

1   Two nights together had these gentlemen,
Marcellus and Bernardo, on their watch,
In the dead vast and middle of the night,
Been thus encounter'd.
Hamlet I, 2
Horatio tells Hamlet about the Ghost

2   'Tis now the very witching time of night,
When churchyards yawn and hell itself breathes out
Contagion to this world.
Hamlet III, 2
Hamlet to himself

3   The day begins to break, and night is fled,
Whose pitchy mantle over-veil'd the earth.
1 Henry VI II, 2
Duke of Bedford at Orleans

4   Is Brutus sick,
And will he steal out of his wholesome bed,
To dare the vile contagion of the night?.
Julius Caesar II, 1
Portia to Brutus

5   Good my lord, enter;
The tyranny of the open night's too rough
For nature to endure.
King Lear III, 4
Kent to Lear, seeking shelter in a hovel

6   Light thickens, and the crow
Makes wing to the rooky wood.
Macbeth III, 2
Macbeth to his wife

7   Go not my horse the better,
I must become a borrower of the night
For dark hour or twain.
Macbeth III, 1
Banquo, setting out for an evening ride

8   The night is long that never finds the day.
Macbeth IV, 3
Macduff to Malcolm

9   Soft stillness and the night
Become the touches of sweet harmony.
The Merchant of Venice V, 1
Lorenzo to Jessica

10   Come, civil night,
Thou sober-suited matron, all in black . . .
Hood my unmann'd blood bating in my cheeks,
With thy black mantle.
Romeo and Juliet III, 2
Juliet, awaiting Romeo

---

121 OATHS

1   'Tis not the many oaths that make the truth,
But the plain single vow that is vow'd true.
All's Well That Ends Well IV, 2
Diana to Bertram

2   When a gentleman is disposed to swear, it is not for any
standers-by to curtail his oaths.
Cymbeline II, 1
Cloten, at bowls

3   Thou art damned for keeping thy word with the
devil.
1 Henry IV I, 2
Poins to Falstaff

4   It is great sin to swear unto a sin,
But greater sin to keep a sinful oath.
2 Henry VI V, 1
Earl of Salisbury to Henry, excusing himself for breaking his
oath of allegiance

5   Having sworn too hard a keeping oath,
      Study to break it, and not break my troth . . .
      Swear me to this, and I will ne'er say no.
      Love's Labour's Lost I, 1
      Biron to King of Navarre

6   What fool is not so wise
      To lose an oath to win a paradise?
      Love's Labour's Lost IV, 3
      Longaville to Biron

7   I'll take thy word for faith, not ask thine oath:
      Who shuns not to break one will sure crack both.
      Pericles I, 2
      Pericles to Helicanus

8   Grant I may never grow so fond
      To trust man on his oath or bond.
      Timon of Athens I, 2
      Part of the cynical philosophy of Apemantus

9 A terrible oath, with a swaggering accent sharply twanged off, gives manhood more approbation than ever proof itself would have earned him.
  Twelfth Night III, 4
  Sir Toby Belch to Sir Andrew Aguecheek

---

122   OFFENCE

---

1 I am very proud, revengeful, ambitious; with more offences at my beck than I have thoughts to put them in.
  Hamlet III, 1
  Hamlet, feigning madness, to Ophelia

2   O, my offence is rank, it smells to heaven.
      Hamlet III, 3
      King Claudius, confessing to himself the crime of killing his brother

3   Where the offence is, let the great axe fall.
    Hamlet IV, 5
    Claudius to Laertes, the offence being the death of Polonius

4   In such a time as this it is not meet
    That every nice offence should bear his comment.
    Julius Caesar IV, 3
    Cassius to Brutus

5   Weaving spiders, come not here;
    Hence, you long-legg'd spinners, hence!
    Beetles black, approach not near;
    Worm nor snail, do no offence.
    A Midsummer Night's Dream II, 2
    Fairy song

6   If we offend, it is with our good will.
    That you should think, we come not to offend,
    But with good will. To show our simple skill,
    That is the true beginning of our end.
    A Midsummer Night's Dream V, 1
    Quince introduces his play

7   If thy offences were upon record,
    Would it not shame thee in so fair a troop
    To read a lecture of them?
    Richard II IV, 1
    Richard to Earl of Northumberland, who has demanded such a
    'lecture'

8   To make a sweet lady sad is a sour offence.
    Troilus and Cressida III, 1
    Helen to Pandarus

9   Put up your sword. If this young gentleman
    Have done offence, I take the fault on me.
    Twelfth Night III, 4
    Antonio comes to the aid of Cesario/Viola

10 With foul offenders thou perforce must bear,
    When they in thee the like offences prove.
    The Rape of Lucrece Stanza 88

123 ORATORY

1 Very good orators, when they are out, they will spit.
   As You Like It IV, 1
   Rosalind/Ganymede to Orlando

2 Be not thy tongue thy own shame's orator.
   The Comedy of Errors III, 2
   Luciana to Antipholus of Syracuse, believing him unfaithful to
   her sister

3 I am no orator, as Brutus is,
   But, as you know me all, a plain blunt man.
   Julius Caesar III, 2
   Antony, proving himself a masterly orator over Caesar's corpse

4   I'll play the orator
   As if the golden fee for which I plead
   Were for myself.
   Richard III III, 5
   Duke of Buckingham, agreeing to help Richard gain the crown

5 *Viola:* Say I do speak with her, my lord, what then?
   Orsino: O, then unfold the passion of my love;
                Surprise her with discourse of my dear faith.
   Twelfth Night I, 4
   Viola/Cesario is sent to plead with Countess Olivia

6 I would be loath to cast away my speech, for besides that it is
   excellently well penned, I have taken great pains to con it.
   Twelfth Night I, 5
   Viola to Olivia

7 Bid me discourse, I will enchant thine ear.
   Venus and Adonis Stanza 25

124 PARDON

1   Love that comes too late,
   Like a remorseful pardon slowly carried,
   To the great sender turns a sour offence
   All's Well That Ends Well V, 3
   King to Bertram

2 I will o'ertake thee, Cleopatra, and
   Weep for my pardon.
   Antony and Cleopatra IV, 14
   Antony had cursed Cleopatra before being told of her death

3 I minded him how royal 'twas to pardon
   When it was less expected.
   Coriolanus V, 1
   Cominius concerning Coriolanus

4   That comfort comes too late;
   'Tis like a pardon after execution.
   Henry VIII IV, 2
   Queen Katherine, dying, on a message of comfort from the king

5 O pardon me, thou bleeding piece of earth,
   That I am meek and gentle with these butchers.
   Julius Caesar III, 1
   Antony over Caesar's body

6 I humbly do beseech you of your pardon
   For too much loving you.
   Othello III, 3
   Iago, hypocritically, to Othello

7 My tongue cleave to my roof within my mouth,
   Unless a pardon ere I rise or speak.
   Richard II V, 3
   Duke of Aumerle, guilty of conspiracy against King Henry IV

8 Say 'pardon', king; let pity teach thee how:
The word is short, but not so short as sweet;
No word like 'pardon' for kings' mouths so meet.
Richard II V, 3
Duchess of York, Aumerle's mother, to Henry IV

9 God pardon all oaths that are broke to me.
Richard II IV, 1
Richard at his abdication

10   Let me not,
Since I have my dukedom got,
And pardon'd the deceiver, dwell
In this bare island.
The Tempest Epilogue
Prospero

125   PATIENCE

1 They can be meek that have no other cause . . .
So thou, that hast no unkind mate to grieve thee,
With urging helpless patience wouldst relieve me.
The Comedy of Errors II, 1
Adriana to her unmarried sister

2 For who would bear the whips and scorns of time . . .
The insolence of office, and the spurns
That patient merit of the unworthy takes.
Hamlet III, 1
Hamlet on suicide

3 Though patience be a tired mare, yet she will plod.
Henry V II, 1
Nym to Bardolph

4   What you have to say
     I will with patience hear.
     Julius Caesar I, 2
     Brutus to Cassius

5 In the Rialto you have rated me
     About my moneys and my usances:
     Still I have borne it with a patient shrug.
     The Merchant of Venice I, 3
     Shylock to Antonio

6   I do oppose
     My patience to his fury; and am arm'd
     To suffer, with a quietness of spirit.
     The Merchant of Venice IV, 1
     Antonio concerning Shylock's bond

7 'Tis all men's office to speak patience
     To those that wring under the load of sorrow.
     Much Ado About Nothing V, 1
     Leonato to Antonio

8 How poor are they that have not patience!
     What wound did ever heal but by degrees.
     Othello II, 3
     Iago to Roderigo

9 That which in mean men we entitle patience
     Is pale cold cowardice in noble breasts.
     Richard II I, 2
     Duchess of Gloucester to John of Gaunt

10 With a green and yellow melancholy
     She sat like patience on a monument
     Smiling at grief.
     Twelfth Night II, 4
     Viola/Cesario to Orsino, describing an imaginary sister

11 There's some ill planet reigns:
I must be patient till the heavens look
With an aspect more favourable.
The Winter's Tale II, 1
Hermione to Leontes

126 PEACE

1 Our peace we'll ratify; seal it with feasts.
Set on there! Never was a war did cease,
Ere bloody hands were washed, with such a feast.
Cymbeline V, 5
Cymbeline, King of Britain, makes peace with the Romans

2 A peace is in the nature of a conquest;
For then both parties nobly are subdued,
And neither party loser.
2 Henry IV IV, 2
Archbishop of York, referring to a supposed peace between king
and rebels

3 In peace there's nothing so becomes a man
As modest stillness and humility.
Henry V III, 1
Henry, speech before Harfleur

4 Poor and mangled Peace,
Dear nurse of arts, plenties, and joyful births.
Henry V V, 2
Duke of Burgundy to French and English nobles and royalty

5 Still in thy right hand carry gentle peace,
To silence envious tongues.
Henry VIII III, 2
Wolsey to Thomas Cromwell

6   I feel within me
A peace above all earthly dignities,
A still and quiet conscience.
Henry VIII III, 2
Wolsey to Thomas Cromwell

7   Good grows with her;
In her days every man shall eat in safety,
Under his own vine, what he plants, and sing
The merry songs of peace to all his neighbours.
Henry VIII V, 5
Cranmer, praising the infant princess who was to become Queen
Elizabeth

8 In this seat of peace tumultuous wars
Shall kin with kin and kind with kind confound.
Richard II IV, 1
Bishop of Carlisle, prophesying doom if Bolingbroke replaces
Richard II as king

9 I, in this weak piping time of peace,
Have no delight to pass away the time.
Richard III I, 1
Richard, soliloquizing

10 In God's name, cheerly on, courageous friends,
To reap the harvest of perpetual peace
By this one bloody trial of sharp war.
Richard III V, 2
Earl of Richmond, rallying forces opposed to Richard

11 I am ashamed that women are so simple
To offer war where they should kneel for peace.
The Taming of the Shrew V, 2
Katherina, tamed, offers domestic advice

127   PEOPLE

1 That's a brave fellow; but he's vengeance proud, and loves not the common people.
Coriolanus II, 2
One officer to another, discussing Coriolanus

2 You common cry of curs! whose breath I hate
As reek o' the rotten fens, whose loves I prize
As the dead carcasses of unburied men.
Coriolanus III, 3
Coriolanus to citizens of Rome, which has just banished him

3 It offends me to the soul to hear a robustious periwig-pated fellow tear a passion to tatters, to very rags, to split the ears of the groundlings.
Hamlet III, 2
Hamlet to the Players

4   The people muddied,
Thick and unwholesome in their thoughts and whispers.
Hamlet IV, 5
Claudius, apt to be blamed for the death of Polonius

5 The commons, like an angry hive of bees
That want their leader, scatter up and down,
And care not who they sting.
2 Henry VI III, 2
Earl of Warwick, after the murder of Humphrey Duke of Gloucester

6 The common people swarm like summer flies.
3 Henry VI II, 6
Lord Clifford to himself, lamenting that Henry's enemies receive popular support

7 The common people by numbers swarm to us.
3 Henry VI IV, 2
Unlike Clifford, Earl of Warwick is pleased

8   I have bought
Golden opinions from all sorts of people,
Which would be worn now in their newest gloss.
Macbeth I, 7
Macbeth at war with himself over the contemplated murder of
Duncan

9   How beauteous mankind is! O brave new world,
That hath such people in't!
The Tempest V, 1
Miranda, on first seeing people from the normal world

128   PERFECTION

1   He lost a wife . . .
Whose dear perfection hearts that scorn'd to serve
Humbly call'd mistress.
All's Well That Ends Well V, 3
Lafeu to King of France, concerning Bertram and Helena

2   I saw her once
Hop forty paces through the public street;
And having lost her breath, she spoke, and panted,
That she did make defect perfection.
Antony and Cleopatra II, 2
Enobarbus concerning Cleopatra

3   Those about her
From her shall read the perfect ways of honour.
Henry VIII V, 5
Archbishop Cranmer, offering fulsome praise to an infant – the
future Elizabeth I

4   How many things by season season'd are
To their right praise and true perfection.
The Merchant of Venice V, 1
Portia to Nerissa

5   One entire and perfect chrysolite.
     Othello V, 2
     Othello to Emilia, concerning Desdemona's worth

6   O heaven, were man
     But constant, he were perfect!
     The Two Gentlemen of Verona V, 4
     Proteus, far from perfect, to Julia

7   Right perfection, wrongfully disgraced.
     Sonnet 66

129   PHILOSOPHY

1   Hast any philosophy in thee, shepherd?
     As You Like It III, 2
     Touchstone to Corin

2   There are more things in heaven and earth, Horatio,
     Than are dreamt of in your philosophy.
     Hamlet I, 5
     Hamlet, after seeing his father's ghost

3   There is something in this more than natural, if philosophy
     could find it out.
     Hamlet II, 2
     Hamlet to Rosencrantz and Guildenstern, concerning child actors

4   Of your philosophy you make no use.
     Julius Caesar IV, 3
     Cassius to Brutus, after a quarrel

5   I fear he will prove the weeping philosopher when he grows
     old, being so full of unmannerly sadness in his youth.
     The Merchant of Venice I, 2
     Portia concerning her suitor, the Count Palatine

6   There was never yet philosopher
     That could endure the toothache patiently.
     Much Ado About Nothing V, 1
     Leonato to Antonio

7   I'll give thee armour to keep off that word,
     Adversity's sweet milk, philosophy,
     To comfort thee, though thou art banished.
     Romeo and Juliet III, 3
     Friar Laurence deals with the word 'banishment'

8   Hang up philosophy!
     Unless philosophy can make a Juliet.
     Romeo and Juliet III, 3
     Romeo to Friar Laurence

9   That part of philosophy
     Will I apply that treats of happiness.
     The Taming of the Shrew I, 1
     Lucentio to Tranio

10   I am . . .
     Glad that you thus continue your resolve
     To suck the sweets of sweet philosophy.
     The Taming of the Shrew I, 1
     Tranio to Lucentio

11   You have both said well . . .
                   but superficially; not much
     Unlike young men, whom Aristotle thought
     Unfit to hear moral philosophy.
     Troilus and Cressida II, 2
     Hector to Paris and Troilus

130 PITY

1 If ever you have looked on better days . . .
   If ever from your eyelids wiped a tear
   And know what 'tis to pity and be pitied,
   Let gentleness my strong enforcement be.
   As You Like It II, 7
   Orlando, almost starving, to Duke Senior and his companions

2 My pity hath been balm to heal their wounds.
   3 Henry VI IV, 8
   Henry concerning the people

3 O, now you weep, and I perceive you feel
   The dint of pity: these are gracious drops.
   Julius Caesar III, 2
   Antony to citizens, after Caesar's assassination

4 Pity, like a new-born naked babe,
   Striding the blast, or heaven's cherubim horsed
   Upon the sightless couriers of the air,
   Shall blow the horrid deed in every eye.
   Macbeth I, 7
   Macbeth, thinking about the projected murder of Duncan

5 She loved me for the dangers I had pass'd,
   And I lov'd her that she did pity them.
   Othello I, 3
   Othello to senators, on his love for Desdemona

6 My friend, I spy some pity in thy looks;
   O, if thine eye be not a flatterer,
   Come thou on my side, and entreat for me.
   As you would beg, were you in my distress.
   Richard III I, 4
   Duke of Clarence to Second Murderer

7   Is there no pity sitting in the clouds,
     That sees into the bottom of my grief?
     Romeo and Juliet III, 5
     Juliet, secretly married to Romeo, being forced by her parents
     into another marriage

8   I am a humble suitor to your virtues;
     For pity is the virtue of the law,
     And none but tyrants use it cruelly.
     Timon of Athens III, 5
     Alcibiades pleads to senators for the life of a friend

9   Men must learn now with pity to dispense,
     For policy sits above conscience.
     Timon of Athens III, 2
     Strangers discussing the reluctance of Timon's friends to help
     him

131   PLACE

1   There's place and means for every man alive.
     All's Well That Ends Well IV, 3
     Parolles

2   I like this place, and willingly could waste my time in it.
     As You Like It II, 4
     Celia in the Forest of Arden

3   Now I am in Arden, the more fool I. When I was at home I was
     in a better place.
     As You Like It II, 4
     Touchstone to Rosalind and Celia

4   Come, my lord,
     We will bestow you in some better place,
     Fitter for sickness and for crazy age.
     1 Henry VI III, 2
     Lord Talbot to the elderly Duke of Bedford before the enemy
     attack

5   He that stands upon a slippery place
Makes nice of no vile hold to stay him up.
King John III, 4
Cardinal Pandulph to Dauphin

6   My ventures are not in one bottom trusted,
Nor to one place.
The Merchant of Venice I, 1
Antonio to Salarino

7   *First witch:*   When shall we three meet again?
In thunder, lightning, or in rain? . . .
Where the place?
Second witch: Upon the heath.
Macbeth I, 1
Witches plan a meeting with Macbeth

8   All places that the eye of heaven visits
Are to a wise man ports and happy havens.
Richard II I, 3
John of Gaunt to his banished son, Henry Bolingbroke

9   Is there no respect of place, persons, nor time in you?
Twelfth Night II, 3
Malvolio to Sir Toby Belch and his noisy companions

132   PLAYS AND PLAYERS

1   All the world's a stage,
And all the men and women merely players:
They have their exits and their entrances;
And one man in his time plays many parts.
As You Like It II, 7
Jaques to Duke Senior and companions

2   If it be true that good wine needs no bush,
'Tis true that a good play needs no epilogue.
As You Like It Epilogue

3   Like a dull actor now
I have forgot my part and I am out,
Even to a full disgrace.
Coriolanus V, 3
Coriolanus to his wife

4   If you delight not in man, what lenten entertainment the
players shall receive from you.
Hamlet II, 2
Rosencrantz to Hamlet

5   The best actors in the world, either for tragedy, comedy,
history, pastoral, pastoral-comical, tragical-historical, tragical-
comical-historical-pastoral, or poem unlimited.
Hamlet II, 2
Polonius to Hamlet

6   Will you see the players well bestowed? Let them be well used,
for they are the abstract and brief chronicles of the time.
Hamlet II, 2
Hamlet to Polonius

7   Is it not monstrous that this player here,
But in a fiction, in a dream of passion,
Could force his soul so to his own conceit
That from her working all his visage wann'd.
Hamlet II, 2
Hamlet, soliloquizing

8   The play's the thing
Wherein I'll catch the conscience of the king.
Hamlet II, 2
Hamlet, soliloquizing on *The Mousetrap* play

9   Speak the speech, I pray you, as I pronounced it to you,
trippingly on the tongue; but if you mouth it, as many of your
players do, I had as lief the town-crier spoke my lines.
Hamlet III, 2
Hamlet to Players

10   O'erstep not the modesty of nature . . . The purpose of playing
    . . . was and is, to hold, as 'twere, the mirror up to nature.
    Hamlet III, 2
    Hamlet to Players

11   Let those that play your clowns speak no more than is set down
    for them.
    Hamlet III, 2
    Hamlet to Players

12   O Jesu, he does it as like one of these harlotry players as ever I
    see.
    1 Henry IV II, 4
    Hostess of Boar's Head tavern, concerning Falstaff's impersonation of
    Henry IV

        13   How many ages hence
            Shall this our lofty scene be acted over
            In states unborn and accents yet unknown.
            Julius Caesar III, 1
            Cassius, just after Caesar's murder

        14   Life's but a walking shadow, a poor player
            That struts and frets his hour upon the stage,
            And then is heard no more.
            Macbeth V, 6
            Macbeth to himself, on the futility of life

15   Here's a marvellous convenient place for our rehearsal. This
    green plot shall be our stage, this hawthorn-brake our tiring-
    house.
    A Midsummer Night's Dream III, 1
    Quince to his fellows

16   You must not speak that yet; that you answer to Pyramus. You
    speak all your part at once, cues and all!
    A Midsummer Night's Dream III, 1
    Quince to Flute

17 A play there is, my lord, some ten words long,
Which is as brief as I have known a play;
But by ten words, my lord, it is too long.
A Midsummer Night's Dream V, 1
Philostrate to Theseus

18 The actors are at hand; and by their show,
You shall know all that you are like to know.
A Midsummer Night's Dream V, 1
Quince, presenting the 'Pyramus and Thisbe' play

19 If this were played upon a stage now, I should condemn it as an
improbable fiction.
Twelfth Night III, 4
Fabian, on the plot to hoax Malvolio

20 As an unperfect actor on the stage,
Who with his fear is put besides his part . . .
So I, for fear of trust, forget to say,
The perfect ceremony of love's rite.
Sonnet 23

133 POETRY

1 The truest poetry is the most feigning.
As You Like It III, 3
Touchstone to Audrey

2 This is the very false gallop of verses.
As You Like It III, 2
Touchstone, criticizing Orlando's love poems addressed to
Rosalind and fastened to trees

3   Mincing poetry,
'Tis like the forced gait of a shuffling nag.
1 Henry IV III, 1
Hotspur to Glendower

4 O for a Muse of fire, that would ascend
   The brightest heaven of invention.
   Henry V I Prologue
   Chorus

5 The elegancy, facility, and golden cadence of poesy.
   Love's Labour's Lost IV, 2
   Holofernes to Sir Nathaniel

6 Never durst poet touch a pen to write
   Until his ink were temper'd with Love's sighs.
   Love's Labour's Lost IV, 3
   Biron to his companions

7 The poet's eye in a fine frenzy rolling,
   Doth glance from heaven to earth; from earth to
      heaven.
   A Midsummer Night's Dream V, 1
   Theseus to Hippolyta

8 I can find out no rhyme to 'lady' but 'baby', an innocent
   rhyme; for 'scorn', 'horn', a hard rhyme; for 'school', 'fool', a
   babbling rhyme ... No I was not born under a rhyming planet.
   Much Ado About Nothing V, 2
   Benedick

9 Our poesy is as a gum, which oozes
   From whence 'tis nourished.
   Timon of Athens I, 1
   Poet to Painter

10 You must lay lime to tangle her desires
    With wailful sonnets.
    The Two Gentlemen of Verona III, 2
    Proteus to Duke

11 Much is the force of heaven-bred poesy.
    The Two Gentlemen of Verona III, 2
    Duke to Proteus

12 Had my friend's Muse grown with this growing age,
A dearer birth than this his love had brought . . .
But since he died and Poets better prove,
Theirs for their style I'll read, his for his love.
Sonnet 32

134 POISON

1   Now I feed myself
With most delicious poison.
Antony and Cleopatra I, 5
Cleopatra to Charmian, thinking of absent Antony

2   You have
Commanded of me these most poisonous compounds,
Which are the movers of a languishing death.
Cymbeline I, 5
Dr Cornelius to the queen

3 I bought an unction of a mountebank,
So mortal that but dip a knife in it,
Where it draws blood no cataplasm so rare . . .
                    Can save the thing from death
That is but scratch'd withal.
Hamlet IV, 7
Laertes to Claudius, seeking Hamlet's death

4   O, I die, Horatio;
The potent poison quite o'er-crows my spirit.
Hamlet V, 2
Hamlet, slain by Laertes

5 And that same sword-and-buckler Prince of Wales,
But that I think his father loves him not
And would be glad he met with some mischance,
I would have him poison'd with a pot of ale.
1 Henry IV I, 3
Hotspur, working himself into rage against his enemies

6　If you have poison for me, I will drink it.
King Lear IV, 7
Lear, broken and feeble, to Cordelia

7　Do it not with poison, strangle her in her bed.
Othello IV, 1
Iago to Othello, concerning Desdemona

8　They love not poison that do poison need,
Nor do I thee, though I did wish him dead.
Richard II V, 6
Bolingbroke to Exton, who arranged for Richard's murder

9　　　　　　Let me have
A dram of poison: such soon-spending gear
As will disperse itself through all the veins,
That the life-weary taker may fall dead.
Romeo and Juliet V, 1
Romeo to apothecary

10　What if it be a poison which the friar
Subtly hath minister'd to have me dead?
Romeo and Juliet IV, 3
Juliet, momentarily hesitating to take Friar Laurence's sleep-inducing drug

135　POSSESSIONS

1　This is the brief of money, plate, and jewels
I am possessed of: 'tis exactly valued;
Not petty things admitted.
Antony and Cleopatra V, 2
Cleopatra to Octavius Caesar, after her capture

2　Can one desire too much of a good thing?
As You Like It IV, 1
Rosalind/Ganymede to Orlando

3 A poor virgin, sir, an ill-favoured thing, sir, but mine own.
As You Like It V, 4
Touchstone, introducing Audrey to Duke Senior

4 Lo, now my glory smear'd in dust and blood!
My parks, my walks, my manors that I had,
Even now forsake me, and of all my lands
Is nothing left me but my body's length.
3 Henry VI V, 2
The dying Earl of Warwick

5 What piles of wealth hath he accumulated
To his own portion! and what expense by the hour
Seems to flow from him!
Henry VIII III, 2
Henry to himself, regarding Cardinal Wolsey

6 What's mine is yours, and what is yours is mine.
Measure for Measure V, 1
Duke to Isabel

7 So shall you share all that he does possess,
By having him making yourself no less.
Romeo and Juliet I, 3
Lady Capulet, encouraging Juliet to marry Paris

8   My house within the city
Is richly furnished with plate and gold . . .
In ivory coffers I have stuff'd my crowns;
In cypress chests my arras, counterpoints,
Costly apparel, tents, and canopies,
Fine linen, Turkey cushions boss'd with pearl.
The Taming of the Shrew II, 1
Gremio, to Baptista, claiming eligibility as suitor to Bianca

9 Gremio, 'tis known my father had no less
Than three great argosies; besides two galliasses,
And twelve tight galleys: these I will assure her,
And twice as much, whate'er thou offer'st next.
The Taming of the Shrew II, 1
Tranio, as Lucentio, capping Gremio's offer

136 POVERTY

1 'Tis not so well that I am poor, though many of the rich are damned.
All's Well That Ends Well I, 3
Clown to Countess

2 I am as poor as Job, my lord, but not as patient.
2 Henry IV I, 2
Falstaff to Chief Justice

3 There's but a shirt and a half in all my company; and the half-shirt is two napkins tacked together and thrown over the shoulders like a herald's coat without sleeves.
1 Henry IV IV, 2
Falstaff, recruiting on behalf of the king

4 She bears a duke's revenues on her back,
And in her heart she scorns our poverty.
2 Henry VI I, 3
Queen Margaret, speaking of the wealthy and proud Duchess of Gloucester

5 If thou art rich, thou'rt poor;
For, like an ass whose back with ingots bows,
Thou bear'st thy heavy riches but a journey,
And death unloads thee.
Measure for Measure III, 1
Duke to Claudio

6 Fortune shows herself more kind
Than is her custom: it is still her use
To let the wretched man outlive his wealth,
To view with hollow eye and wrinkled brow
An age of poverty.
The Merchant of Venice IV, 1
Antonio, apparently due to die shortly, calmly accepts this as a release from future poverty

7   Poor and content is rich, and rich enough;
But riches fineless is as poor as winter
To him that ever fears he shall be poor.
Othello III, 3
Iago to Othello
fineless 'endless'

8   Art thou so bare and full of wretchedness,
And fear'st to die? famine is in thy cheeks,
Need and oppression starveth in thy eyes,
Contempt and beggary hangs upon thy back.
Romeo and Juliet V, 1
Romeo to apothecary whom he bribes to supply poison

9   O world, how apt the poor are to be proud!
Twelfth Night III, 1
Olivia to Cesario/Viola

137 POWER

1   We, ignorant of ourselves,
Beg often our own harms, which the wise powers
Deny us for our good.
Antony and Cleopatra II, 1
Menecrates to Pompey

2   Now we have shown our power,
Let us seem humbler after it is done.
Coriolanus IV, 2
The tribunes, Brutus and Sicinius, seeking to entrap hasty-tempered Coriolanus

3   The power that I have on you is to spare you.
Cymbeline V, 5
Posthumus to Iachimo

4   The spirit that I have seen
May be the devil; and the devil hath power
To assume a pleasing shape.
Hamlet II, 2
Hamlet, anxious to be sure that his father's ghost is genuine

5 The abuse of greatness is when it disjoins
Remorse from power.
Julius Caesar II, 1
Brutus, considering Caesar's growing strength

6   I could
With bare-faced power sweep him from my sight.
Macbeth III, 1
Macbeth, however, engages secret murderers to dispose of
Banquo

7 Then everything includes itself in power,
Power into will, will into appetite;
And appetite a universal wolf.
Troilus and Cressida I, 3
Ulysses, warning that unchecked and unorganized power can
lead to chaos

8 Most wisely hath Ulysses here discovered
The fever whereof all our power is sick.
Troilus and Cressida I, 3
Nestor to other Greek leaders

138 PRAISE

1 I will spare my praises towards him;
Knowing him is enough.
All's Well That Ends Well II, 1
Helena to King of France, concerning her father, a great
physician no longer living

2   I will praise any man that will praise me.
Antony and Cleopatra II, 6
Enobarbus to Menas

3   First he did praise my beauty, then my speech.
The Comedy of Errors IV, 2
Luciana to Adriana, about the latter's husband

4   My mother,
Who has a charter to extol her blood,
When she does praise me grieves me.
Coriolanus I, 9
Coriolanus dislikes adulation for his war deeds

5   All the priests and friars in my realm
Shall in procession sing her endless praise.
1 Henry VI I, 6
Dauphin on Joan of Arc

6   To dispraise my lord with that same tongue
Which she hath praised him with above compare
So many thousand times.
Romeo and Juliet III, 5
Juliet, condemning the inconsistency of her nurse's attitude to Romeo

7   The worthiness of praise disdains his worth
If that the praised himself brings the praise forth.
Troilus and Cressida I, 3
Aeneas to Agamemnon

8   Thou shalt find that she will outstrip all praise
And make it halt behind her.
The Tempest IV, 1
Prospero to Ferdinand, on Miranda

9   Who is it that says most? which can say more
Than this rich praise, that you alone are you?
Sonnet 84

139 PRAYER

1   And what's in prayer but this twofold force,
    To be forestalled ere we come to fall,
    Or pardon'd being down?
    Hamlet III, 3
    Claudius to himself

2   My words fly up, my thoughts remain below:
    Words without thoughts never to heaven go.
    Hamlet III, 3
    Claudius to himself

3   All his mind is bent to holiness,
    To number Ave-Maries on his beads.
    2 Henry VI I, 3
    Queen concerning Henry

4   Go with me, like good angels, to my end,
    And, as the long divorce of steel falls on me,
    Make of your prayers one sweet sacrifice,
    And lift my soul to heaven.
    Henry VIII II, 1
    Duke of Buckingham, when taken to his execution

5   My prayers
    Are not words duly hallowed, nor my wishes
    More worth than empty vanities; yet prayers and
       wishes
    Are all I can return.
    Henry VIII II, 3
    Anne Bullen to Lord Chamberlain, acknowledging a gift from
    the king

6   I could not say 'Amen'
    When they did say 'God bless us' . . .
    I had most need of blessing, and 'Amen'
    Stuck in my throat.
    Macbeth II, 2
    Macbeth, at the murder of Duncan

7   When I would pray and think, I think and pray
To several subjects. Heaven hath my empty words;
Whilst my invention, hearing not my tongue,
Anchors on Isabel.

Measure for Measure II, 4
Angelo, admitting to himself his weakness

8   We do pray for mercy;
And that same prayer doth teach us all to render
The deeds of mercy.

The Merchant of Venice IV, 1
Portia, as Balthasar, to Shylock

9   His worst fault is that he is given to prayer; he is something peevish that way.

The Merry Wives of Windsor I, 4
Mistress Quickly, concerning a servant

10   If my wind were but long enough to say my prayers, I would repent.

The Merry Wives of Windsor IV, 5
Falstaff to himself

---

140 PRIDE

---

1   My pride fell with my fortunes.

As You Like It I, 2
Rosalind, frankly revealing her interest in Orlando

2   Why, who cries out on pride? . . .
Does it not flow as hugely as the sea?

As You Like It II, 7
Jaques to Duke Senior

3   My high-blown pride
At length broke under me, and now has left me
Weary and old with service.
Henry VIII III, 2
Cardinal Wolsey to himself

4   I will instruct my sorrows to be proud;
For grief is proud and makes his owner stoop.
King John III, 1
Constance to Earl of Salisbury

5   Man, proud man,
Drest in a little brief authority . . .
Plays such fantastic tricks before high heaven
As make the angels weep.
Measure for Measure II, 2
Isabella to Angelo

6   Proud I can never be of what I hate.
Romeo and Juliet III, 5
Juliet, trying to resist a forced marriage

7 He that is proud eats up himself: pride is his own glass, his
own trumpet, his own chronicle.
Troilus and Cressida II, 3
Agamemnon to Ajax

8   The proud lord
That bastes his arrogance with his own seam.
Troilus and Cressida II, 3
Ulysses to Agamemnon
seam 'grease'

141 PRISON

1   They fell upon me, bound me, bore me thence,
And in a dark and dankish vault at home
There left me and my man, both bound together;
Till, gnawing with my teeth my bonds in sunder,
I gain'd my freedom.
The Comedy of Errors V, 1
Antipholus of Ephesus, complaining to the Duke of being
treated as a lunatic by his wife

2   Even like a man new haled from the rack,
So fare my limbs with long imprisonment.
1 Henry VI II, 5
Mortimer to gaolers

3   Go, lead the way; I long to see my prison.
2 Henry VI II, 4
Duchess of Gloucester to Sir John Stanley

4   Let me live in prison all my days,
And when I give occasion of offence
Then let me die.
3 Henry VI I, 3
The youthful Earl of Rutland pleads vainly for his life

5   I take it, by all voices, that forthwith
You be convey'd to the Tower a prisoner;
There to remain till the king's further pleasure
Be known unto us.
Henry VIII V, 3
Lord Chancellor to Archbishop Cranmer in Council

6   I have been studying how I may compare
This prison where I live unto the world.
Richard II V, 5
Richard, soliloquizing after his abdication

7   O Pomfret, Pomfret! O thou bloody prison!
Fatal and ominous to noble peers.
Richard III III, 3
Earl Rivers, on the way to execution

8 The wreck of all my friends, nor this man's threats,
To whom I am subdued, are but light to me,
Might I but through my prison once a day
Behold this maid.

The Tempest I, 2
Ferdinand, consoled by Miranda's charm for Prospero's
pretended harshness

9 We'll have him in a dark room and bound. My niece is already
in the belief that he's mad.

Twelfth Night III, 4
Sir Toby Belch concerning Malvolio

10 Why have you suffer'd me to be imprison'd,
Kept in a dark house, visited by the priest,
And made the most notorious geck and gull?

Twelfth Night V, 1
Malvolio to Countess Olivia

142 PROPHECY

1 And thus I prophesy: that many a thousand
Which now mistrust no parcel of my fear,
Shall rue the hour that ever thou wast born.

3 Henry VI V, 6
Henry to Richard of Gloucester

2 This royal infant . . .
Though in her cradle, yet now promises
Upon this land a thousand thousand blessings,
Which time shall bring to ripeness.

Henry VIII V, 5
Archbishop Cranmer offering a flattering prophecy about Queen
Elizabeth

3   *Soothsayer:* Beware the ides of March.
      Caesar: He is a dreamer; let us leave him.
      Julius Caesar I, 2

4   Now hear me speak with a prophetic spirit.
      King John III, 4
      Cardinal Pandulph to the Dauphin, on the latter's opportunity
      to replace John

5   Is this Ascension-day? Did not the prophet
      Say that before Ascension-day at noon
      My crown I should give off? Even so I have.
      King John V, 1
      John hands the crown to the Pope's representative, to receive it
      back immediately

6   If you can look into the seeds of time,
      And say which grain will grow and which will not,
      Speak then to me.
      Macbeth I, 3
      Banquo to the witches

7   Methinks I am a prophet new inspired,
      And thus expiring do foretell of him:
      His rash fierce blaze of riot cannot last,
      For violent fires soon burn out themselves.
      Richard II II, 1
      John of Gaunt on Richard's excesses

8   Come, Hector, come; go back:
      Thy wife hath dream'd; thy mother hath had visions:
      Cassandra doth foresee; and I myself
      Am like a prophet suddenly enrapt,
      To tell thee that this day is ominous.
      Troilus and Cressida V, 3
      Priam, attempting to dissuade Hector from combat

9   Not my own fears, nor the prophetic soul
      Of the wide world dreaming on things to come,
      Can yet the lease of my true love control.
      Sonnet 107

143   PUNISHMENT

1   To punish me for what you make me do
Seems most unequal.
Antony and Cleopatra II, 5
Messenger who brings news to Cleopatra that Antony has
married Octavia

2   Bid that welcome
Which comes to punish us, and we punish it
Seeming to bear it lightly.
Antony and Cleopatra IV, 14
Antony to followers

3   Almost at fainting under
The pleasing punishment that women bear . . .
There had she not been long but she became
The joyful mother of two goodly sons.
The Comedy of Errors I, 1
Aegeon, speaking of his wife to Duke of Ephesus

4   Disloyal! No:
She's punished for her truth.
Cymbeline III, 2
Pisanio, defending Imogen from a false charge of unfaithfulness

5   Thou dost in thy passages of life
Make me believe that thou art only mark'd
For the hot vengeance and the rod of heaven
To punish me for my misreadings.
1 Henry IV III, 2
The king to his apparently irresponsible son, Prince Hal

6   The Moor's abused by some most villainous knave . . .
O heaven, that such companions thou'dst unfold,
And put in every honest hand a whip
To lash the rascals naked through the world.
Othello IV, 2
Emilia, concerning any knaves who have slandered Desdemona
to Othello

7 Subjects punish'd that ne'er thought offence.
Pericles I, 2
Pericles on the likely behaviour of Antiochus

8 Go charge my goblins that they grind their joints
With dry convulsions; shorten up their sinews
With aged cramps.
The Tempest IV, 1
Prospero, punishing Caliban and companions for plotting to kill him

9 Set him breast-deep in earth, and famish him;
There let him stand and rave and cry for food:
If anyone relieves or pities him,
For the offence he dies.
Titus Andronicus V, 3
Lucius concerning Aaron

144   QUARRELS

1   Beware
Of entrance to a quarrel; but being in
Bear't that the opposed may beware of thee.
Hamlet I, 3
Polonius, giving advice to Laertes

2 You owe me money, Sir John; and now you pick a quarrel to beguile me of it.
1 Henry IV III, 3
Mrs Quickly to Falstaff

3 Be friends, you English fools, be friends: we have French quarrels enow, if you could tell how to reckon.
Henry V IV, 1
Bates to King Henry, incognito, and Williams

4   Thrice is he arm'd that hath his quarrel just.
2 Henry VI III, 2
Henry to courtiers

5   I should forge
Quarrels unjust against the good and loyal
Destroying them for wealth.
Macbeth IV, 3
Malcolm to Macduff, testing him

6   In the managing of quarrels you may say he is wise; for either he avoids them with great discretion, or undertakes them with a most Christian-like fear.
Much Ado About Nothing II, 3
Don Pedro to Claudio, concerning Benedick

7   Thy head is as full of quarrels as an egg is full of meat.
Romeo and Juliet III, 1
Mercutio to Benvolio

8   These quarrels must be quietly debated.
Titus Andronicus V, 3
This peaceful advice by Marcus Andronicus is in fact followed by an orgy of killing

9   He's a great quarreller; and but that he hath the gift of a coward to allay the gust he hath in quarrelling . . . he would quickly have the gift of a grave.
Twelfth Night I, 3
Maria on Sir Andrew Aguecheek

10 I am sure no man hath any quarrel with me: my remembrance is very free and clear from any image of offence done to any man.
Twelfth Night III, 4
Viola/Cesario to Sir Toby Belch

145 QUEEN

1 I must from this enchanting queen break off.
Antony and Cleopatra I, 2
Antony concerning Cleopatra

2 As sweet as ditties highly penn'd,
Sung by a fair queen in a summer's bower.
1 Henry IV III, 1
Mortimer to Glendower's daughter

3 Now, welcome, Kate: and bear witness all
That here I kiss her as my sovereign queen.
Henry V V, 2
Henry in a French palace

4 To be a queen in bondage is more vile
Than is a slave in base servility;
For princes should be free.
1 Henry VI V, 3
Princess Margaret of Anjou to Earl of Suffolk

5 I know I am too mean to be your queen,
And yet too good to be your concubine.
3 Henry VI III, 2
Lady Grey to King Edward IV

6 I am about to weep; but thinking that
We are a queen, or long have dream'd so, certain
The daughter of a king, my drops of tears
I'll turn to sparks of fire.
Henry VIII II, 4
Queen Katherine to Wolsey

7 I would not be a queen
For all the world.
Henry VIII II, 3
Anne Bullen

8 She had all the royal makings of a queen.
As holy oil, Edward the Confessor's crown,
The rod, a bird of peace, and all such emblems
Laid nobly on her.
Henry VIII IV, 1
Gentleman, describing the crowning of Anne Bullen

9 O queen of queens! how far dost thou excel,
No thought can think, no tongue of mortal tell.
Love's Labour's Lost IV, 3
King of Navarre, writing of the Princess of France

10 I had rather be a country servant maid
Than a great queen, with this condition,
To be thus taunted, scorn'd, and baited at.
Richard III I, 3
Queen of Edward IV to Duke of Gloucester

11 As on the finger of a throned queen
The basest jewel will be well esteemed,
So are those errors that in thee are seen
To truths translated and for true things deemed.
Sonnet 96

146   RAIN

1 For raging wind blows up incessant showers,
And when the rage allays, the rain begins.
3 Henry VI I, 4
Duke of York to his enemy, Queen Margaret

2 You cataracts and hurricanoes, spout
Till you have drench'd our steeples, drown'd the cocks!
King Lear III, 2
Lear, addressing the storm

3   Court holy-water in a dry house is better than this rain-water out o' door.

King Lear III, 2
Fool to Lear

    4   The quality of mercy is not strain'd,
       It droppeth as the gentle rain from heaven
       Upon the place beneath.

       The Merchant of Venice IV, 1
       Portia/Balthasar to Shylock

5   Let the sky rain potatoes; let it thunder to the tune of Green Sleeves.

The Merry Wives of Windsor V, 5
Falstaff to Mrs Ford

6   Stand thee close, then, under the pent-house, for it drizzles rain.

Much Ado About Nothing III, 3
Borachio to Conrade

    7   When that I was and a little tiny boy,
       With hey, ho, the wind and the rain,
       A foolish thing was but a toy,
       For the rain it raineth every day.

       Twelfth Night V, 1
       Clown, song to end the play

    8   Rain added to a river that is rank
       Perforce will force it overflow the bank.

       Venus and Adonis Stanza 12

147 REASON

1 (They) no sooner looked but they loved, no sooner loved but they sighed, no sooner sighed but they asked one another the reason, no sooner knew the reason but they sought the remedy.
As You Like It V, 2
Rosalind, telling Orlando about Oliver's strangely sudden romance with Celia

2 Sure, he that made us with such large discourse,
Looking before and after, gave us not
That capability and god-like reason
To fust in us unused.
Hamlet IV, 4
Hamlet, soliloquizing

3 I will lay him down such reasons for this adventure that he shall go.
1 Henry IV I, 2
Poins promises Falstaff to draw Prince Hal into a highwayman escapade

4 Give you a reason on compulsion! If reasons were as plentiful as blackberries, I would give no man a reason upon compulsion.
1 Henry IV II, 4
Falstaff unwilling to give an honest explanation of failure

5 Good reasons must, of force, give place to better.
Julius Caesar IV, 3
Brutus over-rules Cassius in planning a battle

6 Since the affairs of men rest still uncertain,
Let's reason with the worst that may befall.
Julius Caesar V, 1
Cassius to Brutus

7 Strong reasons make strong actions.
King John III, 4
Dauphin to Cardinal Pandulph

8 Gratiano speaks an infinite deal of nothing, more than any man in all Venice. His reasons are as two grains of wheat hid in two bushels of chaff: you shall seek all day ere you find them; and when you have them, they are not worth the search.
The Merchant of Venice I, 1
Bassanio to Antonio

9 I have no other but a woman's reason;
I think him so because I think him so.
The Two Gentlemen of Verona I, 2
Lucetta gives Julia her opinion of Proteus

10 O judgement! thou art fled to brutish beasts,
And men have lost their reason.
Julius Caesar III, 2
Antony over Caesar's dead body

148 REMEDY

1 Our remedies oft in ourselves do lie
Which we ascribe to heaven.
All's Well That Ends Well I, 1
Helena to herself

2 There is a remedy, approved, set down.
To cure the desperate languishings whereof
The king is rendered lost.
All's Well That Ends Well I, 3
Helena, whose father was a notable physician

3 I can get no remedy against this consumption of the purse . . .
the disease is incurable.
2 Henry IV I, 2
Falstaff to his Page

4   Things without all remedy
Should be without regard: what's done is done.
Macbeth III, 2
Lady Macbeth to Macbeth, after the murder of Duncan

5   When remedies are past, the griefs are ended . . .
To mourn a mischief that is past and gone
Is the next way to draw new mischief on.
Othello I, 3
Duke of Venice advising Brabantio concerning his daughter's
marriage to Othello

6   The nature of the sickness found, Ulysses,
What is the remedy?
Troilus and Cressida I, 3
Agamemnon on Achilles's tendency to stay in his tent

7   The remedy indeed to do me good
Is to let forth my foul-defiled blood.
The Rape of Lucrece Stanza 147
Lucrece appears to regard suicide as a remedy for rape

149   REPENTANCE

1   Try what repentance can: what can it not?
Yet what can it when one cannot repent?
Hamlet III, 3
King Claudius to himself

2   Confess yourself to heaven;
Repent what's past, avoid what is to come.
Hamlet III, 4
Hamlet to his mother

3 Well, I'll repent, and that suddenly . . . I shall be out of heart
shortly, and then I shall have no strength to repent.
1 Henry IV III, 3
Falstaff to Bardolph

4 Under your good correction, I have seen,
When, after execution, Judgement hath
Repented o'er his doom.
Measure for Measure II, 2
Provost to Angelo

5 After I have solemnly interr'd
At Chertsey monastery this noble king,
And wet his grave with my repentant tears,
I will with all expedient duty see you.
Richard III I, 2
Richard of Gloucester's insincere repentance for the murders of
King Henry VI and his son is being offered to the latter's
widow, Lady Anne

6 If one good deed in all my life I did,
I do repent it from my very soul.
Titus Andronicus V, 3
The villainous Aaron to Lucius

150 REPUTATION

1 Jealous in honour, sudden and quick in quarrel,
Seeking the bubble reputation
Even in the cannon's mouth.
As You Like It II, 7
Jaques, describing the typical soldier in the Seven Ages of Man

2 I have offended reputation,
A most unnoble swerving.
Antony and Cleopatra III, 11
Antony to Eros

3 I would to God thou and I knew where a commodity of good
names were to be bought.
1 Henry IV I, 2
Falstaff to Prince Hal

4   The purest treasure mortal times afford
    Is spotless reputation.
    Richard II I, 1
    Mowbray to Richard

5   Thy death-bed is no lesser than thy land
    Wherein thou liest in reputation sick.
    Richard II II, 1
    John of Gaunt to Richard

6   Reputation, reputation, reputation! O, I have lost my
    reputation! I have lost the immortal part of myself, and what
    remains is bestial.
    Othello II, 3
    Cassio, guilty of a drunken affray

7   Reputation is an idle and most false imposition; oft got
    without merit and lost without deserving.
    Othello II, 3
    Iago to Cassio

8   I see my reputation is at stake;
    My fame is shrewdly gored.
    Troilus and Cressida III, 2
    Achilles to Patroclus

---

151   REST

---

1   Quietness, grown sick of rest, would purge
    By any desperate change.
    Antony and Cleopatra I, 3
    Antony to Cleopatra

2   Weariness
    Can snore upon the flint, when resty sloth
    Finds the down pillow hard.
    Cymbeline III, 6
    Belarius to Guiderius

3   Rest, rest, perturbed spirit.
     Hamlet I, 5
     Hamlet to his father's ghost

4   Good night, sweet prince,
     And flights of angels sing thee to thy rest.
     Hamlet V, 2
     Horatio, as Hamlet dies

5   Not all these, laid in bed majestical,
     Can sleep so soundly as the wretched slave,
     Who with a body fill'd and vacant mind
     Gets him to rest.
     Henry V IV, 1
     The king is referring to the trappings of kingship

6   So may he rest; his faults lie gently on him.
     Henry VIII IV, 2
     Queen Katherine concerning Cardinal Wolsey

7   She is troubled with thick-coming fancies
     That keep her from her rest.
     Macbeth V, 3
     Doctor concerning Lady Macbeth

8   O here
     Will I set up my everlasting rest.
     Romeo and Juliet V, 3
     Romeo in Juliet's tomb

9   And everyone to rest themselves betake,
     Save thieves and cares and troubled minds that wake.
     The Rape of Lucrece Stanza 18

152   REVENGE

1   O, a kiss
Long as my exile, sweet as my revenge!
Coriolanus V, 3
The kiss is from his wife, the revenge towards Rome, which
banished him

2   If thou didst ever thy dear father love . . .
Revenge his foul and most unnatural murder.
Hamlet I, 5
Ghost of Hamlet's father to his son

3   How all occasions do inform against me
And spur my dull revenge.
Hamlet IV, 4
Hamlet grows impatient with himself over carrying out his task

4   Caesar's spirit, ranging for revenge
With Ate by his side, come hot from hell.
Julius Caesar III, 1
Antony pictures the goddess of vengeance aiding the murdered
Caesar

5   If I can catch him once upon the hip,
I will feed fat the ancient grudge I bear him.
The Merchant of Venice I, 3
Shylock on Antonio

6   If a Jew wrong a Christian, what is his humility? Revenge. If a
Christian wrong a Jew, what should his sufferance be by
Christian example? Why, revenge.
The Merchant of Venice III, 1
Shylock to Salarino

7   My bloody thoughts, with violent pace,
Shall ne'er look back, ne'er ebb to humble love,
Till that a capable and wide revenge
Swallow them up.
Othello III, 3
Othello to Iago

8   Murder's out of tune
And sweet revenge grows harsh.
Othello V, 2
Othello, having murdered his wife, wishes Cassio were dead too

9   Vengeance is in my heart, death in my hand,
Blood and revenge are hammering in my head.
Titus Andronicus II, 3
Aaron on behalf of Tamora, whose eldest son Titus ordered to
be slain

10   I'll be revenged on the whole pack of you.
Twelfth Night V, 1
Malvolio, baited as a madman by Sir Toby Belch and his cronies

153   REWARD

1   I will reward thee
Once for thy sprightly comfort, and ten-fold
For thy good valour.
Antony and Cleopatra IV, 7
Antony to Scarus

2   A man that fortune's buffets and rewards
Hath ta'en with equal thanks.
Hamlet III, 2
Hamlet to and about Horatio

3   Long since we were resolved of your truth,
Your faithful service and your toil in war;
Yet never have you tasted our reward . . .
We here create you Earl of Shrewsbury.
1 Henry VI III, 4
King Henry to Lord Talbot

4   If we thrive, promise them such rewards
    As victors wear at the Olympian games.
    3 Henry VI II, 3
    Duke of Clarence to Earl of Warwick

5   (I'll) make the Moor thank me, love me, and reward me
    For making him egregiously an ass.
    Othello II, 1
    Iago to himself

154   ROARING

1   Alas! poor Yorick . . . Where be your gibes now? . . . Your
    flashes of merriment that were wont to set the table in a roar?
    Hamlet V, 1
    Hamlet, gazing at the skull of a jester

2   I will roar that it will make the duke say, 'Let him roar again,
    let him roar again!'
    A Midsummer Night's Dream I, 2
    Bottom, eager to play the lion in the 'Pyramus and Thisbe' play

3   You ladies . . .
    May now, perchance, both quake and tremble here
    When lion rough in wildest rage doth roar.
    A Midsummer Night's Dream V, 1
    Snug, who actually does play the lion, is anxious to make it clear
    that he is harmless

4   Well roared, Lion!
    A Midsummer Night's Dream V, 1
    Demetrius is appreciative

5   (He) talks as familiarly of roaring lions
    As maids of thirteen do of puppy-dogs.
    King John II, 1
    Philip the Bastard, mocking the bragging of an Angiers citizen

6   Since I was man . . .
Such groans of roaring wind and rain, I never
Remember to have heard.
King Lear III, 2
Lear to Kent

---

155 ROME

---

1   Let Rome in Tiber melt, and the wide arch
Of the ranged empire fall.
Antony and Cleopatra I, 1
Antony, more concerned with Cleopatra than with conquest

2   He'll shake your Rome about your ears.
Coriolanus IV, 6
Cominius, referring to Coriolanus, now banished from Rome

3   Rome, thou hast lost the breed of noble bloods!
Julius Caesar I, 2
Cassius, persuading Brutus to oppose Caesar's seeming ambition

4   Shall Rome stand under one man's awe? what, Rome?
My ancestors did from the streets of Rome
The Tarquin drive, when he was called a king.
Julius Caesar II, 1
Brutus concerning Caesar

5   Those sparks of life
That should be in a Roman you do want.
Julius Caesar I, 3
Cassius to Casca

6   This was the noblest Roman of them all.
All the conspirators, save only he,
Did that they did in envy of great Caesar;
He only, in a general honest thought
And common good to all, made one of them.
Julius Caesar V, 5
Antony to his companions, concerning Brutus

7   I am more an antique Roman than a Dane.
Hamlet V, 2
Horatio, proposing to join Hamlet in death

8   In the most high and palmy state of Rome,
A little ere the mightiest Julius fell,
The graves stood tenantless, and the sheeted dead
Did squeak and gibber in the Roman streets.
Hamlet I, 1
Horatio to Bernardo, after they had seen the ghost of the elder
Hamlet

9   Rome, I have been thy soldier forty years,
And led my country's strength successfully.
Titus Andronicus I, 1
Titus to his followers and others

10   Dost thou not perceive
That Rome is but a wilderness of tigers.
Titus Andronicus III, 1
Titus, condemning Rome for cruelty

---

156   SEASONS

---

1   The icy fang
And churlish chiding of the winter's wind . . .
Even till I shrink with cold.
As You Like It II, 1
Duke Senior to companions

2   The canker galls the infants of the spring
    Too oft before their buttons be disclosed.
    Hamlet I, 3
    Laertes to Ophelia

3   Winter's not gone yet if the wild geese fly that way.
    King Lear II, 4
    Fool to Lear

4   This side is Hiems, Winter, this Ver, the Spring; the one
    maintained by the owl, the other by the cuckoo.
    Love's Labour's Lost V, 2
    Armado, introducing a song

5   At Christmas I no more desire a rose
    Than wish a snow in May's new-fangled shows.
    Love's Labour's Lost I, 1
    Biron to his companions

6   When icicles hang by the wall,
    And Dick the shepherd blows his nail,
    And Tom bears logs into the hall,
    And milk comes frozen home in pail.
    Love's Labour's Lost V, 2
    Song to close play

7   Never, since the middle summer's spring,
    Met we on hill, in dale, forest, or mead . . .
    But with thy brawls thou hast disturb'd our sport.
    A Midsummer Night's Dream II, 1
    Titania to Oberon

8   Now is the winter of our discontent
    Made glorious summer.
    Richard III I, 1
    Richard, Duke of Gloucester, opening the play with soliloquy

9   Shall I compare thee to a summer's day?
    Thou art more lovely and more temperate.
    Sonnet 18

10   From you I have been absent in the spring,
When proud-pied April, dress'd in all his trim,
Hath put a spirit of youth in everything.
Sonnet 98

157   SILENCE

1   Be check'd for silence,
But never tax'd for speech.
All's Well That Ends Well I, 1
Countess to Bertram

2   O Imogen! I'll speak to thee in silence.
Cymbeline V, 4
Posthumus to himself, in prison

3   There are a sort of men . . .
That do a wilful stillness entertain . . .
That therefore only are reported wise
For saying nothing.
The Merchant of Venice I, 1
Gratiano to Antonio

4   Your silence most offends me, and to be merry best becomes
you.
Much Ado About Nothing II, 1
Don Pedro, begging Beatrice not to lose her liveliness

5   Silence is the perfectest herald of joy; I were but little happy, if
I could say how much.
Much Ado About Nothing II, 1
Claudio to Hero

6   What, gone without a word?
Ay, so true love should do; it cannot speak;
For truth hath better deeds than words to grace it.
The Two Gentlemen of Verona II, 2
Proteus to himself, concerning Julia

158 SIN

1   Thus was I, sleeping, by a brother's hand . . .
    Cut off even in the blossoms of my sin.
    Hamlet I, 5
    Ghost of Hamlet's father to Hamlet

2   Self-love, my liege, is not so great a sin
    As self-neglecting.
    Henry V II, 4
    Dauphin, persuading King of France to boast about France's
    strength

3   Revel the night, rob, murder, and commit
    The oldest sins the newest kind of ways.
    2 Henry IV IV, 5
    King Henry to Prince Hal, reproving his way of life

4   I am a man
    More sinn'd against than sinning.
    King Lear III, 2
    Lear to himself

5   Some rise by sin, and some by virtue fall.
    Measure for Measure II, 1
    Escalus to himself

6   O, what authority and show of truth
    Can cunning sin cover itself withal.
    Much Ado About Nothing IV, 1
    Claudio, unjustly accusing Hero of misbehaviour

7   Nothing emboldens sin so much as mercy.
    Timon of Athens III, 5
    Senators refuse plea by Alcibiades for mercy for a condemned
    friend

159 SLANDER

1
Slander lives upon succession,
For ever housed where it gets possession.
The Comedy of Errors III, 1
Balthazar to Antipholus of Ephesus

2   I say thou hast belied mine innocent child;
Thy slander hath gone through and through her heart.
Much Ado About Nothing V, 1
Leonato to Claudio

3
Done to death by slanderous tongues
Was the Hero that here lies.
Much Ado About Nothing V, 3
On a scroll read out by Claudio

4
God knows I loved my niece;
And she is dead, slandered to death by villains.
Much Ado About Nothing V, 1
Antonio to Leonato

5   I will be hang'd, if some eternal villain,
Some busy and insinuating rogue,
Some cogging, cozening slave, to get some office,
Have not devised this slander.
Othello IV, 2
Emilia to Iago and Desdemona

6   I am disgrac'd, impeach'd, and baffled here,
Pierc'd to the soul with slander's venom'd spear.
Richard II I, 1
Mowbray, complaining of Bolingbroke to Richard

7
Slander Valentine
With falsehood, cowardice, and poor descent,
Three things that women highly hold in hate.
The Two Gentlemen of Verona III, 2
Proteus, behaving dishonourably to his friend

160 SLEEP

1 He that sleeps feels not the toothache.
Cymbeline V, 4
Gaoler to Posthumus

2 If thou canst wake by four o' the clock
I prithee, call me. Sleep hath seized me wholly.
Cymbeline II, 2
Imogen to lady attending her

3   To die; to sleep;
No more; and by a sleep to say we end
The heart-ache, and the thousand natural shocks
That flesh is heir to.
Hamlet III, 1
Hamlet, expressing a hope for finality

4   O sleep, O gentle sleep,
Nature's soft nurse, how have I frighted thee,
That thou no more will weigh my eyelids down?
2 Henry IV III, 1
King Henry to himself

5 This sleep is sound indeed; this is a sleep
That from this golden rigol hath divorc'd
So many English kings.
2 Henry IV V, 5
Prince Henry to sleeping king
rigol 'circle, crown'

6 Boy! Lucius! Fast asleep! It is no matter;
Enjoy the honey-heavy dew of slumber.
Julius Caesar II, 1
Brutus to sleeping servant

7   Sleep shall neither night nor day
Hang upon his pent-house lid.
Macbeth I, 3
Witch's curse on a sailor

8   Methought I heard a voice cry 'Sleep no more!
     Macbeth does murder sleep' — the innocent sleep,
     Sleep that knits up the ravell'd sleave of care.
     Macbeth II, 2
     Macbeth to Lady Macbeth

9   Sleep, that sometimes shuts up sorrow's eye,
     Steal me awhile from mine own company.
     A Midsummer Night's Dream III, 2
     Helena to herself

10   Sleep dwell upon thine eyes, peace in thy breast.
     Romeo and Juliet II, 2
     Romeo, as Juliet departs

11   He sleeps by day
     More than the wild-cat.
     The Merchant of Venice II, 5
     Shylock to Jessica, about Launcelot Gobbo

12   Thou art inclined to sleep; 'tis a good dulness,
     And give it way: I know thou canst not choose.
     The Tempest I, 2
     Prospero to Miranda

161   SMILES

1   Nobly he yokes
     A smiling with a sigh.
     Cymbeline IV, 2
     Arviragus on Imogen disguised as a page

2   One may smile and smile, and be a villain.
     Hamlet I, 5
     Hamlet concerning Claudius

3   I saw him fumble with the sheets and play with flowers and smile upon his fingers' ends.
Henry V II, 3
Hostess on the death of Falstaff

4   Seldom he smiles, and smiles in such a sort
As if he mocked himself.
Julius Caesar I, 2
Caesar to Antony, concerning Cassius

5   Those happy smiles
That play'd on her ripe lip seem'd not to know
What guests were in her eyes.
King Lear IV, 3
A gentleman to Lear, talking of Cordelia

6   His flaw'd heart . . .
'Twixt two extremes of passion, joy and grief,
Burst smilingly.
King Lear V, 3
Edgar, speaking of his father

7   Affliction may one day smile again.
Love's Labour's Lost I, 1
Costard to Biron

8   There's daggers in men's smiles.
Macbeth II, 3
Donalbain to Malcolm, after Duncan's murder

9   Nature hath framed strange fellows in her time,
Some . . . of such vinegar aspect
That they'll not show their teeth in way of smile,
Though Nestor swear the jest be laughable.
The Merchant of Venice I, 1
Solanio to Antonio

162   SORROW
see also **Grief** 64

1   Wherever sorrow is, relief would be:
If you do sorrow at my grief in love,
By giving love, your sorrow and my grief
Were both extermined.
As You Like It III, 5
Silvius to Phebe

2   But I have that within which passeth show;
These but the trappings and the suits of woe.
Hamlet I, 2
Hamlet, sorrowing for the death of his father

3   When sorrows come, they come not single spies,
But in battalions.
Hamlet IV, 5
King Claudius to Gertrude

4   I swear, 'tis better to be lowly born
And range with humble livers in content,
Than to be perk'd up in a glistering grief.
Henry VIII II, 3
Anne Bullen to an old lady

5   My grief's so great
That no supporter but the huge firm earth
Can hold it up: here I and sorrows sit.
King John III, 1
Constance to Earl of Salisbury

6   Each new morn
New widows howl, new orphans cry, new sorrows
Strike heaven on the face.
Macbeth IV, 3
Macduff, reporting to Malcolm Scotland's condition under
Macbeth

7　Give sorrow words: the grief that does not speak
Whispers the o'erfraught heart.
Macbeth IV, 3
Malcolm to Macduff, who has just learnt of the murder of his
wife and children

8　　　　　　　　　　　Your cause of sorrow
Must not be measured by his worth, for then
It hath no end.
Macbeth V, 8
Ross to Old Siward, whose son was slain in battle

9　One sorrow never comes but brings an heir,
That may succeed as his inheritor.
Pericles I, 4
Cleon to a Lord

10　　　　　　　　Parting is such sweet sorrow
That I shall say good-night till it be morrow.
Romeo and Juliet II, 2
Juliet to Romeo

11　To weep with them that weep doth ease some deal,
But sorrow flouted at is double death.
Titus Andronicus III, 1
Marcus Andronicus to Lucius

163　SOUL

1　A wretched soul, bruised with adversity,
We bid be quiet when we hear it cry.
The Comedy of Errors II, 1
Adriana to Luciana

2　Those friends thou hast, and their adoption tried,
Grapple them to thy soul with hoops of steel.
Hamlet I, 3
Polonius to Laertes

3   I could a tale unfold, whose lightest word
    Would harrow up thy soul.
    Hamlet I, 5
    Ghost to Hamlet

4   O limed soul, that struggling to be free
    Art more engaged! Help, angels! make assay!
    Hamlet III, 3
    King Claudius, trying to pray

5   Every subject's duty is the king's; but every subject's soul is his
    own.
    Henry V IV, 1
    Henry is arguing that the king is not responsible for the misdeeds of his
    soldiers

6   Within this wall of flesh
         There is a soul counts thee her creditor.
    King John III, 3
    King to Hubert de Burgh

7   Banquo, thy soul's flight,
         If it find heaven, must find it out tonight.
    Macbeth III, 1
    Macbeth, after engaging Banquo's murderers

8   Thinkst thou I'll endanger my soul gratis?
    The Merry Wives of Windsor II, 2
    Falstaff to Pistol

9   Excellent wretch! Perdition catch my soul,
    But I do love thee!
    Othello III, 3
    Othello to himself about Desdemona

10 Good name in man and woman, good my lord,
    Is the immediate jewel of their souls.
    Othello III, 3
    Iago to Othello

11   I count myself in nothing else so happy
As in a soul remembering my good friends.
Richard II II, 3
Henry Bolingbroke on his premature return from banishment

12   Her body sleeps in Capels' monument,
And her immortal part with angels lives.
Romeo and Juliet V, 1
Balthasar to Romeo, on Juliet

13   I think nobly of the soul.
Twelfth Night IV, 2
Malvolio, while being unkindly baited as mad by Sir Toby and
his cronies

164   SPORT

1   Am I so round with you, as you with me,
That like a football you do spurn me thus?
You spurn me hence, and he will spurn me hither:
If I last in this service you must case me in leather.
The Comedy of Errors II, 1
Dromio of Ephesus, driven backwards and forwards between
mistress and master

2   Was ever a man had such luck! when I kissed the jack upon an
up-cast to be hit away! I had a hundred pound on't: and then a
whoreson jackanapes must take me up for swearing.
Cymbeline II, 1
Cloten to a Lord

3   When we have match'd our rackets to these balls,
We will, in France, by God's grace play a set
Shall strike his father's crown into the hazard.
Henry V I, 2
The Dauphin has sent Henry some tennis balls, to suggest he is
fit only for sport

4   I see you stand like greyhounds in the slips,
     Straining upon the start.
     Henry V III, 1
     Henry to his troops, before Harfleur

5   Like an arrow shot
     From a well experienc'd archer hits the mark
     His eye doth level at.
     Pericles I, 1
     Antiochus tells one of his courtiers to kill Pericles

6   What sport shall we devise here in this garden,
     To drive away the heavy thought of care?
     Richard II III, 4
     Richard's queen to a gentlewoman, whose suggestions are all
     rejected

7   Thus the bowl should run,
     And not unluckily against the bias.
     The Taming of the Shrew IV, 5
     Petruchio, satisfied that his taming of Kate is going well

8   Well could he ride, and often men would say,
     'That horse his mettle from his rider takes'.
     A Lover's Complaint Stanza 16

165   STARS

1   Two stars keep not their motion in one sphere.
     1 Henry IV V, 4
     Prince Henry to Hotspur

2   I am constant as the northern star,
     Of whose true-fix'd and resting quality
     There is no fellow in the firmament.
     Julius Caesar III, 1
     Caesar to Cassius

3   The skies are painted with unnumber'd sparks;
They are all fire and every one doth shine.
Julius Caesar III, 1
Caesar to Cassius

4   It is the stars,
The stars above us govern our condition.
King Lear IV, 3
Earl of Kent to a gentleman

5   The unfolding star calls up the shepherd.
Measure for Measure IV, 2
Duke to the Provost

6   Look how the floor of heaven
Is thick inlaid with patines of bright gold:
There's not the smallest orb which thou behold'st
But in his motion like an angel sings.
The Merchant of Venice V, 1
Lorenzo to Jessica

7   Those blessed candles of the night.
The Merchant of Venice V, 1
Bassanio to Portia

8   I find my zenith doth depend upon
A most auspicious star, whose influence
If now I court not, but omit, my fortunes
Will ever after droop.
The Tempest I, 2
Prospero to Miranda

9   It (love) is the star to every wandering bark.
Sonnet 116

166   STONE

1   Sparkles this stone as it was wont? or is't not
Too dull for your good wearing?
Cymbeline II, 4
Posthumus to Iachimo

2   The bishop and the Duke of Gloucester's men,
Forbidden late to carry any weapon,
Have filled their pockets full of pebble stones . . .
Our windows are broke down in every street,
And we for fear compell'd to shut our shops.
1 Henry VI III, 1
Lord Mayor of London to king and nobles

3   Hear not my steps, the way they walk, for fear
The very stones prate of my whereabout.
Macbeth II, 1
Macbeth, on his way to murder Duncan

4   Her salt tears fell from her, and softened the stones.
Othello IV, 3
Desdemona's song

5   This precious stone set in the silver sea.
Richard II II, 1
John of Gaunt's speech on England

6   A stone is soft as wax, tribunes more hard than stones,
A stone is silent and offendeth not.
Titus Andronicus III, 1
Titus, whose two sons have been condemned to death by the tribunes

7   He is a stone, a very pebble stone, and has no more pity in him than a dog.
The Two Gentlemen of Verona II, 3
Launce, speaking of his dog, Crab

8   'Tis time: descend: be stone no more.
The Winter's Tale V, 3
Paulina tells the apparent statue of Hermione to come to life

9   His falchion on a flint he softly smiteth,
That from the cold stone sparks of fire do fly.
The Rape of Lucrece Stanza 26

10   Stones dissolved to water do convert.
The Rape of Lucrece Stanza 85

167   STORM

1   As far as I could ken thy chalky cliffs,
When from thy shore the tempest beat us back,
I stood upon the hatches in the storm.
2 Henry VI III, 2
Queen Margaret to Henry

2   I have seen tempests, when the scolding winds
Have rived the knotty oaks, and I have seen
The ambitious ocean swell and rage and foam,
To be exalted with the threatening clouds.
Julius Caesar I, 3
Casca to Cicero

3   Blow wind, swell billow, and swim bark!
The storm is up, and all is on the hazard.
Julius Caesar V, 1
Cassius to Brutus, in battle against Antony and Octavius

4   Blow, winds, and crack your cheeks! rage! blow!
King Lear III, 2
Lear, addressing the storm

5   Thou all-shaking thunder,
Strike flat the thick rotundity o' th' world.
King Lear III, 2
Lear, addressing the storm

6　Poor naked wretches, whereso'er you are
That bide the pelting of this pitiless storm,
How shall your houseless heads, and unfed sides . . .
　　　　Defend you
From seasons such as these?
King Lear III, 4
Lear to his own conscience

7　　　　Since I was man
Such sheets of fire, such bursts of horrid thunder,
Such groans of roaring wind and rain, I never
Remember to have heard.
King Lear III, 2
Earl of Kent to Lear

8　Small showers last long, but sudden storms are short.
Richard II II, 1
John of Gaunt, forecasting England's future condition

9　If by your art, my dearest father, you have
Put the wild waters in this roar, allay them . . .
　　　　Oh, I have suffer'd
With those that I saw suffer.
The Tempest I, 2
Miranda to Prospero

10　I pray now keep below . . . You mar our labour, keep your
cabins; you do assist the storm.
The Tempest I, 1
Boatswain to Alonso, Gonzalo, and others

168　STORY

1　Let us from point to point this story know,
To make the even truth in pleasure flow.
All's Well That Ends Well V, 3
King of France, seeking final explanations

2   Absent thee from felicity awhile,
     And in this harsh world draw thy breath in pain,
     To tell my story.
     Hamlet V, 2
     Hamlet, dying, persuades Horatio to continue living

3   If you be not too much cloyed with fat meat, our humble
     author will continue the story, with Sir John in it.
     2 Henry IV Epilogue
     Spoken by a dancer, promising more Falstaff

4   In her bosom I'll unclasp my heart,
     And take her hearing prisoner with the force
     And strong encounter of my amorous tale.
     Much Ado About Nothing I, 1
     Don Pedro's tale to Hero is the story of Claudio's love for her

5   Her father loved me, oft invited me,
     Still questioned me the story of my life.
     Othello I, 3
     Othello to senators, concerning Brabantio

6   I'll hear you more, to the bottom of your story,
     And never interrupt you.
     Pericles V, 1
     Pericles to Marina

7   Never was a story of more woe
     Than this of Juliet and her Romeo.
     Romeo and Juliet V, 3
     Prince of Verona

8   I long
     To hear the story of your life, which must
     Take the ear strangely.
     The Tempest V, 1
     Alonso to Prospero

9 I'll to thy closet; and go read with thee
Sad stories chanced in the times of old.
Titus Andronicus III, 2
Titus to Lavinia

10 She told him stories to delight his ear.
The Passionate Pilgrim

11 Their copious stories, oftentimes begun,
End without audience, and are never done.
Venus and Adonis Stanza 141
The reference is to lovers' tales

169   SUICIDE

1   There is left us
Ourselves to end ourselves.
Antony and Cleopatra IV, 14
Antony to Eros

2   Is it sin
To rush into the secret house of death
Ere death dare come to us?
Antony and Cleopatra IV, 15
Cleopatra to Iras and Charmian

3   It is great
To do that thing that ends all other deeds.
Antony and Cleopatra V, 2
Cleopatra to her women

4   Against self-slaughter
There is a prohibition so divine
That cravens my weak hand.
Cymbeline III, 4
Imogen to Pisanio

5 Whether 'tis nobler in the mind to suffer
The slings and arrows of outrageous fortune,
Or to take arms against a sea of troubles,
And by opposing, end them.
Hamlet III, 1
Hamlet, soliloquizing

6 O . . . that the Everlasting had not fix'd
His canon 'gainst self-slaughter!
Hamlet I, 2
Hamlet, unhappy even before meeting his father's ghost

7 Life, being weary of these worldly bars,
Never lacks power to dismiss itself.
Julius Caesar I, 3
Cassius to Casca

8 Impatient of my absence . . . she fell distract,
And, her attendants being absent, swallowed fire.
Julius Caesar IV, 3
Brutus concerning his wife, Portia

9 You ever gentle gods, take my breath from me;
Let not my worser spirit tempt me again
To die before you please.
King Lear IV, 6
Earl of Gloucester, blind, who has failed in one suicide attempt

10 'To kill myself,' quoth she, 'alack, what were it,
But with my body my poor soul's pollution?'
The Rape of Lucrece Stanza 166

170   SUN

1 At length the sun, gazing upon the earth,
Dispersed those vapours that offended us.
The Comedy of Errors I, 1
Aegeon to Duke of Ephesus

2 When the sun shines let foolish gnats make sport,
   But creep in crannies when he hides his beams.
   The Comedy of Errors II, 2
   Antipholus of Syracuse warns his servant to take note of his
   master's mood

3 I am too much i' the sun.
   Hamlet I, 2
   Hamlet gives a vague reply to Claudius's attempt to converse

4 I 'gin to be aweary of the sun,
   And wish the estate o' the world were now undone.
   Macbeth V, 5
   Macbeth to a messenger bringing bad news

5 When from under this terrestrial ball
   He fires the proud tops of the eastern pines,
   And darts his light through every guilty hole,
   Then murders, treasons, and detested sins,
   The cloak of night being plucked from off their backs,
   Stand bare and naked, trembling at themselves.
   Richard II III, 2
   Richard to Duke of Aumerle

6   This must my comfort be,
   The sun that warms you here shall shine on me.
   Richard II I, 3
   Bolingbroke, banished for a period, to Richard, who sentenced
   him

7 When the sun sets, who doth not look for night?
   Richard III II, 3
   A citizen sees trouble ahead on the death of King Edward IV

8 When the golden sun salutes the morn,
   And, having gilt the ocean with his beams,
   Gallops the zodiac in his glistering coach.
   Titus Andronicus II, 1
   Aaron to himself

9   Men shut their doors against a setting sun.
Timon of Athens I, 2
Apemantus to himself

171 TALK

1   If I chance to talk a little wild, forgive me,
I had it from my father.
Henry VIII I, 4
Lord Sands, a lively courtier, to the ladies

2   The red wine first must rise
In their fair cheeks, my lord, then we shall have 'em
Talk us to silence.
Henry VIII I, 4
Lord Sands concerning the ladies

3   What cracker is the same that deafs our ears
With this abundance of superfluous breath?
King John II, 1
Duke of Austria concerning Philip the Bastard

4   Let it serve for table-talk;
Then, howsoe'er thou speak'st, 'mong other things,
I shall digest it.
The Merchant of Venice III, 5
Lorenzo in light-hearted conversation with Jessica

5 I wonder that you will still be talking, Signior Benedick: nobody marks you.
Much Ado About Nothing I, 1
Beatrice to her mental sparring-partner

6   My lord shall never rest;
I'll watch him tame and talk him out of patience.
Othello III, 3
Desdemona promises Cassio to persuade Othello to pardon a drunken lapse

7 Fear not, my lord, we will not stand to prate;
Talkers are no good doers: be assured
We come to use our hands and not our tongues.
Richard III I, 3
A sinister murderer promises Gloucester, later Richard III, to
murder the Duke of Clarence

8 A gentleman, nurse, that loves to hear himself talk, and will
speak more in a minute than he will stand to in a month.
Romeo and Juliet II, 4
Romeo tells Juliet's nurse about Mercutio

172 TEACHING

1   Thus may poor fools
Believe false teachers.
Cymbeline III, 4
Imogen to Pisanio

2 We'll teach you to drink deep ere you depart.
Hamlet I, 2
Hamlet to Horatio

3 I can easier teach twenty what were good to be done, than be
one of the twenty to follow my own teaching.
The Merchant of Venice I, 2
Portia to Nerissa

4 O! she doth teach the torches to burn bright!
Romeo and Juliet I, 5
Romeo to himself, on first seeing Juliet

5 Schoolmasters will I keep within my house,
Fit to instruct her youth.
The Taming of the Shrew I, 1
Baptista concerning Bianca

6   I must begin with rudiments of art;
    To teach you gamut in a briefer sort,
    More pleasant, pithy, and effectual,
    Than hath been taught by any of my trade.
    The Taming of the Shrew III, 1
    Hortensio, posing as a musician, offers a love note under the
    guise of tonic sol-fa

7   You taught me language; and my profit on't
    Is, I know how to curse.
    The Tempest I, 2
    Caliban to Prospero

173   TEARS
see also **Weeping** 189

1   If ever you have look'd on better days . . .
    If ever from your eyelids wip'd a tear.
    As You Like It II, 7
    Orlando, asking Duke Senior and his companions for food

2   What would he do,
    Had he the motive and the cue for passion
    That I have? He would drown the stage with tears.
    Hamlet III, 2
    Hamlet, after watching an actor's sham weeping

3   Cromwell, I did not think to shed a tear
    In all my miseries; but thou hast forc'd me,
    Out of thy honest truth, to play the woman.
    Henry VIII III, 2
    Wolsey, after his downfall, to sympathetic Cromwell

4   If you have tears, prepare to shed them now.
    Julius Caesar III, 2
    Antony to citizens over Caesar's body

5 Thou shouldst please me better wouldst thou weep.
Richard II III, 4
Richard's unhappy Queen, to a friend

6 Mine eyes do itch; doth that bode weeping?
Othello IV, 3
Desdemona to Emilia

---

174   THEFT

---

1 A plague upon it when thieves cannot be true one to another.
1 Henry IV II, 2
Falstaff to Prince Hal

2 'Tis my vocation, Hal; 'tis no sin for a man to labour in his vocation.
1 Henry IV I, 2
Falstaff to Prince, referring to his robberies

3 The jury, passing on the prisoner's life,
May in the sworn twelve have a thief or two
Guiltier than him they try.
Measure for Measure II, 1
Angelo to Escalus

4 Thieves for their robbery have authority
When judges steal themselves.
Measure for Measure II, 2
Angelo to himself

5 The most peaceable way for you, if you do take a thief, is to let him show himself what he is, and steal out of your company.
Much Ado About Nothing III, 3
Constable Dogberry to a Watchman

6 The robb'd that smiles steals something from the thief;
He robs himself that spends a bootless grief.
Othello I, 3
Duke of Venice to Brabantio

7 He that is robb'd, not wanting what is stolen,
Let him not know it and he's not robb'd at all.
Othello III, 3
Othello to Iago

8   Thanks I must you con
That you are thieves profess'd, that you work not
In holier shapes: for there is boundless theft
In limited professions.
Timon of Athens IV, 3
Timon to bandits

9 I am . . . a snapper up of unconsidered trifles.
The Winter's Tale IV, 3
Autolycus has a euphemism for his activities

---

175 THOUGHT

---

1 Give thy thoughts no tongue,
Nor any unproportion'd thought his act.
Hamlet I, 3
Polonius to Laertes

2 There is nothing either good or bad, but thinking makes it so.
Hamlet II, 2
Hamlet to Rosencrantz

3 Thus conscience doth make cowards of us all,
And thus the native hue of resolution
Is sicklied o'er with the pale cast of thought.
Hamlet III, 1
From Hamlet's most famous soliloquy, 'To be or not to be'

4   Some craven scruple
Of thinking too precisely on the event.
Hamlet IV, 4
Hamlet urging himself towards action

5   My thoughts are whirled like a potter's wheel;
I know not where I am, nor what I do.
1 Henry VI I, 5
Lord Talbot, baffled by Joan of Arc

6 Never a man's thought in the world keeps the road-way better than thine.
2 Henry IV II, 2
Prince Henry believes Poins's thoughts to be typical of most men's

7   The wish was father, Harry, to that thought.
2 Henry IV IV, 5
Henry IV supposes, wrongly, that his son wishes him dead

8   So swift a pace hath thought, that even now
You may imagine him upon Blackheath.
Henry V V, Prologue
Chorus concerning King Henry

9   I cannot tell what you and other men
Think of this life, but, for my single self,
I had as lief not be as live to be
In awe of such a thing as I myself.
Julius Caesar I, 2
Cassius, making known to Brutus his enmity to Caesar

---

176 TIME
see also **Hours** 80

---

1   The inaudible and noiseless foot of Time.
All's Well That Ends Well V, 3
King of France to Bertram

2 'Thus we may see,' quoth he, 'how the world wags:
    'Tis but an hour ago since it was nine,
    And after one hour more 'twill be eleven;
    And so, from hour to hour, we ripe and ripe,
    And then, from hour to hour, we rot and rot.'
    As You Like It II, 7
    Jaques, quoting Touchstone

3 Time travels in divers paces with divers persons.
    As You Like It III, 2
    Rosalind to Orlando

4 Time, that takes survey of all the world,
    Must have a stop.
    1 Henry IV V, 4
    Hotspur, dying, to Prince Henry

5 Thereby to see the minutes how they run,
    How many make the hour full complete;
    How many hours bring about the day;
    How many days will finish up the year;
    How many years a mortal man may live.
    3 Henry VI II, 5
    Henry, alone on the battlefield

6   How many ages hence
    Shall this our lofty scene be acted over
    In states unborn and accents yet unknown.
    Julius Caesar III, 1
    Cassius to Brutus and others

7 Time shall unfold what plaited cunning hides.
    King Lear I, 1
    Cordelia to her sisters

8   Come what come may,
    Time and the hour runs through the roughest day.
    Macbeth I, 3
    Macbeth to himself

9   Time goes on crutches till love have all the rites.
    Much Ado About Nothing II, 1
    Claudio to Don Pedro

10   I see that Time's the king of men:
    He's both their parent, and he is their grave,
    And gives then what he will, not what they crave.
    Pericles II, 3
    Pericles to himself

11   Time hath set a blot upon my pride.
    Richard II III, 2
    Richard returned from Ireland just too late to hold his forces
    together

12   O! call back yesterday, bid time return,
    And thou shalt have twelve thousand fighting men:
    Today, today, unhappy day too late!
    Richard II III, 2
    Earl of Salisbury brings the bad news of a disbanded army

13   What seest thou else
    In the dark backward and abysm of time?
    The Tempest I, 2
    Prospero to Miranda

14   Time hath, my lord, a wallet at his back
    Wherein he puts alms for oblivion.
    Troilus and Cressida III, 3
    Ulysses to Achilles

15   The end crowns all;
    And that old common arbitrator, Time,
    Will one day end it.
    Troilus and Cressida IV, 5
    Hector to Ulysses

16   Thus the whirligig of time brings in his revenges.
    Twelfth Night V, 1
    Feste, earlier criticized by Malvolio, has now helped to make a
    fool of him

17   Cease to lament for that thou canst not help . . .
Time is the nurse and breeder of all good.
The Two Gentlemen of Verona III, 1
Proteus to banished Valentine

18   O fearful meditation! where, alack,
Shall Time's best jewel from Time's chest lie hid?
Sonnet 65

19   Yet do thy worst, old Time: despite thy wrong,
My love shall in my verse ever live young.
Sonnet 19

20   Make use of time; let not advantage slip;
Beauty within itself should not be wasted.
Fair flowers that are not gathered in their prime
Rot and consume themselves in little time.
Venus and Adonis Stanza 22

---

177 TOMORROW

---

1   Tomorrow, good Sir Michael, is a day
Wherein the fortune of ten thousand men
Must bide the touch.
1 Henry IV IV, 4
Archbishop of York to a fellow rebel against King Henry

2   He that shall live this day, and see old age,
Will yearly on the vigil feast his neighbours,
And say, 'Tomorrow is Saint Crispian'.
Henry V IV, 3
Henry to Earl of Westmoreland

3   Tomorrow, and tomorrow, and tomorrow,
Creeps in this petty pace from day to day,
To the last syllable of recorded time.
Macbeth V, 5
Macbeth, on learning of his wife's death

4   Up with my tent there! here I will lie tonight.
    But where tomorrow? Well, all's one for that.
    Richard III V, 3
    Richard to Duke of Norfolk before the battle of Bosworth

5   Let's want no discipline, make no delay;
    For, lords, tomorrow is a busy day.
    Richard III V, 3
    Richard to Duke of Norfolk before the battle of Bosworth

6   Methought the souls of all that I had murder'd
    Came to my tent, and every one did threat
    Tomorrow's vengeance on the head of Richard.
    Richard III V, 3
    Richard, after a bad dream the night before battle

7   We were . . .
    Two lads that thought there was no more behind,
    But such a day tomorrow as today,
    And to be boy eternal.
    The Winter's Tale I, 2
    Polixenes, telling Hermione how he and Leontes spent a
    carefree boyhood together

8   Kind is my love today, tomorrow kind,
    Still constant in a wondrous excellence.
    Sonnet 105

178   TOUCH

1   A little touch of Harry in the night.
    Henry V Prologue IV
    Chorus, indicating Henry's influence before battle

2   What, doth my lord of Suffolk comfort me? . . .
Lay not thy hands on me; forbear, I say,
Their touch affrights me as a serpent's sting.
2 Henry VI III, 2
Henry to Suffolk

3   Duncan is in his grave . . .
Malice domestic, foreign levy, nothing
Can touch him further.
Macbeth III, 2
Macbeth to his wife

4   He loves us not;
He wants the natural touch.
Macbeth IV, 2
Lady Macduff, left unguarded in her husband's eagerness to
seek English help

5   But for my bonny Kate, she must with me . . .
And here she stands, touch her whoever dare.
The Taming of the Shrew III, 2
Petruchio regards Kate as his property

6   O touch me not; – I am not Stephano but a cramp.
The Tempest V, 1
Prospero has used magic to inflict him with pain

7   One touch of nature makes the whole world kin.
Troilus and Cressida III, 3
Ulysses to Achilles

8   Ruffian, let go that rude uncivil touch,
Thou friend of an ill fashion.
The Two Gentlemen of Verona V, 4
Valentine, whose love, Silvia, is pestered by his friend, Proteus

179   TRAVEL

1   It is a melancholy of mine own, extracted from many objects, and indeed the sundry contemplation of my travels.
As You Like It IV, 1
Jaques to Rosalind

2   A traveller! By my faith, you have great reason to be sad: I fear you have sold your own lands to see other men's.
As You Like It IV, 1
Rosalind to Jaques

3   Now am I in Arden; the more fool I: when I was at home I was in a better place: but travellers must be content.
As You Like It II, 4
Touchstone to Ganymede

4   The dread of something after death,
The undiscover'd country from whose bourn
No traveller returns.
Hamlet III, 1
Hamlet, soliloquizing on suicide

5   Travell'd gallants
That fill the court with quarrels, talk, and tailors.
Henry VIII I, 3
Sir Thomas Lovell to the Lord Chamberlain and others

6   The west yet glimmers with some streaks of day;
Now spurs the lated traveller apace
To gain the timely inn.
Macbeth III, 3
Banquo's First Murderer

7   I spake of most disastrous chances,
Of moving accidents by flood and field . . .
Rough quarries, rocks, and hills whose heads touch heaven.
Othello I, 3
Othello, telling senators how he first enthralled Desdemona

180   TREASON

1   Though those that are betray'd
Do feel the treason sharply, yet the traitor
Stands in worse case of woe.
Cymbeline III, 4
Imogen to Pisanio

2 Treason is but trusted like the fox,
Who, ne'er so tame, so cherish'd and lock'd up,
Will have a wild trick of his ancestors.
1 Henry IV V, 2
Worcester to Vernon

3 Some guard these traitors to the block of death,
Treason's true bed and yielder up of breath.
2 Henry IV IV, 2
John of Lancaster, treacherously, after agreeing to a peace with
three rebel leaders

4 Treason and murder ever kept together,
As two yoke-devils sworn to either's purpose.
Henry V II, 2
King Henry in the council-chamber

5 Smooth runs the water where the brook is deep;
And in his simple show he harbours treason.
2 Henry VI III, 1
Earl of Suffolk to Queen Margaret, concerning Richard of
Gloucester

6 Witness the loving kiss I give the fruit.
(*Aside*) To say the truth, so Judas kissed his master,
And cried 'All hail!' when as he meant all harm.
3 Henry VI V, 7
Richard of Gloucester to King Edward IV

7 O what a fall was there, my countrymen!
Then I, and you, and all of us fell down,
Whilst bloody treason flourish'd over us.
Julius Caesar III, 2
Antony's oration over Caesar's murdered body

8 My name is lost
By treason's tooth bare-gnawn and canker-bit.
King Lear V, 3
Edgar to Duke of Albany

9 After life's fitful fever he sleeps well;
Treason has done his worst.
Macbeth III, 2
Macbeth, himself the traitor, talking of King Duncan to Lady
Macbeth

10 The man that hath no music in himself,
Nor is not mov'd with concourse of sweet sounds,
Is fit for treasons, stratagems, and spoils.
The Merchant of Venice V, 1
Lorenzo to Jessica

181   TREES

1 Under the greenwood tree
Who loves to lie with me . . .
Come hither, come hither, come hither.
As You Like It II, 5
Amiens, song

2 These trees shall be my books
And in their barks my thoughts I'll character.
As You Like It III, 2
Orlando in the Forest carves Rosalind's name on trees

3 I pray you, mar no more trees with writing love-songs in their
barks.
As You Like It III, 2
Jaques to Orlando

4   There is a willow grows aslant a brook,
    That shows his hoar leaves in the glassy stream.
    Hamlet IV, 7
    Queen Gertrude to Laertes, describing where Ophelia was
    drowned

5   Many strokes, though with a little axe,
    Hew down and fell the hardest-timbered oak.
    3 Henry VI II, 1
    A messenger telling of the slaughter of the Duke of York

6   Thus yields the cedar to the axe's edge,
    Whose arms gave shelter to the princely eagle.
    3 Henry VI V, 2
    Earl of Warwick compares the cedar's fall to his own in battle

7   Orpheus with his lute made trees,
    And the mountain-tops that freeze,
    Bow themselves when he did sing.
    Henry VIII III, 1
    Song to Queen Katherine

8   Under the cool shade of a sycamore
    I thought to close mine eyes some half an hour.
    Love's Labour's Lost V, 2
    Boyet to Princess of France

9   You may as well forbid the mountain pines
    To wag their high tops, and to make no noise,
    When they are fretten with the gusts of heaven.
    The Merchant of Venice IV, 1
    Antonio to Bassanio, concerning Shylock and his bond

182   TRUTH

1   That truth should be silent I had almost forgot.
    Antony and Cleopatra II, 2
    Enobarbus to Antony

2 If circumstances lead me, I will find
Where truth is hid, though it were hid indeed
Within the centre.
Hamlet II, 2
Polonius to Claudius

3 This above all: to thine own self be true,
And it must follow, as the night the day,
Thou canst not then be false to any man.
Hamlet I, 3
Polonius to Laertes

4 Doubt truth to be a liar;
But never doubt I love.
Hamlet II, 2
Written by Hamlet to Ophelia

5 Is not the truth the truth?
1 Henry IV II, 4
Falstaff, detected by Prince Hal in a gross falsehood

6 I can teach thee, coz, to shame the devil
By telling truth: tell truth and shame the devil.
1 Henry IV III, 1
Hotspur to Owen Glendower

7 What, can the devil speak true?
Macbeth I, 3
Banquo, as a witches' prophecy proves correct

8   Truth is truth
To the end of reckoning.
Measure for Measure V, 1
Isabella to the Duke

9 The seeming truth which cunning times put on
To entrap the wisest.
The Merchant of Venice III, 2
Bassanio, putting aside the gold casket

10   As gentle and as jocund as to jest
     Go I to fight: truth has a quiet breast.
     Richard II I, 3
     Mowbray, before an arranged combat with Bolingbroke

11   Simple truth miscall'd simplicity.
     Sonnet 66

183   UNKINDNESS

1   We see how mortal an unkindness is to them (our women); if
    they suffer our departure, death's the word.
    Antony and Cleopatra I, 2
    Enobarbus to Antony

2   Henry, though he be infortunate,
    Assure yourselves, will never be unkind.
    2 Henry VI IV, 9
    Henry to his soldiers

3   This was the most unkindest cut of all.
    Julius Caesar III, 2
    Antony refers to the dagger thrust Caesar received from his
    friend Brutus

4   Give me a bowl of wine.
    In this I bury all unkindness, Cassius.
    Julius Caesar IV, 3
    Brutus, after a brief quarrel

5   Redeem thy brother
    By yielding up thy body to my will:
    Or else he must not only die the death,
    But thy unkindness shall his death draw out
    To lingering sufferance.
    Measure for Measure III, 1
    Angelo to Isabella

6   Join with the present sickness that I have;
    And thy unkindness be like crooked age,
    To crop at once a too-long wither'd flower.
    Richard II II, 1
    John of Gaunt to Richard

7   In nature there's no blemish but the mind;
    None can be call'd deform'd but the unkind.
    Twelfth Night III, 4
    Antonio, upset by the apparent ingratitude of Sebastian

8   For if you were by my unkindness shaken,
    As I by yours, you've passed a hell of time.
    Sonnet 120

---

184   VALOUR
see also **Courage** 27

---

1   When valour plays on reason,
    It eats the sword it fights with.
    Antony and Cleopatra III, 13
    Enobarbus, deciding to leave Antony

2   It is held
    That valour is the chiefest virtue, and
    Most dignifies the haver.
    Coriolanus II, 2
    Cominius, praising Coriolanus

3   Valour becomes thee well enough.
    Cymbeline IV, 2
    Belarius to Guiderius

4   The better part of valour is discretion; in the which better part
    I have saved my life.
    1 Henry IV V, 4
    Falstaff, after shamming dead

5 Valiant Jack Falstaff, and therefore more valiant, being as he is, old Jack Falstaff.
1 Henry IV II, 4
Falstaff to Prince Hal

6 I never knew yet but rebuke and check was the reward to valour.
2 Henry IV IV, 3
Falstaff to John of Lancaster, on being reproved for tardiness

7 You may as well say, that's a valiant flea that dare eat his breakfast on the lip of a lion.
Henry V III, 7
Duke of Orleans denying that the English were valiant

8 What valour were it, when a cur doth grin,
For one to thrust his hand between his teeth,
When he might spurn him with his foot away.
3 Henry VI I, 4
Earl of Northumberland concerning Duke of York

9 Cowards die many times before their deaths:
The valiant never taste of death but once.
Julius Caesar II, 2
Caesar to Calpurnia

10 He is now (regarded) as valiant as Hercules that only tells a lie, and swears it.
Much Ado About Nothing IV, 1
Beatrice to Benedick

11 They were red-hot with drinking;
So full of valour that they smote the air
For breathing in their faces.
The Tempest IV, 1
Ariel on Stephano, Trinculo, and Caliban

12 There is no love-broker in the world can more prevail in man's commendation with women than report of valour.
Twelfth Night III, 2
Sir Toby to Sir Andrew

185 VICTORY

1   Nothing can seem foul to those that win.
1 Henry IV V, 1
King Henry to Prince Hal

2   I may justly say, with the hooked-nose fellow of Rome, 'I came, saw, and overcame'.
2 Henry IV IV, 3
Falstaff compares himself with Caesar because an enemy officer surrendered to him

3   To whom God will, there be the victory.
3 Henry VI II, 5
Henry to himself

4   Thus far our fortune keeps an upward course,
And we are graced with wreaths of victory.
3 Henry VI V, 3
King Edward IV to nobles

5   A victory is twice itself when the achiever brings home full numbers.
Much Ado About Nothing I, 1
Leonato to a messenger

6   Now are our brows bound with victorious wreaths.
Richard III I, 1
Richard, none the less unhappy with idle peace

7   The painful warrior, famoused for fight,
After a thousand victories, once foil'd
Is from the book of honour razed quite,
And all the rest forgot for which he toil'd.
Sonnet 25

186   VILLAINY

1   There's ne'er a villain dwelling in all Denmark
But he's an arrant knave.
Hamlet I, 5
Hamlet to Horatio in the ghost scene

2   I like not fair terms and a villain's mind.
The Merchant of Venice I, 3
Bassanio has misgivings about Shylock's bond with Antonio

3   We make guilty of our disasters the sun, the moon, and stars,
as if we were villains by necessity.
King Lear I, 2
Edmund, scornful of supposed astrological influences

4   The villainy you teach me I will execute; and it shall go hard
but I will better the instruction.
The Merchant of Venice III, 1
Shylock, claiming that his desire for revenge follows Christian example

5   Since I cannot prove a lover . . .
I am determined to prove a villain.
Richard III I, 1
Richard, being candid with himself

187   VIRTUE

1   In the fatness of these pursy times
Virtue itself of vice must pardon beg.
Hamlet III, 4
Hamlet to his mother

2   The purpose of playing . . . (is) to show virtue her own feature.
Hamlet III, 2
Hamlet to First Player

3   Assume a virtue if you have it not.
Hamlet III, 4
Hamlet to his mother

4   Men's evil manners live in brass: their virtues
We write in water.
Henry VIII IV, 2
Griffith to Queen Katherine

5   According to his virtue let us use him,
With all respect and rites of burial.
Julius Caesar V, 5
Octavius Caesar concerning Brutus

6   His virtues
Will plead like angels trumpet-tongued against
The deep damnation of his taking-off.
Macbeth I, 7
Macbeth, weighing up reasons for not murdering Duncan

7   Virtue is bold and goodness never fearful.
Measure for Measure III, 1
Duke to Isabella

8   There is no vice so simple, but assumes
Some mark of virtue on his outward parts.
The Merchant of Venice III, 2
Bassanio to himself, while choosing a casket

9   Therefore is it most expedient for the wise ... to be the
trumpet of his own virtues, as I am to myself.
Much Ado About Nothing V, 2
Benedick to Beatrice

10   Virtue itself turns vice, being misapplied,
And vice sometime's by action dignified.
Romeo and Juliet II, 3
Friar Laurence, soliloquizing

11 Virtue that transgresses is but patched with sin.
Twelfth Night I, 5
Feste to Olivia

188 WAR

1 Your honour calls you hence . . .
And all the gods go with you! Upon your sword
Sit laurel victory.
Antony and Cleopatra I, 3
Cleopatra to Antony

2 Away, boy, from the troops, and save thyself;
For friends kill friends, and the disorder's such
As war were hoodwink'd.
Cymbeline V, 2
Lucius to Imogen, in male disguise

3 Great the slaughter is
Here made by the Roman; great the answer be
Britons must take.
Cymbeline V, 3
Posthumus to himself

4 Caesar's spirit, ranging for revenge,
With Ate by his side come hot from hell,
Shall in these confines with a monarch's voice
Cry 'Havoc', and let slip the dogs of war.
Julius Caesar III, 1
Antony, soliloquizing over Caesar's body

5 Now for the bare-picked bone of majesty
Doth dogged war bristle his angry crest.
King John IV, 3
Philip the Bastard to Hubert de Burgh

6   We must have bloody noses and cracked crowns,
And make them current too.
1 Henry IV II, 3
Hotspur on the coming battle

7   Sound all the lofty instruments of war,
And by that music let us all embrace;
For, heaven to earth, some of us never shall
A second time do such a courtesy.
1 Henry IV V, 2
Hotspur to a messenger

8   They come like sacrifices in their trim,
And to the fire-eyed maid of smoky war
All hot and bleeding will we offer them.
1 Henry IV IV, 1
Hotspur, speaking of his enemies to Sir Richard Vernon

9   From camp to camp through the foul womb of night
The hum of either army stilly sounds.
Henry V Prologue IV
Chorus

10   When the blast of war blows in our ears
Then imitate the action of the tiger,
Stiffen the sinews, summon up the blood,
Disguise fair nature with ill-favour'd rage.
Henry V III, 1
King to his troops, before Harfleur

11   O God of battles! steel my soldiers' hearts.
Henry V IV, 1
King Henry at Agincourt

189 WEEPING
see also **Tears** 176

1 The tears live in an onion that should water this sorrow.
Antony and Cleopatra I, 2
Enobarbus to Antony, relating to the death of his wife, Fulvia

2   The big round tears
Coursed one another down his innocent nose.
As You Like It II, 1
A lord pitying a hunted stag

3 All my mother came into mine eyes
And gave me up to tears.
Henry V IV, 6
Duke of Exeter to Henry, on the death of the Duke of York in
battle

4 To weep is to make less the depth of grief;
Tears then for babes; blows and revenge for me.
3 Henry VI II, 1
Richard of Gloucester

5 Weep, wretched man, I'll aid thee tear for tear,
And let our hearts and eyes, like civil war,
Be blind with tears, and break o'ercharged with grief.
3 Henry VI II, 5
Henry to a son who has unknowingly killed his father in battle

6 Lords, knights, and gentlemen, what I should say
My tears gainsay; for every word I speak,
You see, I drink the water of mine eyes.
3 Henry VI V, 4
Queen Margaret to followers

7 O, now you weep, and I perceive you feel
The dint of pity.
Julius Caesar III, 2
Antony, in his speech to the citizens over Caesar's body

8 And let not woman's weapons, water-drops,
Stain my man's cheeks.
King Lear II, 4
Lear to Goneril and Regan

9   No, I'll not weep.
I have full cause of weeping; but this heart
Shall break into a hundred thousand flaws
Or ere I'll weep.
King Lear II, 4
Lear to Goneril and Regan

10   My plenteous joys,
Wanton in fullness, seek to hide themselves
In drops of sorrow.
Macbeth I, 4
King Duncan to Macbeth and Banquo for their success on the
battlefield

190 WELCOME

1 All strange and terrible events are welcome,
But comforts we despise.
Antony and Cleopatra IV, 15
Cleopatra to Charmian, as Antony is dying

2   Pray God our cheer
May answer my good will and your good welcome here.
The Comedy of Errors III, 1
Antipholus of Ephesus to Balthazar

3 Small cheer and great welcome makes a merry feast.
The Comedy of Errors III, 1
Balthazar to Antipholus

4   I have heard it said, unbidden guests
    Are often welcomest when they are gone.
    1 Henry VI II, 2
    Duke of Bedford to Lord Talbot

5   Good company, good wine, good welcome,
    Can make good people.
    Henry VIII I, 4
    Sir Henry Guildford to the king's guests

6   Bear welcome in your eye,
    Your hand, your tongue: look like the innocent flower,
    But be the serpent under it.
    Macbeth I, 5
    Lady Macbeth, advising Macbeth how to act when King
    Duncan comes

7   Sir, you are very welcome to our house:
    It must appear in other ways than words.
    The Merchant of Venice V, 1
    Portia to Antonio

8   Welcome ever smiles,
    And farewell goes out sighing.
    Troilus and Cressida III, 3
    Ulysses to Achilles

9   His worth is warrant for his welcome hither,
    If this be he you oft hath wish'd to hear from.
    The Two Gentlemen of Verona II, 4
    Silvia, as Valentine introduces his friend Proteus

191   WIFE
see also **Marriage** 106

1   A soldier is better accommodated than with a wife.
    2 Henry IV III, 2
    Bardolph to Justice Shallow

2   Dwell I but in the suburbs
Of your good pleasure? If it be no more,
Portia is Brutus' harlot, not his wife.
Julius Caesar II, 1
Portia to Brutus

3   A light wife maketh a heavy husband.
The Merchant of Venice V, 1
Portia to Bassanio

4   Antonio, I am married to a wife
Which is as dear to me as life itself;
But life itself, my wife, and all the world
Are not with me esteemed above thy life:
I would lose all, ay, sacrifice them all
Here to this devil, to deliver you.
The Merchant of Venice IV, 1
Bassanio to Antonio

5   Your wife would give you little thanks for that,
If she were by, to hear you make the offer.
The Merchant of Venice IV, 1
Portia, disguised as Balthasar, *is* by to hear Bassanio make the
offer

6   Honest company, I thank you all,
That have beheld me give away myself
To this most patient, sweet, and virtuous wife.
The Taming of the Shrew III, 2
Petruchio, with ironic reference to Katherina

7   This is a way to kill a wife with kindness.
The Taming of the Shrew IV, 1
Petruchio, alone, concerning his method of subduing Katherina

8
                                When the priest
Should ask, if Katherine should be his wife,
'Ay, by gogs wouns', quoth he, and swore so loud,
That, all amazed, the priest let fall the book.
The Taming of the Shrew III, 2
Gremio, describing the wedding of his eccentric acquaintance,
Petruchio

9 Should all despair
That have revolted wives, the tenth of mankind
Would hang themselves.
The Winter's Tale I, 2
Leontes to himself

192 WIT

1 Make the doors upon a woman's wit and it will out at the
casement; shut that and 'twill out at the key-hole; stop that,
'twill fly with the smoke out at the chimney.
As You Like It IV, 1
Rosalind to Orlando

2 The satirical rogue says here that old men have grey beards . . .
and that they have a plentiful lack of wit.
Hamlet II, 2
Hamlet, reading, mocks Polonius

    3 Brevity is the soul of wit.
      Hamlet II, 2
      Polonius to Queen Gertrude

4 I am not only witty in myself, but the cause that wit is in other
men.
2 Henry IV I, 2
Falstaff to his page

5   This rudeness is a sauce to his good wit;
Which gives men stomach to digest his words
With better appetite.

Julius Caesar I, 2
Cassius on Casca

6   His eye begets occasion for his wit;
For every object that the one doth catch,
The other turns to a mirth-moving jest.

Love's Labour's Lost II, 1
Rosaline, describing Biron

7   Great men may jest with saints, 'tis wit in them,
But in the less, foul profanation.

Measure for Measure II, 2
Isabella to Angelo

8   He doth indeed show some sparks that are like wit.

Much Ado About Nothing II, 3
Don Pedro, teasing Benedick

9   Thy wit is as quick as the greyhound's mouth.

Much Ado About Nothing V, 2
Benedick to Margaret

10   Look, he's winding up the watch of his wit; by and by it will
strike.

The Tempest II, 1
Sebastian concerning Gonzalo

11   Better a witty fool than a foolish wit.

Twelfth Night I, 5
Feste to Maria, quoting

193   WOMAN

1   Age cannot wither her, nor custom stale
Her infinite variety.
Antony and Cleopatra II, 2
Enobarbus, describing Cleopatra

2   If ladies be but young and fair
They have the gift to know it.
As You Like It II, 7
Jaques to Duke Senior, quoting Touchstone

3   I thank God I am not a woman, to be touched with so many
giddy offences.
As You Like It III, 2
Rosalind, as a youth, to Orlando

4   Do you not know that I am a woman? When I think, I must
speak.
As You Like It III, 2
Rosalind to Celia

5   Frailty, thy name is woman.
Hamlet I, 2
Hamlet concerning his mother

6   Is not my hostess of the tavern a most sweet wench?
1 Henry IV I, 2
Falstaff to Prince Hal

7   She's beautiful and therefore to be woo'd;
She is a woman, therefore to be won.
1 Henry VI V, 3
Earl of Suffolk concerning Margaret of Anjou

8   Women are soft, mild, pitiful and flexible;
Thou stern, obdurate, flinty, rough, remorseless.
3 Henry VI I, 4
Duke of York to Margaret

9 'Tis beauty that doth oft make women proud.
3 Henry VI I, 4
Duke of York to Margaret

10 Two women plac'd together makes cold weather.
Henry VIII I, 4
Lord Chamberlain, arranging guests at table

11   Ay me, how weak a thing
The heart of woman is.
Julius Caesar II, 4
Portia to herself

12 I grant I am a woman, but withal
A woman that Lord Brutus took to wife.
Julius Caesar II, 1
Portia to Brutus

13 There was never yet fair woman, but she made mouths in a glass.
King Lear III, 2
Fool to Lear

14   Her voice was ever soft,
Gentle, and low, an excellent thing in woman.
King Lear V, 3
Lear over Cordelia's dead body

15 A child of our grandmother Eve, a female, or, for thy more sweet understanding, a woman.
Love's Labour's Lost I, 1
King of Navarre, reading a letter from Armado

16 I am ashamed that women are so simple
To offer war where they should kneel for peace.
The Taming of the Shrew V, 2
Katherina to a Widow

17 For women are as roses, whose fair flower
Being once displayed, doth fall that very hour.
Twelfth Night II, 4
Orsino to Viola

18 Women will love her, that she is a woman
More worth than any man; men, that she is
The rarest of all women.
The Winter's Tale V, 1
A servant describing Perdita

194 WOOING

1 A heaven on earth I have won by wooing thee.
All's Well That Ends Well IV, 2
Betram to Diana

2 Come, woo me, woo me, for now I am in a holiday humour and
like enough to consent.
As You Like It IV, 1
Rosalind/Ganymede to Orlando

3 Will you vouchsafe to teach a soldier terms
Such as will enter at a lady's ear
And plead his love-suit to her gentle heart?
Henry V V, 2
Henry to Princess Katherine

4 Albeit I will confess thy father's wealth
Was the first motive that I woo'd thee, Anne:
Yet, wooing thee, I found thee of more value
Than stamps in gold or sums in sealed bags.
The Merry Wives of Windsor III, 4
Fenton to Anne Page

5   We cannot fight for love, as men may do;
We should be woo'd, and were not made to woo.
A Midsummer Night's Dream II, 1
Helena to Demetrius

6   I was not born under a rhyming planet, nor I cannot woo in festival terms.
Much Ado About Nothing V, 2
Benedick to himself

7   (She) bade me, if I had a friend that loved her,
I should but teach him how to tell my story,
And that would woo her.
Othello I, 3
Othello to Duke and Senators

8   Was ever woman in this humour woo'd?
Was ever woman in this humour won?
Richard III I, 2
Richard, who successfully wooed Lady Anne despite having murdered her well-loved husband

9   If thou think'st I am too quickly won,
I'll frown and be perverse and say thee nay,
So thou wilt woo.
Romeo and Juliet II, 2
Juliet to Romeo

10   I am rough, and woo not like a babe.
The Taming of the Shrew II, 1
Petruchio to Baptista, concerning Katherina

11   Women are angels, wooing.
Troilus and Cressida I, 2
Cressida to herself

195 WORDS

1   Thither write, my queen,
And with mine eyes I'll drink the words you send,
Though ink be made of gall.
Cymbeline I, 1
Posthumus, just banished, to his wife Imogen, left behind

2 *Polonius:* What do you read, my lord?
Hamlet: Words, words, words.
Hamlet II, 2

3 Why, what an ass I am! This is most brave,
That I, the son of a dear father murdered,
Prompted to my revenge by heaven and hell,
Must, woman-like, unpack my heart with words.
Hamlet II, 2
Hamlet, soliloquizing

4 That ever this fellow should have fewer words than a parrot,
and yet the son of a woman.
1 Henry IV II, 4
Prince Hal to Poins about a young barboy

5 My words fly up, my thoughts remain below;
Words without thoughts never to heaven go.
Hamlet III, 3
Claudius to himself, trying to pray

6 And 'tis a kind of good deed to say well;
And yet words are no deeds.
Henry VIII III, 2
Henry, displeased with Cardinal Wolsey

7 But yesterday the word of Caesar might
Have stood against the world: now lies he there,
And none so poor to do him reverence.
Julius Caesar III, 2
Antony to citizens

8 For your words, they rob the Hybla bees,
   And leave them honeyless.
   Julius Caesar V, 1
   Cassius to Antony in a battle of words

9 Good words are better than bad strokes.
   Julius Caesar V, 1
   Brutus to Octavius Caesar

10 He draweth out the thread of his verbosity finer than the staple
of his argument.
Love's Labour's Lost V, 1
Holofernes to Sir Nathaniel, concerning Don Armado

11 Madam, you have bereft me of all words,
    Only my blood speaks to you in my veins.
    The Merchant of Venice III, 2
    Bassanio to Portia, after choosing the right casket

12 Here are a few of the unpleasant'st words
    That ever blotted paper.
    The Merchant of Venice III, 2
    Bassanio to Portia, concerning Antonio's financial disasters

13 I know thou'rt full of love and honesty
    And weigh'st thy words before thou giv'st them breath.
    Othello III, 3
    Othello, impressed by Iago

14 How long a time lies in one little word!
    Richard II I, 3
    Bolingbroke, whose banishment has been reduced by four years

15 Words pay no debts.
    Troilus and Cressida III, 2
    Pandarus to Troilus

16 Words are grown so false I am loath to prove reason with them.
Twelfth Night III, 1
Feste to Viola/Cesario

17 A fine volley of words, gentlemen, and quickly shot off.
The Two Gentlemen of Verona II, 4
Silvia on backchat between Valentine and Thurio

196   THE WORLD

1 All the world's a stage,
And all the men and women merely players.
As You Like It II, 7
Jaques to his companions

2 Fare you well:
Hereafter, in a better world than this,
I shall desire more love and knowledge of you.
As You Like It I, 2
Le Beau to Orlando

3 How weary, stale, flat and unprofitable,
Seem to me all the uses of this world.
Hamlet I, 2
Hamlet, concerned about his mother's early remarriage

4 He doth bestride the narrow world
Like a Colossus.
Julius Caesar I, 2
Cassius, criticizing Caesar to Brutus

5 I am one, my liege,
Whom the vile blows and buffets of the world
Have so incensed that I am reckless what
I do to spite the world.
Macbeth III, 1
Second Murderer to Macbeth

6 I hold the world but as the world, Gratiano;
A stage where every man must play a part.
The Merchant of Venice I, 1
Antonio to Gratiano

7   Why, then the world's mine oyster,
      Which I with sword will open.
      The Merry Wives of Windsor II, 2
      Pistol to Falstaff, who has refused to lend him money

8   O monstrous world! take note, take note, O world!
      To be direct and honest is not safe.
      Othello III, 3
      Iago, deceiving Othello

9   The world is grown so bad
      That wrens make prey where eagles dare not perch.
      Richard III I, 3
      Richard on the advancement of commoners

10   The world is not thy friend, nor the world's law.
      Romeo and Juliet V, 1
      Romeo to desperately poor apothecary

11   The cloud-capp'd Towers, the gorgeous Palaces,
      The solemn Temples, the great Globe itself,
      Yea, all which it inherit, shall dissolve,
      And like this insubstantial pageant faded,
      Leave not a wrack behind.
      The Tempest IV, 1
      Prospero, after a visual performance by spirits, muses on life's
      transience

197   YOUTH

1   He wears the rose of youth upon him.
      Antony and Cleopatra III, 13
      Antony on Octavius Caesar, now his enemy

2   In the morn and liquid dew of youth
      Contagious blastments are most imminent.
      Hamlet I, 3
      Laertes to Ophelia

3 To flaming youth let virtue be as wax
   And melt in her own fire.
   Hamlet III, 4
   Hamlet to his mother

4 A very riband in the cap of youth.
   Hamlet IV, 7
   Claudius to Laertes

5   Youth no less becomes
   The light and careless livery that it wears
   Than settled age his sables and his weeds.
   Hamlet IV, 7
   Claudius to Laertes

6 He was indeed the glass
   Wherein the noble youth did dress themselves.
   2 Henry IV II, 3
   Hotspur's widow, Lady Percy, talking of him to his father

7   My thrice-puissant liege
   Is in the very May-morn of his youth,
   Ripe for exploits and mighty enterprises.
   Henry V I, 2
   Bishop of Ely to King Henry

8 (I) often did beguile her of her tears
   When I did speak of some distressful stroke
   That my youth suffered.
   Othello I, 3
   Othello to Senators, concerning his talks with Desdemona

9 Home-keeping youth have ever homely wits.
   The Two Gentlemen of Verona I, 1
   Valentine to Proteus

10 Crabbed age and youth cannot live together:
   Youth is full of pleasance, age is full of care.
   The Passionate Pilgrim Stanza 12

DICTIONARY OF
CHARACTERS

A

Aaron *Titus Andronicus* Villainous Moor, lover of Tamora, and partly responsible for atrocities against Titus and his family. Finally punished by being buried alive up to the neck.

Abbess *see* **Aemilia**

Abhorson *Measure for Measure* Executioner who considers himself a craftsman.

Achilles *Troilus and Cressida* Greek warrior who tends to sulk in his tent.

Adam *As You Like It* Faithful old servant of Orlando.

Adriana *The Comedy of Errors* Wife of Antipholus of Ephesus. She confuses her husband with his twin brother.

Aegeon *The Comedy of Errors* Elderly merchant of Syracuse, who comes to Ephesus looking for his lost son.

Aemilia *The Comedy of Errors* Wife of Aegeon and mother of twins; she had lost touch with her family. At the time of the play, she is abbess of an Ephesus convent, where **Antipholus** of Syracuse seeks shelter.

Aeneas *Troilus and Cressida* Trojan officer.

Agamemnon *Troilus and Cressida* Greek commanding officer.

Agrippa *Antony and Cleopatra* Friend of Octavius Caesar.

Aguecheek, Sir Andrew *Twelfth Night* Rather foolish and cowardly companion of Sir Toby Belch. Inveigled by Sir Toby into challenging Viola/Cesario to a duel which both are very reluctant to fight.

Ajax *Troilus and Cressida* Greek officer.

Albany, Duke of *King Lear* Goneril's husband, but an honourable man.

Alcibiades *Timon of Athens* Athenian officer, banished by the Senate. Friendly to Timon.

Aliena *As You Like It* Name assumed by Celia when she flees to Arden Forest with Rosalind.

Alonso *The Tempest* King of Naples, wrecked with Antonio and others on Prospero's island. Father of Ferdinand.

Amiens   *As You Like It*   Lord attending Duke Senior; a singer.

Angelo   *Measure for Measure*   Duke's deputy, regarded as rigidly moral. But virtuous Isabella, pleading for pardon for her brother Claudio, so fascinates him that he demands her surrender to his lust. She resists, and the Duke discovers his evil behaviour.

Anne, Lady   *Richard III*   Widow of Edward Prince of Wales. Although she hates Richard for murdering her husband, he inveigles her, astonishingly, into marrying him. Later he discards her.

Anne Page   *The Merry Wives of Windsor*   Daughter of Page. Her father wishes her to marry Slender; her mother's choice is Dr Caius; but it is the more romantic Fenton whom she loves and secretly marries.

Antiochus   *Pericles*   King of Antioch. Enemy to Pericles.

Antipholus   *The Comedy of Errors*   Identical twin brothers with the same name. Though long separated, they remain exactly alike, and the confusing of the one with the other, by wife and neighbours, is the basis of the play. One, married, lives at Ephesus, the scene of the play; the other is a stranger from Syracuse.

Antonio   *The Merchant of Venice*   Wealthy merchant, close friend to Bassanio, for whose benefit he borrows money from Shylock. The bond allows Shylock a pound of Antonio's flesh if repayment is not made at the due time. Losses at sea destroy Antonio's fortune, and Shylock demands his due.

Antonio   *Much Ado About Nothing*   Uncle of Hero; brother of Leonato. He is pugnaciously angry at Claudio's readiness to slander Hero.

Antonio   *The Tempest*   Brother of Prospero, whose place he has usurped. After being wrecked and is at Prospero's mercy, he repents and restores the dukedom.

Antonio   *Twelfth Night*   Sea captain devoted to Sebastian. Mistaking Viola for him, he is disgusted when she will not, as he supposes, return his purse when he needs it.

Antonio   *The Two Gentlemen of Verona*   Father of Proteus.

Antony   *Julius Caesar* and *Antony and Cleopatra*   In the first play he is chief opponent of Caesar's killers, and rouses the citizens against them by a subtle and powerful speech. In the second play he is the dominating character, a fine soldier weakened by his passion for Cleopatra. Finally kills himself.

Apemantus   *Timon of Athens*   A cynical acquaintance of Timon.

Ariel *The Tempest* Lively spirit who assists Prospero's magical activities, and is finally given his freedom.

Armado, Don Adriano de *Love's Labour's Lost* A fantastical Spaniard.

Arragon, Prince of *The Merchant of Venice* Portia's second suitor, who wrongly chooses the silver casket.

Arthur *King John* Young nephew of the king and rightful heir to the throne. *See* **Hubert de Burgh**

Arviragus *Cymbeline* Supposedly the son of Belarius, but his father is really Cymbeline.

Audrey *As You Like It* Country wench courted by Touchstone, who marries her.

Aufidius, Tullus *Coriolanus* General of the Volscians, Rome's enemies. When Rome banishes Coriolanus, he joins Aufidius in a threatened attack on the city, but the friendship is brief.

Aumerle, Duke of *Richard II* Son of Duke of York, and supporter of Richard. Conspires against Bolingbroke, but his mother wins pardon for him, against his father's wishes.

Austria, Duke of *King John* Supporter of Arthur as rightful king of England.

Autolycus *The Winter's Tale* A thieving pedlar.

B

Bagot *Richard II* Follower of Richard.

Balthasar *The Merchant of Venice* Name assumed by Portia when she impersonates a lawyer to defend Antonio from Shylock's bond.

Balthasar *Romeo and Juliet* Servant to Romeo.

Balthazar *The Comedy of Errors* Friend of Antipholus of Ephesus.

Banquo *Macbeth* Fellow officer of Macbeth in King Duncan's army. Murdered by Macbeth after the witches prophesy that Banquo's desendants will be kings. His bloody ghost appears to Macbeth at a banquet.

Baptista *The Taming of the Shrew* Father of the 'Shrew'.

Bardolph *1 Henry IV* Red-faced follower of Falstaff.

Lord Bardolph *2 Henry IV* Supporter of Earl of Northumberland.

Bassanio *The Merchant of Venice* Venetian nobleman, a friend of Antonio. In love with and loved by Portia. Fortunately he chooses the right casket (lead), and weds her.

Bates *Henry V* English soldier at Agincourt who talks with Henry (incognito).

Beatrice *Much Ado About Nothing* Light-hearted niece of Leonato. She and Benedick are constantly sparring, but finally fall in love, aided by friends.

Beaufort, Cardinal *1* and *2 Henry VI* Bishop of Winchester.

Belarius *Cymbeline* Lord banished by Cymbeline many years earlier. In revenge he stole Cymbeline's two sons, and brought them up as his own (see **Arviragus** and **Guiderius**). Finally reconciled with Cymbeline.

Belch, Sir Toby *Twelfth Night* Olivia's uncle, and a roisterous member of her household, at loggerheads with her steward, Malvolio.

Bellario *The Merchant of Venice* Erudite lawyer who (off stage) assists Portia. *See* **Balthasar** and **Portia**.

Benedick *Much Ado About Nothing* Lively and humorous young gentleman, coaxed by friends into falling in love with his sparring partner, Beatrice.

Benvolio *Romeo and Juliet* Friend of Romeo.

Bernardo *Hamlet* Danish officer who sees the ghost of Hamlet's father.

Berowne *see* **Biron**.

Bertram *All's Well That Ends Well* Young Count of Roussillon. Forced by the King of France to marry a charming girl whom he considers socially inferior, he refuses to accept the marriage. At length he is tricked into sleeping with her, and finally acknowledges her as his wife.

Bianca *Othello* Cassio's mistress.

Bianca *The Taming of the Shrew* Younger sister of Katherina, but sweet-natured. She is successfully wooed by Lucentio.

Blanch *King John* John's niece, married to the Dauphin.

Bolingbroke, Henry *Richard II* Banished by Richard, he returns in order to claim his inheritance on the death of his father. From defending his property from Richard, Bolingbroke goes on to usurp the kingship. In *1* and *2 Henry IV* he appears as King Henry IV.

Biron/Berowne *Love's Labour's Lost* Lively lord attending the King of Navarre.

Borachio *Much Ado About Nothing* Follower of Don John. He plays a part in the plot to suggest Hero's infidelity.

Bottom, Nick *A Midsummer Night's Dream* A very self-confident weaver, who plays the leading part in the 'Pyramus and Thisbe' play. By magic, Oberon causes his head to be temporarily changed into an ass's head, to humiliate Titania, who falls in love with the creature through a magic charm.

Boult *Pericles* Brothel door-keeper, rather improbably converted by Marina's virtue.

Boyet *Love's Labour's Lost* Attendant on Princess of France.

Brabantio *Othello* Venetian senator, father of Desdemona. He encourages Othello to talk about his life, but is outraged when Desdemona falls in love with and marries him.

Brakenbury, Sir Robert *Richard III* Lieutenant of the Tower of London.

Brutus, Junius *Coriolanus* One of the two Roman tribunes, both unfavourable to Coriolanus.

Brutus, Marcus *Julius Caesar* The most honourable of Caesar's assassins. Later in the play he quarrels with Cassius, but friendship is restored. Finally kills himself after defeat in battle.

Bullen, Anne *Henry VIII* (Anne Boleyn) One of Queen Katherine's ladies-in-waiting, and later King Henry's second wife (mother of Queen Elizabeth I). An elaborate and dignified coronation procession takes place in Act IV.

Bushy *Richard II* Follower of King Richard.

C

Cade, Jack *2 Henry VI* Leader of a rebel mob.

Caesar *see* **Julius** and **Octavius.**

Caius, Dr *The Merry Wives of Windsor* French doctor wanting to marry Anne Page, whose mother was favourable (although Anne was not).

Caithness *Macbeth* Scottish thane.

Caliban *The Tempest* Deformed and repulsive creature, made Prospero's slave by his magic power. With Stephano, he tries to plan Prospero's death.

Calpurnia *Julius Caesar* Caesar's wife, who tries to dissuade him from going out on the day of his death.

Camillo *The Winter's Tale* A trusted noble at the court of Leontes, whose baseless jealousy he is unwilling to support.

Capucius *Henry VIII* Ambassador from Emperor Charles V. He visits Queen Katherine when she is seriously ill.

Capulet   *Romeo and Juliet*   Juliet's father, brutally harsh and unsympathetic over her unwillingness to be forced into a sudden marriage. The fierce enmity between the Capulet and Montague families, and the love of Capulet daughter for Montague son, is the basis of the play.

Casca   *Julius Caesar*   One of the conspirators against Caesar.

Cassius   *Julius Caesar*   One of the two chief members of the conspiracy against Julius Caesar. Unlike Brutus, however, Cassius was partly inspired by jealousy.

Cassio   *Othello*   Othello's lieutenant, coaxed by Iago into becoming involved in a drunken brawl, thereby losing favour. Iago also persuades the gullible Moor that Cassio is Desdemona's lover.

Catesby, Sir William   *Richard III*   A follower of Richard.

Celia   *As You Like It*   Devoted cousin of Rosalind and daughter of the usurping duke. When Rosalind is banished by the duke, Celia unhesitatingly goes with her, taking the name Aliena.

Cerimon   *Pericles*   A gentleman of Ephesus.

Ceres   *The Tempest*   A spirit summoned by Prospero.

Cesario   *Twelfth Night*   Name assumed by Viola when pretending to be a male page.

Charles   *As You Like It*   Professional wrestler, defeated by Orlando.

Charmian   *Antony and Cleopatra*   One of Cleopatra's two chief female attendants.

Chiron   *Titus Andronicus*   Malicious son of Tamora, who, with his brother Demetrius, rapes and mutilates Titus's daughter, Lavinia.

Clarence, Duke of   *Richard III*   Brother of Edward IV. Richard is responsible for his death, by preventing a reprieve.

Claudio   *Measure for Measure*   Young gentleman condemned to death by Angelo for immorality. Brother of Isabella, who tries to get him pardoned.

Claudio   *Much Ado About Nothing*   Young lord of Florence, betrothed to Hero. He rejects her unkindly at the wedding ceremony, having received false information about her. Ultimately the misunderstanding is cleared up, and they marry.

Claudius, King   *Hamlet*   Hamlet's uncle, King of Denmark and husband of Hamlet's mother Gertrude, after having murdered his brother, Hamlet's father. Afraid that Hamlet may be seeking revenge, Claudius attempts, unsuccessfully, to have him murdered on a voyage to England.

Cleon *Pericles* Governor of Tharsus, where Pericles is cast ashore after shipwreck.

Cleopatra *Antony and Cleopatra* Heroine of the play, which deals with the fascination she exercises on Antony, and her love for him. When he dies she commits suicide by allowing a poisonous snake to bite her.

Clifford, Lord *2 Henry VI* Supporter of Henry against his opponents; killed by Duke of York in battle. His son, Young Clifford, vows revenge, and kills both York and his son.

Cloten *Cymbeline* Queen's foolish son by a former husband. He constantly pesters Imogen. He attempts to kill Guiderius, but is himself the victim.

Cominius *Coriolanus* Roman general, on good terms with Coriolanus.

Conrade *Much Ado About Nothing* Follower of Don John.

Constance *King John* Mother of Arthur.

Cordelia *King Lear* Youngest daughter of Lear, disowned because she fails to flatter him. She marries the King of France. When in due course they come to England to support Lear, she is captured and murdered.

Corin *As You Like It* An old shepherd.

Coriolanus (Caius Marcius) *Coriolanus* Fine Roman army leader, unpopular because of his arrogance. Banished from Rome, in revenge he joins the city's enemies, the Volscians, to fight against it.

Cornelius *Cymbeline* Physician who saves the life of Imogen, whom the Queen wishes to kill. Cornelius gives her (secretly) not poison but a sleep-inducing drug.

Cornwall, Duke of *King Lear* Husband of Regan, ruthless and cruel. He is responsible for the blinding of Gloucester.

Cranmer, Thomas *Henry VIII* Archbishop of Canterbury, favoured by the King.

Cressida *Troilus and Cressida* Trojan girl having in a love affair with Troilus. She proves faithless, however, when sent to the Greek camp.

Cromwell, Thomas *Henry VIII* Wolsey's servant.

Cymbeline *Cymbeline* King of Britain, whose present Queen is stepmother to his daughter, Imogen

D

Demetrius *Antony and Cleopatra* A friend of Antony.

Demetrius   *A Midsummer Night's Dream*   Grecian gentleman attracted by Hermia but loved by Helena, who becomes the object of his affection when a magic liquid is placed in his eyes by Oberon.

Desdemona   *Othello*   Devoted wife of Othello, wrongly believed by him to be unfaithful, and murdered by him.

Diana   *All's Well That Ends Well*   Young woman to whom Bertram is greatly attracted. She agrees to an assignation with him, but allows his neglected wife, Helena, secretly to take her place.

Dionyza   *Pericles*   Wife of Cleon. She attempts to have Pericles's daughter, Marina, murdered because her beauty and virtue make her outshine Dionyza's daughter.

Donalbain   *Macbeth*   Son of King Duncan, who flees to Ireland for safety after Duncan's murder.

Douglas, Earl of   *1 Henry IV*   Notable Scottish warrior, an ally of Hotspur.

Dromio   *The Comedy of Errors*   Twins of the same name, servants respectively of the twin brothers Antipholus of Ephesus and of Syracuse.

Duke Frederick   *As You Like It*   Younger brother of Duke Senior, and usurper of his dukedom.

Duke Senior   *As You Like It*   Father of Rosalind. Driven into exile in Arden Forest by his younger brother, Frederick.

Dumain   *Love's Labour's Lost*   One of the three French lords attending the King of Navarre. He falls in love with Katherine.

Duncan   *Macbeth*   King of Scotland, murdered by Macbeth and his wife when he visits their castle, so that Macbeth can achieve the crown.

E

Edgar   *King Lear*   Legitimate son of Earl of Gloucester, banished by his father as a result of a plot by his bastard brother, Edmund. Acts as a mad beggar (Tom o' Bedlam) to hide his real identity.

Edmund   *King Lear*   Gloucester's bastard son, who conspires against his brother, and later intrigues with Goneril and Regan separately. Finally he is killed by Edgar in a duel.

Edward, Earl of March   *3 Henry VI* and *King Richard III*   Becomes king as Edward IV, and marries Lady Grey.

Egeus   *A Midsummer Night's Dream*   Father of Hermia, unreasonably opposed to her desire to marry Lysander.

Emilia   *Othello*   Wife of Iago and faithful servant to Desdemona.

Enobarbus *Antony and Cleopatra*   Follower of Antony, blunt and outspoken.

Eros *Antony and Cleopatra*   Freed slave and devoted servant to Antony.

Escalus *Measure for Measure*   Elderly lord who urges Angelo to be lenient in sentencing offenders.

Exton, Sir Pierce of *Richard II*   Lord responsible for the murder of Richard.

Evans, Sir Hugh *The Merry Wives of Windsor*   Parson and schoolmaster, who educates Page's son, William.

F

Fabian *Twelfth Night*   Servant to Olivia, friendly with Sir Toby Belch.

Falstaff, Sir John *1 Henry IV, 2 Henry IV, The Merry Wives of Windsor*   Rascally but genial companion of Prince Hal in the first play, rejected by him in the second, and a mere butt in the third. Notable for his fatness and his ready wit. He is a rather unscrupulous recruiting officer in the second play.

Fastolf, Sir John *1 Henry VI*   Cowardly knight who flees from the battle of Rouen, and is later denounced by Lord Talbot.

Feeble *2 Henry IV*   One of Falstaff's recruits, who belies his name.

Fenton *The Merry Wives of Windsor*   Young man in love with and loved by Anne Page, whom he secretly marries.

Ferdinand *The Tempest*   Son of the King of Naples. He falls deeply in love with Miranda when wrecked on Prospero's island.

Feste *Twelfth Night*   Countess Olivia's clown.

Fidele *Cymbeline*   Name assumed by Imogen as a boy.

Flaminius *Timon of Athens*   Servant to Timon.

Flavius *Timon of Athens*   Timon's steward, who disapproves of his reckless generosity.

Fluellen *Henry V*   Fiery but knowledgeable Welsh captain in Henry's army.

Florizel *The Winter's Tale*   Son of Polixenes; Prince of Bohemia, in love with Perdita.

Fool *King Lear*   Lear's rather serious clown, who keeps him company in his wanderings.

Ford *The Merry Wives of Windsor*   Well-to-do, jealous husband of Mrs Ford. She encourages Falstaff's attentions only to make a fool of him.

Francis, Friar   *Much Ado About Nothing*   Friar who was to have married Claudio and Hero but is prevented by Claudio's slanderous charges against her. Subsequently he remains the most level-headed of those concerned.

Francisco   *Hamlet*   Soldier on sentry duty.

Francisco   *The Tempest*   Lord wrecked with Alonso.

G

Ganymede   *As You Like It*   Name assumed by Rosalind as a male.

Gardiner   *Henry VIII*   Secretary to the king, later Bishop of Winchester and opponent of Archbishop Cranmer.

Gertrude, Queen   *Hamlet*   Hamlet's mother, who (after the death of her first husband) married his persuasive brother.

Ghost   *Hamlet*   Hamlet's father, murdered by his brother Claudius. He appears as a ghost to persuade Hamlet to avenge the crime. He appears first on the castle battlements, later while Hamlet is reproaching his mother.

Glendower, Owen   *1 Henry IV*   Welsh ally of Henry's opponents. He believes strongly in the supernatural, and is lightly mocked by Hotspur.

Gloucester, Humphrey, Duke of   *1* and *2 Henry VI*   King Henry's uncle, who for a while ruled as Protector.

Gloucester, Richard, Duke of   *2* and *3 Henry VI*, and *Richard III*   Brother of Edward IV; hypocritical and ruthlessly ambitious; became king as Richard III. Defeated and killed by Earl of Richmond (later Henry VII) at Bosworth.

Gloucester, Earl of   *King Lear*   Father of Edgar and Edmund, but banishes the former through Edmund's scheming. He is blinded by the Duke of Cornwall for helping King Lear.

Gobbo, Launcelot   *The Merchant of Venice*   Shylock's servant, and later Bassanio's.

Goneril   *King Lear*   One of Lear's two eldest daughters, between whom he unwisely divides his kingdom, only to discover that they are cruelly unwilling to offer him the hospitality he expects. Later, she and her sister quarrel over Gloucester's son, Edmund. Finally Goneril commits suicide.

Gonzalo   *The Tempest*   Old courtier among those wrecked on Prospero's island, friendly to Prospero.

Gower   *2 Henry IV* and *Henry V*   Officer in the king's army.

Gratiano   *The Merchant of Venice*   Lively companion of Bassanio. He marries Nerissa.

Gratiano   *Othello*   Uncle of Desdemona.

Gremio   *The Taming of the Shrew*   Elderly suitor to Bianca.

Green   *Richard II*   A servant of the king.

Grey, Lady   *3 Henry VI* and *Richard III*   Widow of Sir John Grey. Becomes the wife of King Edward IV.

Griffith   *Henry VIII*   Gentleman usher to Queen Katherine, a fair and honest judge of character.

Grumio   *The Taming of the Shrew*   Petruchio's servant.

Guildenstern   *Hamlet*   Acquaintance (with Rosencrantz) of Hamlet's schooldays, friendly with Claudius. The pair are sent with Hamlet to England, carrying a letter giving instructions for Hamlet to be killed. He unseals the letter and substitutes their names for his.

Guiderius   *Cymbeline*   Supposed son of Belarius, but actually he and Arviragus are sons of King Cymbeline himself, stolen in infancy.

Guildford, Sir Henry   *Henry VIII*   A courtier.

H

Hal, Prince   *1* and *2 Henry IV*   Popular name of Henry Prince of Wales (later Henry V), rather dissolute in the first play, but becoming serious in the second.

Hamlet   *Hamlet*   Prince of Denmark, and Shakespeare's most famous character. Burdened with the task of avenging his father's murder, he cannot at first find the right occasion. He is killed with a duelling weapon treacherously poisoned by Laertes, but first forces Claudio to drink poison.

Hastings, Lord   *3 Henry VI* and *Richard III*   Supporter of King Edward IV. He imagines himself on good terms with Richard, but is executed by him on a false charge.

Hecate   *Macbeth*   Chief of the witches.

Hector   *Troilus and Cressida*   Noble Trojan warrior, treacherously killed by Achilles.

Helena   *All's Well That Ends Well*   Physician's daughter who cures the King of France. Her strong desire to be married to Bertram (very unwilling) is achieved with the king's help, but Bertram at first refuses to recognize the marriage.

Helena   *A Midsummer Night's Dream*   Athenian girl in love with Demetrius, who loves Hermia (in vain). Through magic, his affections change to Helena, but at first she thinks he is mocking her.

Helicanus   *Pericles*   Faithful minister of Pericles.

Henry IV   *Richard II*, and *1* and *2 Henry IV*   Henry Bolingbroke forces Richard to abdicate, and becomes king himself as Henry IV.

Henry V   *Henry V*   The casual, rather dissolute Prince Hal of *1 Henry IV* who becomes a strong but human king as Henry V, always ready to talk (incognito) with his common soldiers. He campaigns for the French throne, and marries Princess Katherine of France.

Henry VI   *1, 2*, and *3 Henry VI*   A weak king in turbulent times, finally (in the play) murdered by Richard of Gloucester (Richard III).

Henry VIII   *Henry VIII*   While retaining respect for Queen Katherine, he has his marriage to her annulled (against Cardinal Wolsey's wishes), and marries Anne Bullen.

Hermia   *A Midsummer Night's Dream*   Athenian girl who loves and is loved by Lysander. They elope when her father tries to force her to marry Demetrius.

Hermione   *The Winter's Tale*   Queen to Leontes, unjustly accused by her husband of unfaithfulness. Many years later, Leontes, now penitent, embraces what is presented to him as a statue of her – to find that it is her living body.

Hero   *Much Ado About Nothing*   Daughter to Leonato. Betrothed to Claudio, but wrongly suspected of immoral conduct, and rejected and slandered by him. In the end, however, they are reconciled.

Hippolyta   *A Midsummer Night's Dream*   Queen of the Amazons, betrothed to Theseus.

Holofernes   *Love's Labour's Lost*   A pedantic schoolmaster.

Horatio   *Hamlet*   Hamlet's chief friend and confidant.

Hortensio   *The Taming of the Shrew*   Unsuccessful suitor to Bianca.

Hotspur   *1 Henry IV*   Henry Percy, son of Earl of Northumberland. Notable for his vigorous personality and passion for honour.

Hubert de Burgh   *King John*   The king's Chamberlain ordered to kill John's nephew, Arthur. He secretly disobeys, arranging for false reports of the boy's death to be put about.

I

Iachimo   *Cymbeline*   Roman courtier who tricks Posthumus, foolishly jealous, into believing his wife Imogen to be unfaithful.

Iago *Othello* Malicious villain who sets out to destroy happiness. His superior officer, Othello, is sublimely happy with his devoted wife, Desdemona, but allows himself to be persuaded by Iago that she is false. After murdering her, Othello realizes the truth, and kills both Iago and himself.

Imogen *Cymbeline* Cymbeline's daughter, married to Posthumus, who, easily persuaded by Iachimo that she is unchaste, tries to have her killed.

Iras *Antony and Cleopatra* One of Cleopatra's two chief female attendants.

Iris *The Tempest* Character in a masque.

Isabel *Henry V* French Queen, mother of Princess Katherine.

Isabella *Measure for Measure* Sister of Claudio. Angelo demands her surrender as the price for reprieving her brother from execution. Her indignant refusal, and somewhat casual acceptance of her brother's fate, may seem to some rather cold-blooded.

J

Jaques *As You Like It* Cynical but philosophical companion of Duke Senior in the Forest of Arden. He delivers the famous speech 'All the world's a stage . . .'

Jessica *The Merchant of Venice* Shylock's daughter, who elopes with Lorenzo, and steals her father's treasure.

Joan of Arc *1 Henry VI* Known in the play as La Pucelle.

John, Don *Much Ado About Nothing* Bastard brother of Don Pedro. Villain responsible for the false accusation against Hero.

John of Gaunt *Richard II* Father of Bolingbroke.

John of Lancaster *1 and 2 Henry IV* Younger brother of Prince Hal.

Julia *The Two Gentlemen of Verona* A lady of Verona, in love with Proteus, one of the gentlemen.

Juliet *Romeo and Juliet* Young heroine of the play, in love with and loved by Romeo, though her family, the Capulets, and his, the Montagues, are bitter enemies. The two lovers become secretly married; but when Romeo is banished and Juliet herself about to be forced into another marriage, Friar Laurence helps them to plan a way out. The plan miscarries, and they both kill themselves in her family vault.

Julius Caesar   *Julius Caesar*   Ruler of Rome. Ignoring superstitious warnings, he is murdered by a group of politicians afraid that his power may grow too great.

K

Katherina   *The Taming of the Shrew*   Sharp-tempered and obstinate daughter of a wealthy Paduan citizen. Petruchio, from Verona, marries her and achieves her subjugation by pretending to follow her wishes while doing the opposite.

Katherine   *Henry V*   Daughter of French King, successfully wooed by Henry.

Katherine   *Love's Labour's Lost*   Lady waiting on Princess of France, and wooed by Dumain.

Katherine   *Henry VIII*   The king's first wife. The marriage was annulled, when the king wished to marry Anne Bullen, on the ground that Katherine was his sister-in-law.

Kent, Earl of   *King Lear*   Honest and outspoken follower of Lear.

L

Laertes   *Hamlet*   Ophelia's brother. Hamlet, in Act V, is persuaded to fence with him, and both men die after being wounded by a rapier, poisoned treacherously by Laertes.

Lafeu   *All's Well That Ends Well*   A wise old courtier.

La Pucelle   *1 Henry VI*   Joan of Arc.

Launce   *The Two Gentlemen of Verona*   Servant of Proteus, and owner of the dog, Crab.

Laurence, Friar   *Romeo and Juliet*   Franciscan friar, who gives advice and help to the two lovers.

Lear, King   *King Lear*   King of Britain who foolishly gives up his kingdom to his two elder daughters, Goneril and Regan, who repay him with unkindness. *See also* **Cordelia**.

Le Beau   *As You Like It*   Courtier of Duke Frederick.

Leonato   *Much Ado About Nothing*   Father of Hero.

Leontes   *The Winter's Tale*   King of Sicilia, insanely jealous concerning his wife, Hermione.

Lavinia   *Titus Andronicus*   Daughter of Titus, raped and left without hands or tongue by the sons of Queen Tamora.

Lepidus   *Julius Caesar*   One of the three Roman leaders after the murder of Caesar, together with Antony and Octavius Caesar. Slightingly referred to by Antony as a mere messenger.

Lodovico   *Othello*   Brabantio's kinsman, to whom Othello makes his final speech.

Lorenzo   *The Merchant of Venice*   Young man in love with Shylock's daughter, Jessica, with whom he elopes.

Lovell, Sir Thomas   *Henry VIII*   Gentleman at the king's court.

Lucentio   *The Taming of the Shrew*   Young man whose wooing of Bianca forms the play's sub-plot. *See* **Tranio.**

Lucetta   *The Two Gentlemen of Verona*   Julia's lady-in-waiting.

Luciana   *The Comedy of Errors*   Adriana's sister, admired by Antipholus of Syracuse.

Lucio   *Measure for Measure*   Garrulous friend of Claudio. He unwisely talks to the duke (incognito), slandering him, and is punished by having to marry a girl he has wronged.

Lucius   *Julius Caesar*   Brutus's serving-boy.

Lucius   *Cymbeline*   Roman general who befriends Imogen (who is posing as a boy).

Lucius   *Timon of Athens*   Flattering but hypocritical lord.

Lucius   *Titus Andronicus*   Son of Titus. He finally becomes ruler of Rome.

Lucullus   *Timon of Athens*   Flatterer not prepared to reciprocate Timon's generosity.

Lysander   *A Midsummer Night's Dream*   Young Athenian man eloping with Hermia because of her father's obstinate opposition. A magic eye-drop makes Lysander fall temporarily in love with Helena.

M

Macbeth   *Macbeth*   Originally a brave Scottish lord, and a member of King Duncan's army, but incited by witches' prophecies to murder in order to achieve and maintain kingship. The murders of King Duncan and Banquo, a fellow officer, are among his crimes.

Macbeth, Lady   *Macbeth*   Wife of Macbeth. She encourages her husband to murder Duncan. Later she suffers nightmares from guilt.

Macduff   *Macbeth*   Scottish nobleman who suspects Macbeth. While he is in England gathering support, Macbeth slaughters his wife and children.

Maecenas   *Antony and Cleopatra*   Friend of Octavius Caesar.

Malcolm   *Macbeth*   Son of King Duncan. He becomes king of Scotland after Macbeth's defeat (at the end of the play), having found safety in England meanwhile.

Malvolio   *Twelfth Night*   Countess Olivia's self-important steward, who reproves Sir Toby Belch and his cronies for unseemly behaviour. In revenge they forge a letter to make him believe that Olivia loves him, and then pretend he is mad and shut him away.

Marcellus   *Hamlet*   Soldier on watch who sees the ghost of Hamlet's father.

Marcus Andronicus   *Titus Andronicus*   Brother of Titus, and a tribune of the people.

Mardian   *Antony and Cleopatra*   Eunuch in attendance on Cleopatra.

Margaret   *Much Ado About Nothing*   Gentlewoman attending Hero, whom she impersonates in a pretended assignation with Borachio.

Margaret of Anjou   *1, 2* and *3 Henry VI* and *Richard III*   After being captured by Earl of Suffolk, who becomes her lover, she is married to Henry VI. In later years a bitter enemy of York.

Maria   *Twelfth Night*   Waiting-woman to Countess Olivia, and one of Sir Toby Belch's companions. Instigator of the plot against Malvolio.

Mariana   *Measure for Measure*   Formerly betrothed to Angelo, then rejected, but finally married to him.

Marina   *Pericles*   Beautiful daughter of Pericles and Thaisa. After being captured by pirates, she is bought by a brothel-keeper, but remarkably retains her virtue. She finally marries the city Governor.

Marullus   *Julius Caesar*   Tribune opposed to Caesar.

Menas   *Antony and Cleopatra*   Friend to Pompey.

Menecrates   *Antony and Cleopatra*   Friend to Pompey.

Menenius Agrippa   *Coriolanus*   Friend and sometimes adviser of Coriolanus, critical of the tribunes who oppose him.

Menteith   *Macbeth*   Scottish nobleman.

Mercutio   *Romeo and Juliet*   Lively friend of Romeo, killed by the Capulet Tybalt in a fight provoked by the latter, who himself was killed by Romeo a little later through his own fault.

Milan, Duke of   *The Two Gentlemen of Verona*   Father of Silvia. He banishes Valentine for trying to elope with her.

Miranda   *The Tempest*   Prospero's daughter, who falls in love with Ferdinand when he is wrecked on her island.

Montague   *Romeo and Juliet*   The family to which Romeo belongs, and which has long been at enmity with the Capulets, Juliet's family.

Moor   Name by which Othello is often known. The sub-title of *Othello* is *The Moor of Venice*. Aaron in *Titus Andronicus* is also a Moor.

Morocco, Prince of   *The Merchant of Venice*   Suitor to Portia. He chooses, wrongly, the gold casket.

Mortimer *1 Henry IV* Prisoner of Owen Glendower, but marries his daughter.

Mortimer, Edmund *1 Henry VI* Elderly nobleman with a claim to the throne. He has spent much of his life in prison, and appears in this play only to die.

Mowbray, Thomas *Richard II* Duke of Norfolk. Accused of treason by Bolingbroke, and banished for life.

Moth *Love's Labour's Lost* Lively page of Armado.

N

Nathaniel, Sir *Love's Labour's Lost* A curate.

Navarre, King of *Love's Labour's Lost* He attempts, with three members of his court, to avoid women for three years. They all fail, and fall in love.

Nerissa *The Merchant of Venice* Clever waiting-maid to Portia. When the latter disguises herself as a lawyer, Nerissa becomes her clerk.

Norfolk, 2nd Duke of *Henry VIII* Opponent of Cardinal Wolsey.

Northumberland, Earl of *Richard II, and 1 and 2 Henry VI* Father of Hotspur. Supports Bolingbroke on the latter's return to England to claim his inheritance.

Nurse *Romeo and Juliet* Nurse who looks after Juliet, and acts in some degree as her confidante.

O

Oberon *A Midsummer Night's Dream* King of the Fairies, who quarrels with his wife, Titania. His magic causes her to fall in love with a rough workman bearing an ass's head. *See* **Bottom.**

Octavius Caesar *Julius Caesar* and *Antony and Cleopatra* Julius Caesar's nephew. Antony, who married Octavius's sister, Octavia, is sometimes his ally, sometimes his enemy.

Oliver *As You Like It* Orlando's ill-natured elder brother. Towards the end of the play he suddenly changes character, and Celia marries him.

Olivia, Countess *Twelfth Night* A leading character, who rejects Orsino but falls in love with the supposed youth Cesario (really Viola). She believes she has succeeded in marrying 'him', but her husband is really Viola's identical twin Sebastian.

Ophelia   *Hamlet*   Daughter of Polonius, previously courted by Hamlet, but rejected when avenging his father's murder occupies his mind. She goes mad, after Hamlet kills her father, and later drowns.

Orlando   *As You Like It*   Hero of the play. Hated by his elder brother Oliver, he wanders into the Forest of Arden, where he encounters Rosalind, acting as the youth Ganymede. They play a game of make-believe, she pretending to be the Rosalind she really is, he pretending to accept her as such; but finally her sex is revealed and they marry.

Orleans, Duke of   *Henry V*   Companion of the Dauphin, unwisely contemptuous of the English army before the battle of Agincourt.

Orsino   *Twelfth Night*   Duke of Illyria, in love with but rejected by Olivia. He employs Viola, posing as a youth, as page; but he is quite happy to marry her when her identity is disclosed.

Osric   *Hamlet*   A rather affected courtier.

Othello   *Othello*   A Moor, a distinguished officer of wide experience, but gullible and easily roused. His favourite lieutenant, Iago, easily and maliciously tricks him into murdering his devoted wife, Desdemona.

P

Page   *The Merry Wives of Windsor*   Easy-going husband of Mrs Page, who is courted by Falstaff.

Pandarus   *Troilus and Cressida*   Cressida's uncle, who enjoys encouraging her sexual activities.

Pandulph, Cardinal   *King John*   Papal legate, engaging in political activity.

Paris   *Romeo and Juliet*   Young nobleman whom Juliet's parents wish her to marry immediately (entirely against her will), unaware of her secret marriage to Romeo. In the end he forces Romeo to fight him, and is killed.

Parolles   *All's Well That Ends Well*   Pompous braggart, friendly with Bertram. He has the virtue of accepting his eventual exposure philosophically.

Patroclus   *Troilus and Cressida*   Greek officer, friend to Achilles.

Paulina   *The Winter's Tale*   Lady at the court of Leontes, and a strong supporter of Hermione, not afraid to speak her mind.

Pedant   *The Taming of the Shrew*   Visitor to Padua who agrees, for plausible reasons, to pretend to be Lucentio's father, to help forward the marriage with Bianca.

Pedro, Don   *Much Ado About Nothing*   Prince of Arragon, and friend of Claudio, on whose behalf he begins the wooing of Hero.

Percy, Henry   *See* **Hotspur.**

Perdita   *The Winter's Tale*   Daughter of Hermione and Leontes. As a baby, cruelly abandoned by her father, she is cared for by a shepherd. As a shepherdess she meets Florizel, and they fall in love.

Pericles   *Pericles*   Prince of Tyre, an upright man who suffers many vicissitudes, including the supposed death of his wife; but he finds happiness at last.

Peto   *1 Henry IV*   An associate of Falstaff.

Petruchio   *The Taming of the Shrew*   Veronese gentleman who marries a shrewish and wilful young woman for money, and by physical domination manages to turn her into an obedient and devoted wife.

Phebe   *As You Like It*   Young shepherdess who falls in love with Rosalind posing as a youth, and scorns her honest shepherd lover, Silvius. Rosalind rebukes her.

Philip The Bastard (Faulconbridge)   *King John*   Illegitimate son of King Richard I, witty and brave leader of King John's army against France.

Philo   *Antony and Cleopatra*   Friend of Antony.

Pinch   *The Comedy of Errors*   Schoolmaster called in by Adriana to deal with the supposed madness of Antipholus of Ephesus, whom he orders to be shut away.

Pisanio   *Cymbeline*   Servant of Posthumus, who orders him to kill Imogen, believing her to be unfaithful. Pisanio disobeys, and helps her to safety in disguise.

Pistol   *2 Henry IV, King Henry V,* and *The Merry Wives of Windsor*   Rascally braggart, a hanger-on of Falstaff.

Plantagenet, Richard   *1 Henry VI*   Head of the House of York, and third Duke.

Player King/Queen   *Hamlet*   Members of a travelling group of actors, who perform the 'Mousetrap' play at Hamlet's request; Hamlet hopes that Claudius will be trapped into giving himself away.

Poins, Ned   *1 Henry IV*   Friend of Prince Hal and Falstaff. He often instigates as well as shares their activities.

Polixenes   *The Winter's Tale*   Father of Florizel and King of Bohemia, falsely suspected by Leontes of making love to the latter's wife.

Polonius   *Hamlet*   King's Chamberlain, and father of Laertes and Ophelia. Sententious and a busybody, he is killed by Hamlet while hiding in order to spy on Gertrude's meeting with her son.

Pompey   *Antony and Cleopatra*   Sometime ally, sometime enemy of Antony.

Portia   *Julius Caesar*   Wife of Brutus, who worries about her husband's activities, and in the end commits suicide.

Portia   *The Merchant of Venice*   Heiress, and chief female character of the play. Makes a happy marriage with Bassanio, despite her father's peculiar provision. Disguised as a lawyer, and after consulting a legal expert, she successfully defends Antonio against a contract which seems to allow Shylock to take a pound of his flesh.

Posthumus   *Cymbeline*   Husband of Imogen. His false belief that she is unfaithful makes him order Pisanio to kill her—an order which is indignantly put aside.

Priam   *Troilus and Cressida*   King of Troy.

Prospero   *The Tempest*   Rightful Duke of Milan, driven by his usurping brother to exile on an island, where he studies and practises magic.

Proteus   *The Two Gentlemen of Verona*   One of the two gentlemen, though he hardly deserves the term. Despite his loving attachment to Julia, in Valentine's absence Proteus attempts (unsuccessfully) to seduce his friend's betrothed, Silvia. Moreover, he betrays to her father their plan to elope.

Provost   *Measure for Measure*   Prison custodian who tries to influence Angelo towards mercy.

Puck   *A Midsummer Night's Dream*   Light-hearted sprite, Oberon's servant.

Q

Queen   *Richard II*   Isabel of France, Richard's wife.

Quickly, Mistress   *1* and *2 Henry IV,* and *The Merry Wives of Windsor*   Hostess of the Boar's Head tavern, which Falstaff frequents. She claims that he has agreed to marry her. In *The Merry Wives of Windsor* she has become housekeeper to Dr Caius.

Quince, Peter   *A Midsummer Night's Dream*   A carpenter, and producer of the 'Pyramus and Thisbe' play.

R

Rambures   *Henry V*   French lord at Agincourt.

Ratcliff, Sir Richard   *Richard III*   Follower of Richard.

Regan *King Lear* Second daughter of King Lear, as ungrateful as Goneril, and as cruel as her husband, Cornwall, in the blinding of Gloucester. Later she is in competition with her sister over the attentions of Edmund, and Goneril poisons her.

Reignier *1 Henry VI* Duke of Anjou, father of Margaret.

Richard of Gloucester *see* **Gloucester.**

Richmond, Earl of *Richard III* Henry Tudor, later Henry VII. Defeats Richard at Bosworth, to become king.

Rivers, Earl *3 Henry VI* and *Richard III* Brother of Edward IV's queen, Elizabeth. Unwilling to help Richard become king, and executed by him.

Roderigo *Othello* Foolish gentleman in love (vainly) with Desdemona.

Romeo *Romeo and Juliet* Young member of the Montague family who falls deeply in love with Juliet, a girl of the rival Capulet family. They are secretly married. Romeo is forced into a fight with a quarrelsome Capulet (Tybalt), and kills him. He is banished from Verona, which leads to the death of both lovers.

Rosalind *As You Like It* Daughter of the exiled Duke Senior, and in love with Orlando. After being banished by the usurping duke, she flees with Celia to the Forest of Arden, disguised as a youth.

Rosaline *Love's Labour's Lost* Princess of France's attendant, with whom Biron falls in love.

Rosencrantz *see* **Guildenstern.**

Ross *Macbeth* Scottish nobleman.

Roussillon, Countess of *All's Well That Ends Well* Mother of Bertram; well disposed towards Helena.

Rutland, Earl of *3 Henry VI* Young son of Duke of York, murdered by Clifford.

S

Salanio/Solanio *The Merchant of Venice* Friend of Antonio.

Salarino *The Merchant of Venice* Friend of Antonio.

Sands/Sandys, Lord *Henry VIII* Lively courtier.

Saturninus *Titus Andronicus* Emperor of Rome, married to Tamora, and unfriendly to Titus.

Scarus *Antony and Cleopatra* Friend of Antony.

Sebastian *The Tempest* Brother of the King of Naples, prepared to murder the king to obtain the crown.

Sebastian   *Twelfth Night*   Twin brother of Viola, easily persuaded to marry the lovely Countess Olivia (who mistakes him for Cesario).

Seyton   *Macbeth*   Officer attending Macbeth.

Shallow, Justice   *2 Henry IV*   A country justice.

Shylock   *The Merchant of Venice*   Jewish money-lender, with a grievance against the Venetian merchant, Antonio. A supposedly light-hearted contract gives him what seems to be a fatal hold over the Venetian. *See* **Antonio.**

Sicinius   *Coriolanus*   Roman tribune of the people, unfavourable to Coriolanus.

Silence   *2 Henry IV*   Simple country justice.

Silvia   *The Two Gentlemen of Verona*   Daughter of the Duke of Milan, reciprocating the love of Valentine, against her father's choice — the feeble Thurio.

Silvius   *As You Like It*   Shepherd in love with Phebe.

Simonides   *Pericles*   King of Pentapolis. Pericles marries his daughter Thaisa.

Simple   *The Merry Wives of Windsor*   Servant to Slender.

Slender   *The Merry Wives of Windsor*   Cousin to Shallow, and suitor, favoured by her father, to an unwilling Anne Page.

Sly, Christopher   *Taming of the Shrew*   A tinker who is found, very drunk, by a lord. As a jest he persuades Sly that he is really a nobleman who has lost his memory. *The Taming of the Shrew* is performed for his entertainment.

Snug   *A Midsummer Night's Dream*   A joiner who acts as a lion in the 'Pyramus and Thisbe' play.

Solanio   *see* **Salanio.**

Speed   *The Two Gentlemen of Verona*   Valentine's servant.

Stafford, Sir Humphrey   *2 Henry VI*   A leader of an armed force that attempted to turn back a mob led by Jack Cade. Stafford was killed in the fighting.

Stanley, Sir John   *2 Henry VI*   Nobleman who escorts the Duchess of York into exile.

Stephano   *The Tempest*   Drunken butler wrecked on Prospero's island. He makes Caliban his servant.

Strato   *Julius Caesar*   Servant of Brutus.

Suffolk, Earl of   *1 Henry VI*   He arranges Henry's marriage with Margaret of Anjou, and becomes her lover.

T

Talbot, Lord *1 Henry VI* Commander of the English army, a vigorous leader.

Tamora *Titus Andronicus* Queen of the Goths. She marries the Roman emperor, Saturninus, and has Aaron, the Moor, as lover. Despite her pleas, Titus kills her eldest son as a ritual sacrifice, and there is bitter enmity between the two families, with Titus's suffering vile treament.

Thaisa *Pericles* Daughter of Simonides and wife of Pericles.

Thersites *Troilus and Cressida* Cynical and bawdy Greek.

Theseus *A Midsummer Night's Dream* Duke of Athens about to marry Hippolyta. He reminds Hermia of an ancient law that a girl must marry according to her father's wish.

Thurio *The Two Gentlemen of Verona* Foolish rival to Valentine for the hand of Silvia, but her father's choice at first.

Timon *Timon of Athens* Over-generous noble Athenian who loses his fortune, and is so disgusted at the ingratitude of his former friends that he becomes a bitter misanthrope.

Titania *A Midsummer Night's Dream* Queen of the fairies, for a while at enmity with her husband, Oberon. To humiliate her, he uses magic to make her fall temporarily in love with a villager (Bottom) bearing an ass's head.

Titinius *Julius Caesar* Friend of Brutus and Cassius.

Titus Andronicus *Titus Andronicus* Quick-tempered and ruthless chief character, who is both killer and victim in a play of violence, brutality and horror. Titus's daughter, Lavinia, is chief sufferer.

Touchstone *As You Like It* Family jester who joins Celia and Rosalind in their flight to Arden Forest. He meets and marries a country girl, Audrey.

Tribunes The people's representatives in Rome, usually two. *See* **Brutus** and **Sicinius** (*Coriolanus*).

Tranio *The Taming of the Shrew* Servant of Lucentio. He changes places with his master, who wishes to woo Bianca in the guise of a tutor.

Trinculo *The Tempest* Jester wrecked with Stephano on Prospero's island. Caliban joins them in a futile plan to murder Prospero and take over the island.

Troilus *Troilus and Cressida* Youngest son of King Priam of Troy, and lover of Cressida. He is deeply upset by her unfaithfulness when she is sent to the Greek camp.

Tybalt   *Romeo and Juliet*   Quarrelsome nephew of Lady Capulet. He forces a fight on Romeo and is killed, which leads to Romeo's banishment from Verona.

Tyrrel, Sir James   *Richard III*   Paid by Richard to arrange the murder of the two young princes in the Tower of London.

U

Ulysses   *Troilus and Cressida*   The most articulate of the Greek commanders.

Ursula   *Much Ado About Nothing*   One of Hero's gentlewomen.

V

Valentine   *The Two Gentlemen of Verona*   Lover of Silvia. He is banished by her father, Duke of Milan, for attempting to elope with her. He then falls in with outlaws, and becomes their leader; but the banishment is later repealed, and the Duke accepts Valentine as Silvia's husband.

Ventidius   *Timon of Athens*   False friend of Timon.

Verges   *Much Ado About Nothing*   Elderly assistant constable to Dogberry.

Vernon, Sir Richard   *1 Henry IV*   One of the rebels against Henry IV.

Viola   *Twelfth Night*   Chief female character of the play. After being wrecked, she disguises herself as a page, under the name Cesario, and is employed by Count Orsino, with whom she falls in love. She believes her identical twin brother, Sebastian, to have been drowned, but he is in fact in the same town as herself.

Virgilia   *Coriolanus*   Wife of Coriolanus.

Volumnia   *Coriolanus*   Mother of Coriolanus, who spares Rome at her entreaty, and thereby meets his end.

Vincentio   *The Taming of the Shrew*   Lucentio's father, who almost upsets his son's romance with Bianca by paying an unexpected visit.

W

Warwick, Earl of   *2* and *3 Henry VI*   Powerful nobleman, sometimes known as 'the Kingmaker'.

William   *As You Like It*   A country bumpkin.

Williams   *Henry V*   Soldier with whom the king, incognito, has a long and friendly argument before the battle of Agincourt.

Winchester, Bishop of *1* and *2 Henry VI* A son of John of Gaunt, and at enmity with Humphrey, Duke of Gloucester.

Witches *Macbeth* At their first appearance, three witches whom Macbeth meets on a heath, who encourage his ruthless ambition by promising future kingship. Later they offer him hopes of a safety that is in fact illusory.

Wolsey, Cardinal *Henry VIII* Statesman and cardinal who, in the first part of the play, is in the king's favour; but a careless disclosure of his greedy activities brings about his downfall.

SHAKESPEARE
AND THE STAGE

1   There is an upstart crow, beautified with our feathers, that with his Tiger's heart wrapt in a Player's hide, supposes that he is as well able to bombast out a blank verse as the best of you . . . and is in his own conceit the only Shake-scene in a country.
Robert Greene   1592

2   The applause! delight! the wonder of our Stage!
Ben Jonson   1623

3   He was not of an age, but for all time.
Ben Jonson   1623

4   The Players have often mentioned it as an honour to Shakespeare, that in his writing he never blotted out a line. My answer hath beene, would he had blotted a thousand.
Ben Jonson   1640

5   What he thought he uttered with that easinesse that wee have scarse received from him a blot in his papers.
John Heminge, Henry Condell   1623

6   He was an eminent instance of the Truth of that Rule . . . one is not *made* but *born* a Poet.
Thomas Fuller   c.1660

7   But Shakespeare's magic could not copied be; Within that circle none durst walk but he.
John Dryden   1667

8   He was the man of all Modern, and perhaps Ancient Poets, with the largest and most comprehensive soul.
John Dryden   1668

9   With us a Black-amoor might rise to be a Trumpeter; but Shakespeare would not have him less than a Lieutenant-General.
Thomas Rymer   1677

10   I may venture to maintain that the fury of his fancy often transported him, beyond the bounds of judgement.
John Dryden   1679

11   As for his Jingling sometimes, and playing upon Words, it was the common Vice of the age he lived in.
Nicholas Rowe   1709

12   I could never meet with any further account of Shakespeare this way (as an actor) than that the top of his performance was the Ghost in his own *Hamlet*.
Nicholas Rowe   1709

13   No Dramatic Writer ever succeeded better in raising Terror in the Minds of an audience than Shakespeare has done. The whole Tragedy of Macbeth . . . is a noble Proof of that manly Spirit with which he writ.
Nicholas Rowe   1709

14   Shakespeare (whom you and ev'ry Play-house bill Style the divine, the matchless, what you will) For gain, not glory, wing'd his roving flight, And grew Immortal in his own despight.
Alexander Pope   1737

15   Narration in dramatic poetry is naturally tedious . . . Shakespeare found it an encumbrance, and instead of lightening it with brevity, endeavoured to recommend it by dignity and splendour.
Samuel Johnson   1765

16   Shakespeare has no heroes; his scenes are occupied only with men.
Samuel Johnson   1765

17   Many years ago I was so shocked by Cordelia's death, that I know not whether I ever endured to read the last scenes of the play till I undertook to revise them as an editor.
Samuel Johnson   1765

18   In the sleep-walking scene (*Macbeth*), when I argued the impracticality of washing out that '*damned spot*' while holding the candle in my hand, Sheridan insisted that if I put the candle out of my hand, it would be thought a presumptuous innovation, as Mrs Pritchard had always retained it in hers.
Sarah Siddons   c.1785

19   It is difficult for a frequent playgoer to disembarrass the idea of Hamlet from the person and voice of Mr Kemble. And we speak of Lady Macbeth, while we are in reality thinking of Mrs Siddons.
Charles Lamb   1811

20   To see Lear acted – to see an old man tottering about the stage, turned out of doors by his daughters in a rainy night, has nothing in it but what is painful and disgusting.
Charles Lamb   1811

21   It was said of Garrick and Spranger Barry in this balcony scene (*Romeo and Juliet*), that the one acted as if he would jump up to the lady, the other as if he would make the lady jump down to him.
William Hazlitt   1815

22   There is a perpetual undulation of feeling in the character of Hamlet; but . . . Mr Kemble played it like a man in armour.
William Hazlitt   1815

23   To see Edmund Kean act is like reading Shakespeare by flashes of lightning.
S T Coleridge   1818

24   Of late years Mr Kean had always so much exhausted himself in the previous acts that he was obliged to rest on a sofa during his fearful dialogue with Desdemona, to gather strength for the murder.
John Forster   1835

25   We shall never forget the tone with which Mr Macready broke into 'What a piece of work is man!' so earnest in its faith, so passionate in its sorrow. Here is the true Hamlet.
John Forster   1835

26   Shakespeare is not our poet but the world's.
W S Landor   1846

27   It may be questioned whether the people in the reign of Elizabeth, or indeed the queen herself, would have been contented with a drama without a smack of the indecent or the ludicrous.
W S Landor   c.1846

28   Others abide our question. Thou art free We ask and ask. Thou smilest and art still.
Matthew Arnold   1849

29   I have always considered *The Merry Wives* one of the worst plays, if not altogether the worst, that Shakespeare has left us. But of course, protected as it is by the reverence all Englishmen feel for 'the Swan', critics leave it in peace.
G H Lewes   1851

30   Mr Phelps has of late years been the personator of about thirty of the characters of Shakespeare. Great men or small . . . he has taken all as characters that Shakespeare painted, studied them minutely, and embodied each in what he thinks to be a true Shakespearean form.
Henry Morley   1857

31   It is to be wished that . . . the management of Drury Lane would announce that their *Macbeth* would be acted, for a few nights at least, *without* Locke's music and the corps of witches jigging to misfitted rhymes. The very substantial Hecate looks like a cross between a beef-eater from the Tower and a ghost from the Styx . . . By untuning the keynote they spoil the harmonies of the whole play.
Henry Morley   1864

32   Unlike most actors who have played Hamlet, Mr Irving did not make his success by his rendering of any particular scene, but rather by his realization of the entire character. In the soliloquies he accomplished the rare feat of seeming to think aloud.
Austin Brereton   1883

33   The performance of *As You Like It* by a company consisting entirely of women . . . was a purposeless curiosity, and rather ugly than beautiful. There is something uncomely to the eye and unpleasing to the ear in a bearded woman.
William Archer   1894

34   Nothing shall ever reconcile me to the barbarism of opening *Twelfth Night* to a seashore tableau, instead of that bewitching speech of Orsino's, 'If music be the food of love, play on', in which Shakespeare strikes the keynote of the whole comedy.
William Archer   1894

35   It is certain that if Mr Henry Irving were to present himself in as mutilated a condition as he presented King Lear, a shriek of horror would go up from all London.
G Bernard Shaw   1894

36   When the production of a new play has spelt failure, a revival of *Hamlet* has always set me on my feet again.
Sir Johston Forbes-Robertson   1913

37   If Shakespeare merely let us look on, critically observant . . . Lear is an intolerable tyrant. Regan and Goneril have a good case against him.
H Granville-Barker   1927

38   My own frivolous opinion is that Shakespeare may have held in private life very different views from what we extract from his extremely varied public works; that there is no clue in his writings to the way in which he would have voted in the last, or would vote in the next, election.
T S Eliot   1927

39   The story of *The Merchant of Venice* is incredibly puerile, and would ruin the reputation of a contemporary dramatist.
St John Ervine   1928

40   There's a danger that we may become too subtle in our interpretations of Shakespeare. We forget that as a good dramatist he would be unlikely to put more into a play than an audience would be likely to understand in a single performance.
Sir John Gielgud   1939

41   It may be almost a form of blasphemy, treason, and heresy to say of England's hero that he was not a dog-lover: but Shakespeare frequently refers with distaste to fawning dogs, who are his symbol for odious flattery.
Ivor Brown   1949

42   The first and simple fact about Shakespeare is that he was stage-struck, as all of his calling have to be; otherwise they would be driven frantic.
Ivor Brown   1949

43   At the present time in London . . . no work by any living dramatist receives any subsidy at all. The only subsidized dramatist is Shakespeare, though he does not need the money and has never asked for it.
J B Priestley   1955

44   In the last seven years I have seen a major production of every play of Shakespeare's. This is a remarkable situation — never before has there been such a boom in the Bard.
Sir Peter Hall   1956

45   The remarkable thing about Shakespeare is that he is really very good — in spite of all the people who say he is very good.
Robert Graves   1964

46   I find it impossible to think of Shylock as a really a nice chap; he is just better quality stuff than any of the Christians in the play.
Lord Olivier   1970

47   Shakespeare out in front by a mile, and the rest of the field strung out behind, trying to close the gap.
Tom Stoppard   1982

48   My first attempt at Hamlet owed so much to John Gielgud's performance in the part in 1930 that I must have seemed like his understudy.
Sir Michael Redgrave   1983

49   I know he's a great playwright and all that, and I shouldn't be saying this, but I do find him very difficult to understand, let alone play.
Rex Harrison   1990

50   Three of the biggest examination boards offer A-levels in English Language and Literature in which Shakespeare is not compulsory, and students can gain degrees in English Literature from several universities, including York and East Anglia, without studying his plays.
Sunday Telegraph   1992

SHAKESPEARE:
A BRIEF BIOGRAPHY

William Shakespeare (1564–1616) was born in Stratford-upon-Avon in Warwickshire, the eldest son of John Shakespeare, glover and wool dealer. By long-established tradition, his birthday is celebrated on 23 April. The register of Holy Trinity Church, Stratford, records that he was christened there on 26 April 1564. He lived for 52 years, partly in Stratford and partly in London.

His life can be divided into three consecutive periods. The first period, spent wholly in Stratford, included boyhood, education, and early marriage. At the age of 18 he married Anne Hathaway, a farmer's daughter who lived in Shottery, near Stratford. She was 26, and pregnant by him. The second period began when, still a very young man, he left Stratford to work in London as an actor and playwright. It lasted for 25 years, in the course of which he became a permanent and leading member of a great acting company. For that company he then wrote plays that gave it a commanding place in the London theatre.

The beginning of the third period of his life was marked by his carefully planned and gradual withdrawal from his heavy commitments in the theatre. He had long been investing in land and tithes in and around Stratford. In 1611 he freed himself of his major commitment to his company by bringing forward John Fletcher to take over as chief dramatist. By 1612 he had completed his withdrawal, though in 1613, with Fletcher's collaboration, he wrote *Henry VIII*.

Shakespeare died on 23 April 1616. The nature of his fatal illness is not known. In 1623 his monument was erected in Holy Trinity Church. A few months later John Hemminge and Henry Condell – two of his friends and principal colleagues in the King's Men – published his collected plays in the First Folio. But for them much of his work would have been lost, and all subsequent editions of his plays have been based on the text they so diligently and lovingly established.

CHRONOLOGICAL
LIST OF PLAYS

Title	Date	Category
The Two Gentlemen of Verona	1590–1	comedy
Henry VI Part One	1592	history
Henry VI Part Two	1592	history
Henry VI Part Three	1592	history
Titus Andronicus	1592	tragedy
Richard III	1592–3	history
The Taming of the Shrew	1593	comedy
The Comedy of Errors	1594	comedy
Love's Labour's Lost	1594–5	comedy
Richard II	1595	history
Romeo and Juliet	1595	tragedy
A Midsummer Night's Dream	1595	comedy
King John	1596	history
The Merchant of Venice	1596–7	comedy
Henry IV Part One	1596–7	history
The Merry Wives of Windsor	1597–8	comedy
Henry IV Part Two	1597–8	history
Much Ado About Nothing	1598	dark comedy
Henry V	1598–9	history
Julius Caesar	1599	Roman
As You Like It	1599–1600	comedy
Hamlet, Prince of Denmark	1600–1	tragedy
Twelfth Night, or What You Will	1601	comedy
Troilus and Cressida	1602	tragedy
Measure for Measure	1603	dark comedy
Othello	1603–4	tragedy
All's Well That Ends Well	1604–5	dark comedy
Timon of Athens	1605	romantic drama
The Tragedy of King Lear	1605–6	tragedy
Macbeth	1606	tragedy
Antony and Cleopatra	1606	tragedy
Pericles	1607	romance
Coriolanus	1608	Roman
The Winter's Tale	1609	romance
Cymbeline	1610	romance
The Tempest	1611	romance
Henry VIII	1613	history

INDEX

All's Well That Ends Well

Absence 1, Age 5, Cats 32, Chastity 38, Courage 44, Dress 65, Drinking 67, Duty 70, Friendship 94, Heaven 119, Honesty 126, Honour 126, Husband 133, Knowledge 156, Lady 157, Life 161, Marriage 176, Medicine 179, Memory 182, Oaths 204, Pardon 208, Perfection 214, Place 218, Poverty 227, Praise 229, Remedy 244, Silence 255, Story 269, Time 279, Wooing 306.

Antony and Cleopatra

Absence 1, Age 5, Anger 11, Animals 13, Books 28, Conquest 43, Courage 44, Day 50, Deeds 55, Delight 57, Dreams 62, Duelling 69, Fortune 91, Gods 100, Goodness 103, Hair 106, Hand 108, Harm 111, Haste 112, Hate 113, Heart 115, Honesty 125, Honour 126, Horse 129, Ignorance 135, Injury 139, Judgement 146, Kisses 152, Life 161, Love 164, Marriage 176, Moon 189, Music 194, Name 197, Necessity 201, Pardon 208, Perfection 214, Poison 224, Power 228, Praise 230, Punishment 237, Queen 240, Reputation 246, Rest 247, Reward 250, Rome 252, Suicide 271, Truth 288, Unkindness 290, Valour 291, War 296, Weeping 298, Welcome 299, Woman 304, Youth 311.

As You Like It

Age 5–6, Animals 13, Beauty 17, Bells 21, Blood 27, Children 39, Comfort 41, Dancing 45, Dogs 61, Dress 65, Earth 72, Eating 73, Enemy 75, Eyes 78, Face 79, Folly 89, Fortune 91, Friendship 94, Gods 100, Goodness 103, Happiness 109, Hate 114, Heart 115, Honesty 125, Ingratitude 138, Jewels 143, Kisses 152, Lady 157, Life 161, Lips 163, Love 164, Magic 172, Malice 173, Man 174, Money 186, Months 188, Name 197, Oratory 207, Philosophy 215, Pity 217, Place 218, Plays 219, Poetry 222, Pride 232, Reason 243, Reputation 246, Seasons 253, Sorrow 261, Tears 276, Time 280, Travel 285, Trees 287, Weeping 298, Wit 302, Woman 304, Wooing 306, World 310.

The Comedy of Errors

Age 6, Eating 73, Freedom 93, Grief 105, Hair 106, Husband 133, Inconstancy 137, Injury 139, Jealousy 142, Madness 168–9, Magic 172, Marriage 176, Misfortune 185, Name 197, Oratory 207, Patience 209, Praise 230, Prison 234, Slander 257, Soul 262, Sport 264, Sun 272–3, Welcome 299.

Coriolanus

Action 2, Affection 4, Anger 11, Animals 13, Candour 30, Deeds 55, Drinking 67, Gods 100, Hate 114, Ingratitude 138, Kisses 152, Nature 200, Pardon 208, People 213, Plays 220, Power 228, Praise 230, Revenge 249, Rome 252, Valour 291.

Cymbeline

Angel 9, Bed 20, Birds 23, Chastity 38, Comfort 41, Death 52, Dress 65, Duty 70, Fortune 91, Freedom 93, Gods 101, Gold 101, Grief 105, Hand 108, Harm 111, Hate 114, Horse 129, Husband 133, Joy 145, Kisses 152, Knighthood 154, Lady 157, Medicine 179, Money 186, Music 194, Nature 200, Oaths 204, Peace 211, Poison 224, Power 228, Punishment 237, Rest 247, Silence 255, Sleep 258, Smiles 259, Sport 264, Stone 267, Suicide 271, Teaching 275, Treason 286, Valour 291, War 296, Words 308.

Hamlet

Action 2, Affection 4, Age 6, Ambition 8, Angel 10, Animals, 13, Arms 14, Ass 16, Beauty 18, Bed 20, Bells 22, Birds 23, Cause 33, Change 35, Chastity 38, Danger 47, Death 52, Deeds 55, Delight 57, Destiny 58, Devil 59–60, Dogs 61, Dreams 62, Dress 65, Drinking 67, Duelling 69, Earth 72, Face 79, Fate 82, Father 84, Flowers 87, Folly 89, Fortune 91–2, Friendship 95, Gentleman 96, Gifts 97, God 99, Grief 105, Happiness 109, Haste 112, Heaven 120, Honesty 125–6, Honour 127, Horse 130, Hours 131, Husband 133, Hypocrisy 134, Ignorance 136, Jealousy 142, Joy 145, Judgement 146, Justice 147, King 149, Knowledge 156, Love 165, Madness 169,

Hamlet (contd.)
Man 175, Marriage 176–7, Memory 182, Morning 191, Murder 192–3, Music 194, Nature 200, Night 203, Offence 205–6, Patience 209, People 213, Philosophy 215, Plays 220–1, Poison 224, Power 229, Prayer 231, Quarrels 238, Reason 243, Repentance 245, Rest 248, Revenge 249, Reward 250, Roaring 251, Rome 253, Seasons 254, Sin 256, Sleep 258, Smiles 259, Sorrow 261, Soul 262–3, Story 270, Suicide 272, Sun 273, Teaching 275, Tears 276, Thought 278–9, Travel 285, Trees 288, Truth 289, Virtue 294–5, Wit 302, Woman 304, Words 308, World 310, Youth 311–2.

1 Henry IV
Ambition 8, Anger 11, Arms & Armour 15, Bed 20, Birds 23, Blood 27, Cats 32, Cause 33, Children 39, Courage 44, Danger 47, Devil 60, Dress 65, Drinking 68, Earth 72, Face 80, Gentleman 96, God 99, Harm 111, Heat 118, Honour 127, Horse 130, Hours 131, Innocence 140, King 149, Lady 157, Law 158, Life 161, Madness 170, Medicine 179, Moon 189, Nature 200, Oaths 204, Plays 221, Poetry 222, Poison 224, Poverty 227, Punishment 237, Quarrels 238, Queen 240, Reason 243, Repentance 245, Reputation 246, Stars 265, Theft 277, Time 280, Tomorrow 282, Treason 286, Truth 289, Valour 291–2, Victory 293, War 297, Woman 304, Words 308.

2 Henry IV
Age 6, Bells 22, Conquest 43, Danger 48, Day 51, Death 53, Drinking 68, Eating 73, England 76, Fate 83, Folly 89, Fortune 92, Gold 102, Home 124, Hope 128, Innocence 141, Joy 145, King 149, Kisses 153, Medicine 180, Money 186–7, Peace 211, Poverty 227, Remedy 244, Sin 256, Sleep 258, Story 270, Treason 286, Valour 292, Victory 293, Wife 300, Wit 302, Youth 312.

Henry V
Absence 1, Angel 10, Animals 13, Arms & Armour 15, Blood 27, Cause 33–4, Courage 45, Dancing 45, Day 50, Dress 65, Duty 70, Enemy 75, England 76–7, Eyes 78, Fortune 92, Gold 102, Heart 115, Home 124, Honour 127, Horse 130, King 149, Kisses 153, Life 161, Lips 163, Marriage 177, Patience 209, Peace 211, Poetry 223,

Quarrels 238, Queen 240, Rest 248, Sin 256, Smiles 260, Soul 263, Sport 264–5, Tomorrow 282, Touch 283, Treason 286, Valour 292, War 297, Weeping 298, Wooing 306, Youth 312.

1 Henry VI
Beauty 17–18, Bells 22, Birds 24, Charms 36, Danger 48, Daughters 49, Death 53, Hair 107, Hell 122, Hours 132, King 149, Knighthood 155, Law 158, Madness 170, Magic 172, Malice 173, Marriage 177, Morning 191, Name 197, Night 203, Place 218, Prison 234, Queen 240, Reward 250, Stone 267, Welcome 300, Woman 304.

2 Henry VI
Ambition 8, Animals 13, Beauty 18, Birds 24, Care 31, Gifts 97, God 99, Hair 107, Heaven 120, Home 124, Hypocrisy 135, Ignorance 136, Innocence 141, Jewels 144, Judgement 146, Justice 148, King 149, Kisses 153, Knowledge 156, Law 158, Lips 163, Music 194, Oaths 204, People 213, Prayer 231, Prison 234, Quarrels 239, Storm 268, Touch 284, Treason 286, Unkindness 290.

3 Henry VI
Birds 24, Courage 45, Destiny 58, Earth 72, England 77, Face 80, Fate 83, Hand 108, Happiness 110, Harm 111, Heart 116, Hell 123, King 150, Knighthood 155, Life 161, Marriage 177, Morning 191, People 213, Prison 234, Prophecy 235, Queen 240, Rain 241, Reward 251, Time 280, Treason 286, Trees 288, Valour 292, Victory 293, Weeping 298, Woman 304–5.

Henry VIII
Action 3, Affection 4, Age 6, Ambition 8, Angel 10, Anger 12, Beauty 18, Care 31, Cause 34, Change 35, Comfort 41, Dancing 46, Deeds 56, Destiny 58, Dress 66, Drinking 68, Duty 71, Enemy 75, Face 80, Farewell 81, Father 84, Friendship 95, God 99, Grief 105, Happiness 110, Heart 116, Heat 118, Heaven 120, Innocence 141, Lady 157, Law 159, Malice 174, Music 194, Name 197, Nature 200, Pardon 208, Peace 211–2, Perfection 214, Prayer 231, Pride 233, Prison 234, Prophecy 235, Queen 240–1, Rest 248, Sorrow 261, Talk 274,

Henry VIII (contd.)

Travel 285, Trees 288, Virtue 295, Welcome 300, Woman 305, Words 308.

Julius Caesar

Age 7, Ambition 8–9, Angel 10, Anger 12, Ass 16, Blood 27, Candour 30, Care 31, Cause 34, Conquest 43, Danger 48, Day 51, Death 53, Deeds 56, Dogs 61, Dreams 63, Duty 71, Earth 72, Enemy 75, Eyes 78, Farewell 81, Fate 83, Fear 85–6, Fortune 92, Friendship 95, Gods 101, Gold 102, Goodness 104, Hair 107, Hand 108, Harm 111, Heart 116, Heaven 121, Home 124, Honour 127, Horse 130, Hours 132, Ingratitude 138, Judgement 146, Life 162, Madness 170, Man 175, Marriage 177, Months 188, Murder 193, Necessity 201–2, Night 203, Offence 206, Oratory 207, Pardon 208, Patience 210, Pity 217, Plays 221, Power 229, Prophecy 236, Reason 243, Revenge 249, Rome 252–3, Sleep 258, Smiles 260, Stars 265–6, Storm 268, Suicide 272, Time 280, Treason 286, Unkindness 290, Valour 292, Virtue 295, War 296, Weeping 298, Wife 301, Wit 303, Woman 305, Words 308–9, World 310.

King John

Arms & Armour 15, Bells 22, Blood 27, Comfort 41, Courage 45, Danger 48, Death 53, Destiny 59, England 77, Fear 86, Fortune 92, Gentleman 96, Grief 105–6, Harm 111, Haste 112, Heat 119, Knighthood 155, Lady 158, Law 159, Life 162, Madness 170, Medicine 180, Name 198, Place 219, Pride 233, Prophecy 236, Reason 243, Roaring 251, Sorrow 261, Soul 263, Talk 274, War 296.

King Lear

Affection 4, Age 7, Anger 12, Animals 13, Birds 24, Care 31, Change 35, Charms 36, Children 40, Daughters 49, Death 53, Dogs 61, Duty 71, Face 80, Fate 83, Father 84, Folly 89, Fortune 92, God 99, Gods 101, Goodness 104, Heart 116, Hell 123, Inconstancy 137, Ingratitude 138, Injury 140, Justice 148, King 150, Knighthood 155, Knowledge 156, Madness 170, Misfortune 185, Nature 200–1, Necessity 202, Night 203, Poison 225, Rain 241–2, Roaring 252, Seasons 254, Sin 256, Smiles 260, Stars 266, Storm 268–9, Suicide 272, Time 280, Treason 287, Villainy 294, Weeping 299, Woman 305.

Love's Labour's Lost

Beauty 18, Books 28–9, Dancing 46, Day 51, Delight 57, Eating 74, Eyes 78, Friendship 95, Hand 109, Heart 116, Ignorance 136, Knowledge 156, Love 165, Mirth 183, Music 195, Oaths 205, Poetry 223, Queen 241, Seasons 254, Smiles 260, Trees 288, Wit 303, Woman 305, Words 309.

Macbeth

Action 3, Age 7, Ambition 9, Arms & Armour 15, Bells 22, Birds 24–5, Blood 28, Cats 32–3, Cause 34, Charms 36–7, Children 40, Courage 45, Day 51, Death 53–4, Deeds 56, Delight 57, Devil 60, Drinking 68, Earth 72, Eyes 78, Face 80, Fate 83, Father 84, Fear 86, Gentleman 96, Hair 107, Hand 109, Harm 112, Heart 116, Heaven 121, Horse 131, Hypocrisy 135, Ingratitude 139, Joy 145, Justice 148, King 150, Life 162, Madness 170, Magic 172, Medicine 180, Memory 182, Murder 193, Nature 201, Night 203–4, People 214, Pity 217, Place 219, Plays 221, Power 229, Prayer 231, Prophecy 236, Quarrels 239, Remedy 245, Rest 248, Sleep 258–9, Smiles 260, Sorrow 261–2, Soul 263, Stone 267, Sun 273, Time 280, Tomorrow 282, Touch 284, Travel 285, Treason 287, Truth 289, Virtue 295, Weeping 299, Welcome 300, World 310.

Measure for Measure

Ass 16, Chastity 38, Death 54, Drinking 68, Freedom 93, Goodness 104, Haste 112, Heaven 121, Hope 128, Hypocrisy 135, Ignorance 136, Jewels 144, Judgement 147, Justice 148, Kisses 153, Law 159, Life 162, Lips 163, Madness 171, Medicine 180, Music 195, Possessions 226, Poverty 227, Prayer 232, Pride 233, Repentance 246, Sin 256, Stars 266, Theft 277, Truth 289, Unkindness 290, Virtue 295, Wit 303.

The Merchant of Venice

Absence 1, Action 3, Angel 10, Animals 14, Beauty 18, Bells 22, Birds 25, Books 29,

Index

The Merchant of Venice (contd.)

Cats 33, Chastity 38, Children 40, Daughters 49, Day 51, Delight 57, Destiny 59, Devil 60, Dogs 62, Dreams 63, Dress 66, Duelling 70, Eating 74, Father 84, Folly 89, Friendship 95, God 99, Gold 102, Goodness 104, Hair 107, Happiness 110, Haste 113, Hate 114, Honour 128, Husband 133, Joy 145, Judgement 147, Justice 148, King 150, Knowledge 156, Law 159–60, Love 165, Malice 174, Marriage 177, Medicine 180, Mirth 184, Misfortune 185, Months 188, Moon 189, Music 195, Night 204, Patience 210, Perfection 214, Philosophy 215, Place 219, Poverty 227, Prayer 232, Rain 242, Reason 244, Revenge 249, Silence 255, Sleep 259, Smiles 260, Stars 266, Talk 274, Teaching 275, Treason 287, Trees 288, Truth 289, Villainy 294, Virtue 295, Welcome 300, Wife 301, Words 309, World 310.

The Merry Wives of Windsor

Ass 16, Charms 37, Children 40, Destiny 59, Drinking 68–9, Eating 74, Gifts 98, God 100, Heart 117, Hope 128, Inconstancy 137, Jealousy 142, Madness 171, Marriage 178, Money 187, Name 198, Prayer 232, Rain 242, Soul 263, Wooing 306, World 311.

A Midsummer Night's Dream

Angel 10, Anger 12, Animals 14, Ass 17, Birds 25, Charms 37, Dancing 46, Day 51, Delight 57, Devil 60, Dreams 63, Duty 71, Earth 73, Eating 74, Eyes 79, Father 85, Fear 86, Flowers 87–8, Folly 90, Haste 113, Hate 114, Heart 117, Hours 132, Injury 140, Lips 163, Love 165–6, Magic 172, Man 175, Moon 190, Name 198, Offence 206, Plays 221–2, Poetry 223, Roaring 251, Seasons 254, Sleep 259, Wooing 307.

Much Ado About Nothing

Absence 1, Affection 4, Age 7, Arms & Armour 15, Ass 17, Beauty 18, Birds 25, Candour 30, Care 31, Cats 33, Chastity 38, Courage 45, Dancing 46, Dress 66, Eyes 78, Flowers 88, God 100, Grief 106, Hair 107, Happiness 110, Heart 117, Honesty 126, Husband 134, Inconstancy 137, Joy 145, Kisses 153, Lady 158, Love 165, Man 175, Marriage 178, Memory 183, Mirth 184, Months 188, Patience 210, Philosophy 216, Poetry 223, Quarrels 239, Rain 242, Silence 255, Sin 256, Slander 257, Story 270, Talk 274, Theft 277, Time 281, Valour 292, Victory 293, Virtue 295, Wit 303, Wooing 307.

Othello

Absence 1, Affection 4, Ambition 9, Cause 34, Charms 37, Comfort 42, Danger 48, Daughters 49, Drinking 69, Duty 71, Farewell 81, Folly 90, Gifts 98, Happiness 110, Heaven 121, Hell 123, Honesty 126, Jealousy 142–3, Love 166, Magic 172, Malice 174, Medicine 181, Money 187, Moon 190, Name 198, Pardon 208, Patience 210, Perfection 215, Pity 217, Poison 225, Poverty 228, Punishment 237, Remedy 245, Reputation 247, Revenge 249–50, Reward 251, Slander 257, Soul 263, Stone 267, Story 270, Talk 274, Tears 277, Theft 278, Travel 285, Wooing 307, Words 309, World 311, Youth 312.

Pericles

Beauty 18, Blood 28, Books 29, Candour 30, Care 32, Daughters 50, Destiny 59, Dreams 63, Fear 86, Folly 90, Gentleman 96, Gifts 98, Heart 117, Honour 128, Jewels 144, King 150–1, Kisses 153, Misfortune 185, Oaths 205, Punishment 238, Sorrow 262, Sport 265, Story 270, Time 281.

Richard II

Angel 10, Animals 14, Ass 17, Care 32, Cause 34, Change 35, Comfort 42, Conquest 43, Death 54, Earth 73, Eating 74, Enemy 76, England 77, Face 80, Farewell 81, Fear 86, Grief 106, Haste 113, Hate 114, Heart 117, Heat 119, Heaven 121, Hell 123, Honour 128, Hope 128–9, Horse 131, Ignorance 136, Jewels 144, Joy 145, King 151, Knighthood 155, Law 160, Medicine 181, Memory 183, Murder 193, Music 195, Name 198, Nature 201, Necessity 202, Offence 206, Pardon 208–9, Patience 210, Peace 212, Place 219, Poison 225, Prison 234, Prophecy 236, Reputation 247, Slander 257, Soul 264, Sport 265, Stone 267, Storm 269, Sun 273, Tears 277, Time 281, Truth 290, Unkindness 291.

Richard III

Children 40, Comfort 42, Conquest 43, Death 54, Destiny 59, Devil 61, Dogs 62, Dreams 64, Dress 66, Enemy 75, Gentleman 96, Gold 102, Harm 112, Hate 114–5, Heart 117, Heaven 121, Hell 123, Hope 129, Horse 131, Hours 132, Hypocrisy 135, Innocence 141, Judgement 147, Kisses 153, Law 160, Lips 163, Murder 193, Name 198, Oratory 207, Peace 212, Pity 217, Prison 234, Queen 241, Repentance 246, Seasons 254, Sun 273, Talk 275, Tomorrow 283, Victory 293, Villainy 294, Wooing 307, World 311.

Romeo and Juliet

Action 3, Affection 5, Angel 11, Beauty 19, Birds 26, Care 32, Change 35, Dancing 46, Day 51, Death 54, Delight 57, Dreams 64, Dress 66, Duelling 70, Earth 73, Eating 74, Fear 87, Fortune 93, Gentleman 97, Gold 102, Goodness 105, Haste 113, Heaven 122, Hours 132, Inconstancy 137, Jewels 144, Joy 145–6, Kisses 154, Love 166, Marriage 178, Medicine 181, Misfortune 185–6, Money 187, Months 188, Moon 190, Morning 191, Name 199, Night 204, Philosophy 216, Pity 218, Poison 225, Possessions 226, Poverty 228, Praise 230, Pride 233, Quarrels 239, Rest 248, Sleep 259, Sorrow 262, Soul 264, Story 270, Talk 275, Teaching 275, Virtue 295, Wooing 307, World 311.

The Taming of the Shrew

Anger 12, Birds 26, Candour 30, Change 35–6, Daughters 50, Delight 58, Devil 61, Dress 66–7, Eating 74, Father 85, Freedom 94, Heat 119, Hell 123, Honesty 126, Husband 134, Injury 140, Kisses 154, Law 160, Marriage 178, Mirth 184, Money 187, Music 196, Peace 212, Philosophy 216, Possessions 226, Sport 265, Teaching 275–6, Touch 284, Wife 301–2, Woman 305, Wooing 307.

The Tempest

Bed 21, Books 29, Cats 33, Charms 37, Death 55, Delight 58, Dreams 64, Dress 67, Drinking 69, Eyes 79, Father 85, Freedom 93, Innocence 141, Lady 158, Magic 173, Marriage 179, Misfortune 185, Music 196, Pardon 209, People 214, Praise 230, Prison 235, Punishment 238, Sleep 259, Stars 266, Storm 269, Story 270, Teaching 276, Time 281, Touch 284, Valour 292, Wit 303, World 311.

Timon of Athens

Birds 26, Gifts 98, Gold 103, Honesty 126, Ingratitude 139, Man 175, Medicine 181, Oaths 205, Pity 218, Poetry 223, Sin 256, Sun 274, Theft 278.

Titus Andronicus

Age 7, Birds 26, Deeds 56, Gods 101, Gold 103, Grief 106, Heart 118, Heaven 122, Madness 171, Malice 174, Morning 192, Punishment 238, Quarrels 239, Repentance 246, Revenge 250, Rome 253, Sorrow 262, Stone 267, Story 271, Sun 273.

Troilus and Cressida

Arms & Armour 16, Bed 21, Candour 30, Day 52, Deeds 56, Farewell 81, Folly 90, Heart 118, Ignorance 136, King 151, Kisses 154, Lips 163, Madness 171, Man 176, Morning 192, Name 199, Nature 201, Offence 206, Philosophy 216, Power 229, Praise 230, Pride 233, Prophecy 236, Remedy 245, Reputation 247, Time 281, Touch 284, Welcome 300, Wooing 307, Words 309.

Twelfth Night

Affection 5, Beauty 19, Bed 21, Books 29, Change 36, Daughters 50, Death 55, Dress 67, Drinking 69, Duelling 70, Eyes 79, Farewell 82, Fate 84, Folly 90, Gentleman 97, Harm 112, Heat 119, Home 124, Hope 129, Hours 132, Husband 134, Ignorance 136, Jealousy 143, Kisses 154, Knowledge 156, Law 161, Lips 164, Love 167, Madness 171, Music 196, Name 199, Oaths 205, Offence 206, Oratory 207, Patience 210, Place 219, Plays 222, Poverty 228, Prison 235, Quarrels 239, Rain 242, Revenge 250, Soul 264, Time 281, Unkindness 291, Valour 292, Virtue 296, Wit 303, Woman 306, Words 309.

The Two Gentlemen of Verona

Bed 21, Dogs 62, Duty 71, Father 85, Folly 90, Gentleman 97, Gifts 98, Haste 113, Heart 118, Home 124, Hope 129, Jealousy

The Two Gentlemen of Verona (contd.)
143, Jewels 144, Kisses 154, Love 167, Medicine 181, Name 199, Perfection 215, Poetry 223, Reason 244, Silence 255, Slander 257, Stone 267, Time 282, Touch 284, Welcome 300, Words 310, Youth 312.

The Winter's Tale
Change 36, Chastity 39, Dancing 47, Fear 87, Flowers 88, Folly 90–1, Gentleman 97, Gifts 98, Hate 115, Heart 118, Honesty 126, Innocence 142, Jealousy 143, Kisses 154, Love 168, Mirth 184, Months 188, Stone 267, Theft 278, Tomorrow 283, Wife 302, Woman 306.

A Lover's Complaint
Chastity 39, Freedom 94, Hair 107, Jewels 144, Sport 265.

The Passionate Pilgrim
Age 7, Beauty 19, Ignorance 136, Lips 164, Story 271, Youth 312.

The Rape of Lucrece
Age 8, Beauty 19, Bed 21, Birds 26, Chastity 39, Children 40, Duty 71, Eyes 79, Face 80, Hand 109, Happiness 110, Heart 118, King 151, Knighthood 155, Misfortune 186, Offence 206, Remedy 245, Rest 248, Stone 268, Suicide 272.

Sonnets
Absence 2, Angel 11, Beauty 19–20, Bed 21, Birds 26, Books 29, Change 36, Children 40, Death 55, Deeds 56, Delight 58, Dreams 64, Duty 71, Face 81, Farewell 82, Father 85, Flowers 88, Happiness 110, Haste 113, Hate 115, Home 125, Hours 132, Husband 134, Inconstancy 138, Injury 140, Joy 146, Knowledge 156, Love 168, Madness 171, Memory 183, Money 188–9, Morning 192, Name 199, Perfection 215, Plays 222, Poetry 224, Praise 230, Prophecy 236, Queen 241, Seasons 254–5, Stars 266, Time 282, Tomorrow 283, Truth 290, Unkindness 291, Victory 293.

Venus and Adonis
Affection 5, Birds 26, Chastity 39, Dancing 47, Freedom 94, Heart 118, Heat 119, Love 168, Oratory 207, Rain 242, Story 271, Time 282.